PENAL LAW IN ACTION

PENAL LAW IN ACTION

Msgr. Brendan Daly

Paulist Press
New York / Mahwah, NJ

Nihil Obstat: Rev. Francis Poon JCL
Censor Librorum
Imprimatur: +Most Rev. Stephen Lowe,
Bishop of Auckland
February 2022

Scripture quotations are from New Revised Standard Version Bible: Catholic Edition, copyright © 1989, 1993 National Council of the Churches of Christ in the United States of America. Used by permission. All rights reserved worldwide.

Cover design by Sharyn Banks
Book design by Lynn Else

Copyright © 2023 by Brendan Daly

All rights reserved. No part of this publication may be reproduced, stored in a retrieval system, or transmitted in any form or by any means, electronic, mechanical, photocopying, recording, scanning, or otherwise, without either the prior written permission of the Publisher, or authorization through payment of the appropriate per-copy fee to the Copyright Clearance Center, Inc., www.copyright.com. Requests to the Publisher for permission should be addressed to the Permissions Department, Paulist Press, permissions@paulistpress.com.

Library of Congress Cataloging-in-Publication Data
Names: Daly, Brendan, 1952– author.
Title: Penal Law in action / Msgr. Brendan Daly.
Description: Mahwah, NJ : Paulist Press, [2023] | Includes bibliographical references and index. | Summary: "The book states, outlines, and explains the revised penal law (Book 6) in the Code of Canon Law with practical examples"—Provided by publisher.
Identifiers: LCCN 2022057348 (print) | LCCN 2022057349 (ebook) | ISBN 9780809156450 (paperback) | ISBN 9780809188062 (ebook)
Subjects: LCSH: Criminal law (Canon law)
Classification: LCC KBU3510 .D35 2023 (print) | LCC KBU3510 (ebook) | DDC 262.9—dc23/eng/20230403
LC record available at https://lccn.loc.gov/2022057348
LC ebook record available at https://lccn.loc.gov/2022057349

ISBN 978-0-8091-5645-0 (paperback)
ISBN 978-0-8091-8806-2 (e-book)

Published by Paulist Press
997 Macarthur Boulevard
Mahwah, New Jersey 07430
www.paulistpress.com

Printed and bound in the
United States of America

CONTENTS

Foreword by Dr. Rodger J. Austin, JCD, STL vii
Acknowledgments ix
  1. Rationale for Penal Law and the Obligations for Church Leaders 1
  2. Overview of Recent Penal Legislation 19
  3. Removal of the Faculties of a Priest 30
  4. Suspending Priests 40
  5. The Effects of Excommunication 49
  6. Precepts for Clergy and Religious 62
  7. Absolving an Accomplice in a Sin against the Sixth Commandment ... 73
  8. Solicitation in the Sacrament of Penance 81
  9. Vietnamese and Chinese Communism in Canon Law 92
10. Prescription and Its Impact on Crimes of Sexual Abuse 110
11. The Seal of Confession for Victims and Perpetrators 121
12. Dismissal from the Clerical State 130
Notes 147
Selected Bibliography 201
Index 209

FOREWORD

Pope Saint John Paul II promulgated the revised Code of Canon Law on January 25, 1983, bringing to a closure a process of revision spanning some twenty years. In his apostolic constitution *Sacrae Disciplinae Leges*, the pope recalled that "the whole juridical and legislative tradition of the Church derives from that distant heritage of law contained in the Books of the Old and New Testament."

At the time of the revision, there was a view, albeit a minority one, that the Church ought to codify its penal law. In his address to the Tribunal of the Roman Rota on February 17, 1979, the pope responded, "In the vision of a Church which protects the rights of the individual faithful, but likewise promotes and protects the common good as an indispensable condition for the integral development of the human and Christian person, she also positively includes penal discipline."

Book VI of the 1983 Code of Canon Law, entitled "Sanctions in the Church," was very different from its predecessor, Book V of the 1917 Code of Canon Law. However, within the first decade, concerns were raised as to the adequacy of the norms of penal law in the revised Code to address the challenges facing the Church, specifically, the crisis occasioned by sexual abuse. Notwithstanding the promulgation of new laws especially in 2001, a process of revision of Book VI was embarked upon. In 2007, Pope Benedict XVI instructed the Pontifical Council for Legislative Texts to begin the process of revising the penal regulations contained in the 1983 Code. Pope Francis on May 23, 2021, issued the apostolic constitution *Pascite Gregem Dei* whereby he promulgated the new Book VI of the Code of Canon Law and decreed that it would come into force on December 8, 2021. The pope made reference to the fact that the law of the Church "must take account of changes in society and new needs of the People of God."

With the promulgation of this new Book VI, we are reminded that Saint Paul VI called for a new attitude of mind regarding canonical legislation. We are conscious that the new Book VI is the law for the universal Church, the people of God, to be taken up and acted upon in a variety of diverse churches and communities reflecting very different cultural, social, historical, and political settings. There are significant challenges for the Church in its relationship with civil authorities, including the protection of children, in particular, and the processes for dealing with those who harm them. Monsignor Daly's book, *Penal Law in Action*, is published at a most opportune moment for understanding and applying the penal law of the Church. The contents relate to many facets of the application of the law in the administration of justice within the Church. It is said that the application of the law must be faithful to the meaning of the law. However, we know that has not always been the reality regarding penal law.

Monsignor Daly with his gifts of research and teaching, and drawing on his years of experience in the service to the Church both in New Zealand and overseas, has provided in *Penal Law in Action* an understanding of the law and how it is applied. It is a resource for all who are in any way involved, as Pope Francis said, with persons "who have been harmed by the violation of penal laws as well as those who have committed canonical crimes and are themselves in need of the Church's mercy and correction." Monsignor Daly's *Penal Law in Action* is a companion—*vademecum*—that Christ's faithful should have to assist them in their service of the Church in relation to matters pertaining to penal law. It will be a truly worthy companion.

Dr. Rodger J. Austin, JCD, STL
Former President of the Canon Law Society of Australia and New Zealand Canon Law Advocate and Consultant Sydney Australia

ACKNOWLEDGMENTS

Just before printing, I have the happy task of thanking those who have helped with the writing of this book. I thank Doctor Rodger Austin, who wrote the preface. I especially wish to thank Barbara Brown, who spent much time checking the manuscript and making very helpful suggestions. I also wish to thank Myriam Wijlens, Mark Hangartner, and Andrea Schmitz for their proofreading. I thank Good Shepherd College for my sabbaticals, which enabled me to do the enormous research for this book. I thank the Canon Law Society of Australia and New Zealand for allowing me to use articles from *The Canonist* in my revisions and updating.

1

RATIONALE FOR PENAL LAW AND THE OBLIGATIONS FOR CHURCH LEADERS

In an ideal world, we would have a Church that did not require penal law. Sadly, that is not so, and penal law is necessary. On February 21, 2020, in his address to the plenary assembly of the Pontifical Council for Legislative Texts, Pope Francis reflected on the necessary, but subordinate, role of canon law in the life of the Church:

> Making the laws of the Church known and applying them is not a hindrance to the presumed pastoral "effectiveness" of those who want to solve problems without law, but rather a guarantee of the search for solutions that are not arbitrary, but instead truly just and, therefore, truly pastoral.[1]

Canon law is always geared to the salvation of souls as stated in canon 1752, the last canon of the Code.

In 2021, Pope Francis's apostolic constitution *Pascite Gregem Dei* ("Tend the Flock of God") promulgated the revised Book VI of the Code of Canon Law, "Penal Sanctions in the Church," which consists of canons 1311–99.[2] Of these eighty-nine canons, sixty-three have been changed and others have been renumbered. The changed title of Book VI—with the addition of "Penal"—is part of an effort to combat erroneous ideas that ordinaries should be charitable and avoid implementing penal law. The pope has eliminated conflict and confusion over bishops and religious superiors being pastoral by saying the implementation of penal law is pastoral since it is an instrument of mercy and correction.

The sexual abuse crisis has been made significantly worse by religious superiors and bishops not implementing penal law. In this new Book VI, Pope Francis states that this has led to

> tolerating immoral conduct, for which mere exhortations or suggestions are

insufficient remedies. This situation often brings with it the danger that over time such conduct may become entrenched, making correction more difficult and in many cases creating scandal and confusion among the faithful.

Penal law is like a security system around the faithful to protect them, and it also helps to maintain and reinforce minimum standards of behavior for clergy, religious, and laity. As the title of the apostolic constitution suggests, a pastoral bishop pulls members of the faithful away from danger and corrects them when necessary. He protects the faithful from offending clerics and lay officials and should consider the application of penal law as part of his pastoral ministry.

NEW TESTAMENT BASIS FOR PENAL LAW

The Church has always had penal law. Jesus condemned a person who would lead a child astray and warned that their punishment would be worse than being forcibly drowned (see Matt 18:6–7). Offenders could be excommunicated as demonstrated by Matthew 18:15–17 and 1 Corinthians 5:1–5. In the former, Matthew outlines the principles in dealing with a member who sins against another member; in the latter, Paul advises how to deal with a case of incest. Paul also speaks of ending punishment by forgiveness (see 2 Cor 2:5–7); he deals with the case of blasphemous men (see 1 Tim 1:20); and counsels public rebukes of sinful elders (see 1 Tim 5:20); while Titus outlines instructions for dealing with a man who causes divisions (see Titus 3:10). Saint Paul also warned the Corinthians and Ephesians that evildoers such as fornicators, adulterers, and male prostitutes would not enter the kingdom of heaven (see 1 Cor 6:9–10; Eph 5:5–7). In fact, he warns that "the wrath of God" will come down on them (Eph 5:6).

PENALTIES UNJUSTLY APPLIED

From history, we know unjust penalties have sometimes been imposed: in 1431, Saint Joan of Arc was unjustly excommunicated in France; on September 22, 1871, Saint Mary of the Cross, Mary MacKillop, RSJ, was unjustly excommunicated by Bishop Sheil in South Australia.[3] However, a Jesuit priest, who thought Mary was unjustly treated, gave her communion. Bishop Shiel later admitted that he was wrong and lifted the excommunication on February 23, 1872.[4]

However, in October 1955, Archbishop Joseph Francis Rummel of New Orleans placed a justified interdict on the Jesuit Bend parish when white parishioners prevented Father Gerald Lewis, SVD, an African American supply priest, from celebrating Mass in a parish church when the pastor was sick. The penalty prevented any sacraments being celebrated in the parish until a deputation of parishioners apologized to the bishop, who then lifted the interdict.[5] In recent times, the Church has been criticized because penal law has been ignored by some bishops. All too often, penalties have not been applied to abusers, allowing abusive priests to be moved on to another parish where they have been able to continue their ministry and their abusive actions.

REQUIREMENT TO IMPLEMENT LAW

The 1983 Code allowed bishops and religious superiors wide discretion as to whether to impose penalties and many people have complained about clericalism and "cheap mercy" being granted to offending clergy without sufficient account being taken of justice for victims; protection of the community of the faithful; prevention of scandal; and compensation for the harm that has been caused. Offending clergy certainly do have a right to forgiveness, but this does not mean that they can simply be given new appointments with access to future potential victims.[6] In the new Book VI, Pope Francis has outlined the overall purpose of penal law by adding a paragraph to canon 1311:

> The one who is at the head of a Church must safeguard and promote the good of the community itself and of each of Christ's faithful, through pastoral charity, example of life, advice and exhortation and, if necessary, also through the imposition or declaration of penalties, in accordance with the provisions of the law, which are always to be applied with canonical equity and having in mind the restoration of justice, the reform of the offender, and the repair of scandal. (c. 1311 §2)

Restoring justice is stated as the first aim when penalties are imposed. This is followed by the reform of the offender and the repair of scandal. In recent decades, protecting the Church institution from bad publicity has influenced the actions of many bishops and religious superiors. Offending priests have been protected and penal law has not been implemented. Pope Benedict XVI felt obliged to apologize for the failures of the Irish church and replaced some bishops who had been complicit in cover-ups. He said to the bishops,

> It cannot be denied that some of you and your predecessors failed, at times grievously, to apply the long-established norms of canon law to the crime of child abuse. Serious mistakes were made in responding to allegations. I recognize how difficult it was to grasp the extent and complexity of the problem, to obtain reliable information and to make the right decisions in the light of conflicting expert advice. Nevertheless, it must be admitted that grave errors of judgement were made and failures of leadership occurred. All this has seriously undermined your credibility and effectiveness.[7]

There is no doubt that bishops all over the world have failed to act effectively in dealing with sexual abuse crimes. This lack of action has led to these crimes being reserved to the Dicastery of the Doctrine of the Faith to ensure accountability for the way justice is administered in the Church.

In the past, offenders have been moved to new parishes or offices and sometimes bishops did not impose a penalty. Now if a bishop fails to impose a penalty, he can be held accountable by canon law. Therefore, even if the offender could be reformed by other means, an offender must be punished if it is necessary to restore justice and repair scandal (see c. 1344, no. 1).[8] For the most serious offenses there will be scandal in the canonical sense and the imposition of a penalty is required: "The offender, however, must be punished if there is no other way to provide for the restoration of justice and the repair of any scandal that may have been caused" (c. 1345). It must be remembered that some penalties, such as suspension and dismissal from the clerical state, can only be imposed by Church authorities using the procedures of canon law.

Penal law serves an important role in the Church protecting the common good by restoring justice, reforming the offender, and repairing scandal.[9] The sin of scandal is described by the *Catechism of the Catholic Church*:

> Scandal is an attitude or behavior which leads another to do evil. The person who gives scandal becomes his neighbor's tempter. He damages virtue and integrity; he may even draw his brother into spiritual death. Scandal is a grave offense if by deed or omission another is deliberately led into a grave offense.[10]

Therefore, scandal in canon law is different to sensational bad behavior as understood in society.

SACRAMENTORUM SANCTITATIS TUTELA

On April 30, 2001, following the revelation of the extent of the problem of clerical sexual abuse in North America and in many other countries, Pope John Paul II issued *motu proprio* the apostolic letter *Sacramentorum Sanctitatis Tutela*.[11] The pope appointed the Congregation for the Doctrine of the Faith to supervise investigations into credible complaints of sexual abuse of children and how they were handled. In Article 16 of the "Substantive Norms," it states,

> Whenever the Ordinary or Hierarch receives a report of a more grave delict, which has at least the semblance of truth, once the preliminary investigation has been completed, he is to communicate the matter to the Congregation for the Doctrine of the Faith.[12]

Sacramentorum Sanctitatis Tutela required accountability and transparency from bishops and religious superiors. The Congregation was authorized to order penal trials for accused priests. Now when a diocesan bishop receives a complaint of sexual abuse of a minor, he must notify the Congregation for the Doctrine of the Faith that he has received a complaint. The Congregation will then instruct the bishop about how it is to be handled.

However, until 2019, there were no sanctions for ordinaries failing to act, such as Bishop Geoffrey Jarratt of Lismore.[13] *Sacramentorum Sanctitatis Tutela* reiterated that a sin against the sixth commandment with a minor is a grave crime. Pope John Paul II recognized sexual abuse causes grave damage to the normal development of the victim and grave damage to the Church and its credibility. Furthermore, it betrays the trust that people have in priests. He said that this crime deserved the strictest punishments. This document raised the age a person was considered a minor to eighteen years and changed the time limit for laying a complaint until ten years after the minor had reached the age of eighteen years.

On July 15, 2010, the Congregation for the Doctrine of the Faith released "Revised Norms on Dealing with Clerical Sex Abuse of Minors and Other Grave Offenses"[14] approved *in forma specifica* by Pope Benedict XVI. Grave crimes now included sexual abuse of people with mental disabilities and child pornography in article 6:

> The delict against the Sixth Commandment of the Decalogue committed by a cleric with a minor below the age of 18 years; in this case, a person who habitually lacks the use of reason is to be considered equivalent to a minor. (see Art. 6 §1, no. 1)[15]

A person using child pornography is an essential cooperator in the abuse of a child, thereby committing a crime and incurring the same penalty.[16] The time limit for laying a complaint was raised to twenty years after the minor has reached the age of eighteen (i.e., age thirty-eight).

MANDATORY REPORTING

In 2019, Pope Francis, in his apostolic letter *Vos Estis Lux Mundi*, introduced mandatory reporting of sexual abuse by clerics and religious within the Church.[17] Article 3 stated,

> §1. Except as provided for by canons 1548 §2 CIC and 1229 §2 CCEO, whenever a cleric or a member of an Institute of Consecrated Life or of a Society of Apostolic Life has notice of, or well-founded motives to believe that, one of the facts referred to in article 1 has been committed, that person is obliged to report promptly the fact to the local Ordinary where the events are said to have occurred or to another Ordinary among those referred to in canons 134 CIC and 984 CCEO, except for what is established by §3 of the present article.
>
> §2. Any person can submit a report concerning the conduct referred to in article 1, using the methods referred to in the preceding article, or by any other appropriate means.
>
> §3. When the report concerns one of the persons indicated in article 6, it is to be addressed to the Authority identified based upon articles 8 and 9. The report can always be sent to the Holy See directly or through the Pontifical Representative.
>
> §4. The report shall include as many particulars as possible, such as indications of time and place of the facts, of the persons involved or informed, as well as any other circumstance that may be useful in

order to ensure an accurate assessment of the facts.

§5. Information can also be acquired ex officio.

Most importantly the person submitting the report was guaranteed protection as stated in Article 4:

- §1. Making a report pursuant to article 3 shall not constitute a violation of office confidentiality.
- §2. Except as provided for by canons 1390 CIC and 1452 and 1454 CCEO, prejudice, retaliation or discrimination as a consequence of having submitted a report is prohibited and may constitute the conduct referred to in article 1 §1, letter b.
- §3. An obligation to keep silent may not be imposed on any person with regard to the contents of his or her report.

Mandatory reporting has been considered in the changes in Book VI. All clergy and religious brothers and sisters must report sexual abuse by clergy to the Ordinary. They must report even suspicions that abuse is happening. This includes a cleric or religious abusing their authority by having sexual contact with anyone. This requirement is now reinforced in the revised penal law, which provides penalties for clergy and religious who fail to report an offense as required by canon law:

A person who neglects to report an offence, when required to do so by a canonical law, is to be punished according to the provision of canon 1336 §§ 2–4, with the addition of other penalties according to the gravity of the offence. (c. 1371 §6)

ANONYMOUS COMPLAINTS

Reports might be anonymous or only be suspicions that sexual abuse is taking place. The Congregation for the Doctrine of the Faith explained:

At times, a *notitia de delicto* can derive from an anonymous source, namely, from unidentified or unidentifiable persons. The anonymity of the source should not automatically lead to considering the report as false. Nonetheless, for easily understandable reasons, great caution should be exercised in considering this type of *notitia*, and anonymous reports certainly should not be encouraged.

Likewise, when a *notitia de delicto* comes from sources whose credibility might appear at first doubtful, it is not advisable to dismiss the matter *a priori*.[18]

Experience teaches that anonymous complaints often have a basis in fact, especially when the complaint specifies an exact time and place when the alleged offense occurred. Investigations of these anonymous complaints must also be reported to the Dicastery for the Doctrine of the Faith, including those that, according to the Ordinary, lack a semblance of truth.[19]

Concerning the requirement to report, Article 3 of *Vos Estis Lux Mundi* states,

Except as provided for by canons 1548 §2 CIC and 1229 §2 CCEO, whenever a cleric or a member of an Institute of Consecrated Life or of a Society of Apostolic Life has notice of, or well-founded motives to believe that, one of the facts referred to in article 1 has been committed, that person is obliged to report promptly the fact to the local Ordinary.[20]

While the obligation to uphold the seal of confession is not stated explicitly, the seal is included by mentioning canon 1548, which cites canon 1550 and the inability to report:

> Priests regarding all matters which they have come to know from sacramental confession even if the penitent seeks their disclosure; moreover, matters heard by anyone and in any way on the occasion of confession cannot be accepted even as an indication of the truth. (c. 1550 §2)

A priest cannot report sexual abuse that is confessed to him by a perpetrator in confession. However, the priest could help a victim to report or complain about the abuse when they come to him in confession seeking help. If a complaint involves a bishop or religious superior personally abusing someone or failing to act on abuse complaints, then the report would go to the metropolitan,[21] the papal nuncio, or directly to the Holy See. Persons making complaints are protected in canon law, and any discriminatory action against them is a crime in canon law. There is no requirement in *Vos Estis Lux Mundi* that the acts of the investigation be shared with the accused bishop or religious leader before notifying the Congregation for the Doctrine of the Faith about the complaint or accusation.

CIVIL REPORTING LAWS

Observing the civil reporting laws in countries was first addressed canonically on May 3, 2011, in a circular letter[22] sent by the Congregation for the Doctrine of the Faith to Episcopal Conferences:

> Sexual abuse of minors is not just a canonical delict but also a crime prosecuted by civil law. Although relations with civil authority will differ in various countries, nevertheless it is important to cooperate with such authority within their responsibilities. Specifically, without prejudice to the sacramental internal forum, the prescriptions of civil law regarding the reporting of such crimes to the designated authority should always be followed. This collaboration, moreover, not only concerns cases of abuse committed by clerics, but also those cases which involve religious or lay persons who function in ecclesiastical structures.[23]

The Vatican has concerns that a global requirement to report to civil authorities would in some places result in victims being harshly dealt with and the clergy being persecuted.[24] For example, in the Middle East, victims could be severely punished by secular authorities. Occasionally, there are also media reports of rape victims being jailed or punished, such as a rape victim being stoned in Somalia in 2008.[25] Although the revised penal law does not provide a penalty for not reporting to civil authorities, *Vos Estis Lux Mundi* still requires bishops, religious, and clergy to obey civil reporting laws except if the knowledge was under the seal of confession:

> Compliance with state laws. These norms apply without prejudice to the rights and obligations established in each place by state laws, particularly those concerning any reporting obligations to the competent civil authorities. (Article 19)

Bishops and religious superiors can be removed from office or punished for covering up sexual abuse and not cooperating with civil investigations. Not observing civil law requirements is also explicitly covered in *Vos Estis Lux Mundi*:

> These norms apply to reports regarding clerics or members of Institutes of Consecrated Life or Societies of Apostolic Life and concerning…conduct carried out by the subjects referred to in article 6, consisting of actions or omissions intended to interfere with or avoid civil investigations or canonical investigations, whether administrative or penal, against a cleric or a religious regarding the delicts referred to in letter a) of this paragraph.[26]

Although the Doctrine of the Faith's circular letter in 2011 made it clear the Church must obey civil laws regarding abuse and reporting,[27] Archbishop Scicluna claimed *Vos Estis Lux Mundi* was the first time that "compliance with state laws" had become universal law.

Archbishop Scicluna explained it was unacceptable for people to continue trying to protect the Church, because "the good of the church requires truth and transparency, which includes respecting civil law." He added that he hoped people felt "empowered to go to the police" to denounce a crime.[28] People have an obligation[29] to report already existing crimes, negligence, and inappropriate behavior to church authorities.[30] Furthermore, "if people have the right and the duty to denounce something illicit" in the case of abuse, "they also have the right to denounce if, after one year, nothing has been done."[31] The obligation to observe civil reporting laws is clear. However, the Vatican maintains that mandating reporting to civilian authorities would imperil Catholics in some countries where they already face oppression.[32] Also, privacy laws in some countries conflict with universal mandatory reporting. For example, the Italian privacy law allows a family to decide whether they will report a crime to the police and outsiders do not have the right to take the case to the police.[33]

Vos Estis Lux Mundi states that it is a crime for religious leaders failing to act on complaints of sexual abuse:

> The procedural norms referred to in this title concern the conduct referred to in article 1, carried out by:

Rationale for Penal Law and the Obligations for Church Leaders

a) Cardinals, Patriarchs, Bishops and Legates of the Roman Pontiff;

b) clerics who are, or who have been, the pastoral heads of a particular Church or of an entity assimilated to it, Latin or Oriental, including the Personal Ordinariates, for the acts committed *durante munere*;

c) clerics who are or who have been in the past leaders of a Personal Prelature, for the acts committed *durante munere*;

d) those who are, or who have been, supreme moderators of Institutes of Consecrated Life or of Societies of Apostolic Life of Pontifical right, as well as of monasteries *sui iuris*, with respect to the acts committed *durante munere*.[34]

The provisions set out in b), c), and d) above are a dramatic change in approach by the Church. It is now a crime for religious leaders to fail to observe civil law on reporting and failing to cooperate with or obstructing civil investigations.[35] Effectively the Church is canonizing aspects of civil law regarding what constitutes sexual abuse and grooming, as well as civil procedural laws on reporting.[36] This has significance in many countries because of laws regarding grooming, obtaining phone numbers of children, photographing children, and so on. The Congregation for the Doctrine of the Faith went further and encouraged reporting even when there is no legal obligation to do so:

Even in cases where there is no explicit legal obligation to do so, the ecclesiastical authorities should make a report to the competent civil authorities if this is considered necessary to protect the person involved or other minors from the danger of further criminal acts. (*Vademecum*, no. 17)

Church authorities must do everything possible to ensure that there are no more victims. Historic failures of not dealing with complaints are now also encompassed by this legislation. Furthermore, the provisions set out in b), c), and d) include previous leaders by referring to actions or omissions while they were in office. In the revised Book VI, this law specifically applies canon 1378 (c. 1389 in the 1983 Code), which had already made acts, or failures to act, crimes when they constituted an abuse of an office or position:

§1 A person who, apart from the cases already foreseen by the law, abuses ecclesiastical power, office, or function, is to be punished according to the gravity of the act or the omission, not excluding by deprivation of the power or office, without prejudice to the obligation of repairing the harm.

§2 A person who, through culpable negligence, unlawfully and with harm to another or scandal, performs or omits an act of ecclesiastical power or office or function, is to be punished according to the provision of can. 1336 §§ 2–4, without prejudice to the obligation of repairing the harm.[37]

These provisions remove any doubt about the application of this canon concerning sexual abuse cases.

COMPLAINTS ABOUT BISHOPS AND THEIR FAILURE TO ACT

There has been a lot of publicity about the cases of Cardinals Barbarin and McCarrick, among others. Following this publicity and the questions raised about dealing with accusations against bishops, Pope Francis devoted a significant part of *Vos Estis* to procedures for dealing with complaints against bishops and other religious leaders:

§1 The diocesan Bishop or Eparch, or one who even holds a temporary title and is responsible for a Particular Church, or other community of faithful that is its legal equivalent, according to canon 368 CIC or canon 313 CCEO, can be legitimately removed from this office if he has through negligence committed or through omission facilitated acts that have caused grave harm to others, either to physical persons or to the community as a whole. The harm may be physical, moral, spiritual or through the use of patrimony.

§2 The diocesan Bishop or Eparch can only be removed if he is objectively lacking in a very grave manner the diligence that his pastoral office demands of him, even without serious moral fault on his part.

§3 In the case of the abuse of minors and vulnerable adults it is enough that the lack of diligence be grave.

§4 The Major Superiors of Religious Institutes and Societies of Apostolic Life of Pontifical Right are equivalent to diocesan Bishops and Eparchs.[38]

If bishops commit sexual abuse or fail to act on complaints, the metropolitan bishop receives the complaint. The metropolitan must then first inform the Dicastery for the Doctrine of the Faith through the nuncio. The metropolitan is authorized to deal only with the investigative phase of the complaint against a bishop and must inform the Dicastery each month about the progress of the investigation. When the investigation has been completed, the metropolitan gives his opinion (*votum*) about the complaint. If the metropolitan bishop considers the allegation "manifestly unfounded," he is still obliged to inform the papal nuncio of the allegation to ensure accountability in dealing with complaints.[39] If the metropolitan is a friend of the accused, or if he has another conflict of interest in dealing with the case, *Vos Estis Lux Mundi* states,

> The Metropolitan is required to act impartially and free of conflicts of interest. If he considers himself to be in a conflict of interest or is unable to maintain the necessary impartiality to guarantee the integrity of the investigation, he is obliged to recuse himself and report the circumstance to the competent Dicastery.[40]

Under canon law, the judgment of a case involving a bishop is the prerogative of the pope or a tribunal appointed by him. Archbishop Scicluna has noted,

> Procedures have already been in place when it comes to accusations of abuse of minors by priests, so the new norms address what to do when the accused is a bishop, cardinal, patriarch or religious superior and how accusations against the leadership of abuse or misconduct must be reported. For example, "if a priest uses force with an adult, it's the bishop who takes that case," he said, but "when a person in leadership is guilty of misconduct, the jurisdiction pertains to the Holy See."[41]

GRAVE SINS AND CANONICAL CRIMES

A crime is "an external and morally imputable violation of a law to which a canonical sanction is attached."[42] In other words, to receive a penalty, a person must have gravely sinned. Not all grave sins are crimes, but grave sins that seriously affect the individual or the Church community are sometimes classified by the Church as crimes. Crimes are opposed to everything the Church stands for. To commit a mortal sin one needs full knowledge, full consent and "the act" must be a grave matter.[43] The Ten Commandments guide the faithful about the content of grave matter.[44] In canon law "delict" (*delictum*) and "crime" (*crimen*) are used interchangeably.[45] *Delict* is not a term used by civil jurisdictions, and so it cannot be confused with civil crimes.[46]

For delicts or crimes to be committed, there must be a significant amount of all three factors. An offending person must know how wrong an act is, what penalty is attached to it, and must consent to the action relatively freely.[47]

The Church teaches that people are usually free and are morally responsible for their actions. For example, sexual abusers are not determined by the fact that they have been sexually abused themselves or that they have suffered some trauma as a child. It may be a contributing factor as to why they have abused someone, but this does not remove their culpability. If people have serious problems, they need to get help to deal with them.

CANONICAL PUNISHMENT

An offender does not receive the penalty unless he has violated a law in the external forum and is imputable by reason of malice or negligence.[48] *Dolus* or malice is understood to mean a "deliberate violation of a penal law or precept."[49] The law presumes when an external violation of the law occurs that the perpetrator is culpable.[50] Velasio de Paolis explains that the essence of malice "is the positive will to act against the law, humanly and freely, whatever the reasons may be that lead to violating the law or precept, provided that freedom continues during the act."[51] Juan Arias explains that "negligence" is "the omission of due diligence including ignorance, and even inadvertence and error."[52] For clergy, knowledge of canon law is professional knowledge that the Church can reasonably expect them to know, just as accountants can be expected to know financial regulations. Consequently, after there is an external violation of the law, it is presumed that the violator is imputable.

Before he imposes penalties, the ordinary must exhaust all pastoral means available to him.[53] However, canon 1343 (2021) states that the ordinary must consider "the provision of canon 1326 §3, to determine the matter according to his own conscience and prudence, and in accordance with what the restoration of justice, the reform of the offender and the repair of scandal." Correction of an offender is most important for the Church that wants all members of the faithful to live according to the teaching and example of Jesus Christ. Jesus taught this approach to deal with wrongdoers in Matthew 18:15–17.

TYPES OF PENAL SANCTIONS

Canon 1312 describes two types of penal sanctions: medicinal and expiatory. *Medicinal penalties* aim to bring about the reform of the offender. Before a medicinal penalty, such as suspension, is imposed, the offender must receive a warning.[54] The most serious medicinal penalty that a person can receive is "excommunication." While all penalties have the general aim of reforming offenders and saving their souls,[55] *expiatory penalties*[56] specifically aim to re-establish Church order, repair scandal, remedy the damage done to the Church by the offender, as well as deter other offenders.

A warning is not required before expiatory penalties are imposed, and the penalty may be applied temporarily or permanently as in the case of dismissal from the clerical state.[57] Neither a diocesan bishop nor a bishops' conference can threaten dismissal from the clerical state for an action or a failure to act.[58] Canon 1336 was changed in 2021 to provide a wide range of expiatory penalties for perpetrators of crimes. Since they are expiatory penalties rather than medicinal penalties, the perpetrators do not have to be warned before they are imposed.[59] These expiatory penalties include the following:

1. An order to reside in a certain place or territory; and/or to pay a fine or a sum of money according to guidelines of the Episcopal Conference.
2. A prohibition against residing in a certain place; exercising offices, duties, ministries or functions; performing all or some acts of the power of order; performing all or some acts of the power of governance; using any right or privilege or using insignia or titles; holding active or passive voice in canonical elections; wearing ecclesiastical or religious dress.
3. A deprivation of: all or some offices,[60] duties, ministries or functions; the faculty of hearing confessions or of preaching; a delegated power of governance; some right or privilege or insignia or title; all ecclesiastical remuneration or part of it.

4. Dismissal from the clerical state.

This rather long and extensive list of potential penalties directs ordinaries to think about what is possible and make appropriate decisions in imposing penalties on an offender. Penances can also be applied to increase penalties. Repairing harm is a priority in canon law. Ordinaries cannot remit or revoke penalties "until in the prudent judgment of the Ordinary, the offender has repaired any harm caused."[61] The requirement of "repairing harm" for offenses is included in seven canons.[62]

PENALTIES ARE AUTOMATIC OR IMPOSED

Ferendae sententiae or imposed penalties "are applied by a sentence from a judge or a decree from a superior, following a penal procedure (judicial or administrative, depending on the case) to obtain juridical certainty that there was an offense and to ascertain the author's guilt."[63] Automatic or *latae sententiae*[64] penalties allow for the fact that some crimes cannot be effectively punished by *ferendae sententiae* penalties:[65] for example, absolving an accomplice in a sin against the sixth commandment. However, canon law prefers that penalties be imposed after a process and the legislator is encouraged not to threaten *latae sententiae* penalties.[66]

Furthermore, the law does have an educational purpose. In secular law, the laws on alcohol consumption and driving are a good illustration of this. The existence of *latae sententiae* penalties do warn and educate the faithful about the gravity of a particular crime and its consequences. However, when a priest receives an automatic or *latae sententiae* censure that has not been declared by an administrative or judicial process, the prohibition to celebrate the sacrament is suspended whenever a member of the faithful, such as a parishioner, of their own accord asks for a sacrament, a sacramental, or an act of governance.[67]

Automatic or *latae sententiae* penalties include the following excommunications reserved to the Apostolic See:

a. Throwing away the Holy Eucharist, or taking or keeping the Eucharist for a sacrilegious purpose (c. 1382);
b. Physically attacking the Roman Pontiff (c. 1370 §1);
c. Absolving one's accomplice in a sin against the sixth commandment (c. 1384);
d. Attempting to ordain a woman and the woman the person attempted to ordain (c. 1379 §3);[68]
e. Consecration of someone as a bishop without a pontifical mandate (c. 1382);[69]
f. Directly violating of the seal of confession (c. 1386 §1).

As well as these there are three automatic or *latae sententiae* excommunications that are not reserved to the Apostolic See by universal law:

a. Apostasy, heresy and schism (c. 1364 §§1 and 2);

b. Procuring an abortion (c. 1397);
c. Recording or publishing in the media what was said in a sacramental confession by the confessor or penitent, real or in pretense, by him- or herself or another person.[70]

STANDARD OF PROOF

The revised penal law emphasizes the standard of proof required when alleged crimes are investigated. Many jurisdictions use the standard of "probability" for abuse cases, whereas Church investigations are to be conducted according to the standard of proof of moral certainty:

> For the pronouncement of any sentence, the judge must have moral certitude about the matter to be decided by the sentence. (c. 1608 §1)

The changed penal law emphasizes following correct procedures, protecting the cleric's right of defense and making any decision in a penal process according to moral certainty, which is similar to the standard of "beyond reasonable doubt."[71] The revised canon 1342 now states,

> Whenever there are just reasons against the use of a judicial procedure, a penalty can be imposed or declared by means of an extra-judicial decree, observing canon 1720, especially in what concerns the right of defence and the moral certainty in the mind of the one issuing the decree, in accordance with the provision of canon 1608. (c. 1342 §1)

Canon 1321 has been changed so that "any person is considered innocent until the contrary is proved." This change reinforces the requirement that convictions reach the standard of proof of moral certainty for a conviction. However, once it has been proven that someone violated an external law by their action, canon 1321 states culpability is presumed.[72] However, when offenders are deceased, compensation based on probability is usually all that is possible.

WARNINGS BEFORE MEDICINAL PENALTIES ARE IMPOSED

The revised Book VI of the Code of Canon Law carefully develops the procedures necessary before a medicinal penalty is imposed on an offender. The following paragraphs 4 and 5 have been added to canon 1339:

> §4. If on one or more occasions warnings or corrections have been made to someone to no effect, or if it is not possible to expect them to have any effect, the Ordinary is to issue a penal precept in which he sets out exactly what is to be done or avoided.
>
> §5. If the gravity of the case so requires, and especially in a case where someone is in danger of relapsing into an offence, the Ordinary is also to subject the offender, over and above the penalties imposed according to the provision of the

law or declared by sentence or decree, to a measure of vigilance determined by means of a singular decree.

The offender must be given at least one warning, and then a detailed precept must be given in writing to the offender setting out exactly what is to be done or avoided. Canon 1339 §3 states, "The fact that there has been a warning, or a correction must always be proven, at least from some document to be kept in the secret archive of the curia."

CARE OF VICTIMS

Victims have a legal right to restitution and repair of the harm caused:[73] Canon 128 states, "Whoever unlawfully causes harm to another by a juridical act, or indeed by any other act which is malicious or culpable, is obliged to repair the damage done."

Harm could be caused by a bishop or religious superior failing to act. Resolution for the victim requires both financial compensation and doing what is needed to heal or overcome the enormous damage that sexual abuse causes to victims. Recent popes have been most concerned about caring for victims. Pope Benedict XVI, in an address to the American bishops in 2008 reminded them,

> Rightly, you attach priority to showing compassion and care to the victims. It is your God-given responsibility as pastors to bind up the wounds caused by every breach of trust, to foster healing, to promote reconciliation and to reach out with loving concern to those so seriously wronged.[74]

Article 5 on "Care for Persons" of the *motu proprio Vos Estis Lux Mundi* deals specifically with the care of victims:

§1. The ecclesiastical Authorities shall commit themselves to ensuring that those who state that they have been harmed, together with their families, are to be treated with dignity and respect, and, in particular, are to be:

   a) welcomed, listened to and supported, including through provision of specific services;
   b) offered spiritual assistance;
   c) offered medical assistance, including therapeutic and psychological assistance, as required by the specific case.

§2. The good name and the privacy of the persons involved, as well as the confidentiality of their personal data, shall be protected.[75]

Pope Francis emphasizes that the care of victims is much more than a financial payout, but also includes listening, support, spiritual and therapeutic assistance, and they must be informed of the outcome of investigations promptly. *Vos Estis Lux Mundi* recognizes the need for spiritual assistance for victims/survivors. It does not explicitly state that sexual abuse involves the spiritual abuse of victims, and there is scope for this reality to be recognized in revised editions of the *motu proprio*.

Protection of Whistleblowers

Significant measures in the new law provide that accusers and whistleblowers are to be protected from retribution.[76] *Vos Estis Lux Mundi* provides protection for them in article 4 on "Protection of the Person Submitting the Report":

§1. Making a report pursuant to article 3 shall not constitute a violation of office confidentiality.
§2. Except as provided for by canons 1390 CIC and 1452 and 1454 CCEO, prejudice, retaliation, or discrimination as a consequence of having submitted a report is prohibited and may constitute the conduct referred to in article 1 §1, letter b).
§3. An obligation to keep silent may not be imposed on any person with regard to the contents of his or her report.

The person making the report is protected from prejudice, retaliation, or discrimination as a result of submitting that report. This brings the Church legislation into line with most civil jurisdictions.

Obviously, persons making a report could easily be members of a religious institute or diocesan clergy. Paragraph 3 makes it clear that no obligation to silence or secrecy can be imposed on a person about their report or its contents. This eliminates nondisclosure agreements, as well as making it clear that the person making the report is free to report to any police or civil authority concerning the abuse.

PONTIFICAL SECRET

The pontifical secret is one of the most misunderstood concepts in Church legislation. The word *secret* has the connotation of "cover-up" and keeping incidents "hidden." In English, the word *secretary* comes from the Latin word *secretum*, meaning "secret." Secretaries handle the highly confidential information of their employers. On December 6, 2019, Pope Francis promulgated a rescript and an instruction on the confidentiality of cases of sexual abuse of minors.[77] This law now enables jurisprudence of the Dicastery for the Doctrine of the Faith to be published. Officials dealing with sexual abuse cases must still maintain confidentiality with what they have learned regarding the acts of the case:

1. The pontifical secret does not apply to accusations, trials and decisions involving the offences referred to in:

    a) Article 1 of the Motu proprio "*Vos estis lux mundi*" (7 May 2019);
    b) Article 6 of the *Normae de gravioribus delictis* reserved to the judgement of the Congregation for the Doctrine of the Faith, in accordance with the Motu proprio *Sacramentorum Sanctitatis Tutela* of Saint John Paul II (30 April 2001), and subsequent amendments.

2. Nor does the pontifical secret apply when such offenses were committed in conjunction with other offences.
3. In the cases referred to in No. 1, the information is to be treated in such a way as to ensure its security, integrity and confidentiality in accordance with the prescriptions of canons 471, 2° CIC and 244 §2, 2° CCEO, for the sake of protecting the good name, image and privacy of all persons involved.
4. Office confidentiality shall not prevent the fulfilment of the obligations laid down in all places by civil laws, including any reporting obligations, and the execution of enforceable requests of civil judicial authorities.
5. The person who files the report, the person who alleges to have been harmed and the witnesses shall not be bound by any obligation of silence with regard to matters involving the case.[78]

Removing the word *secret* from procedures for handling abuse cases eliminates confusion for victims and others reporting cases to civil authorities.

OTHER RESPONSIBILITIES OF LEADERS

The ordinary has a duty of vigilance, and the canon makes it clear that the ordinary has an obligation to investigate allegations and to impose penalties on offenders. Canon 1339 §5 also speaks of "vigilance." This means ordinaries have a grave obligation to have a detailed safety plan for offenders and to do everything reasonably possible to prevent the offender reoffending and creating more victims. Lack of supervision of offenders has been a grave omission demonstrated by many cases around the world. There must be real accountability and transparency in how offenders are held to account.

The failure of bishops and religious superiors to implement penal law has been a major cause of the sexual abuse crisis. There have been many improvements made in the penal law of the Church with the revisions to Book VI. The changed canons in this revised Book VI address weaknesses in the 1983 Code, made apparent by the sexual abuse crisis and the financial scandals that have occurred since 2000. After abuse problems by lay leaders in organizations such as the Sodalitium Christianae Vitae—a society of apostolic life, which was founded in 1971 in Peru and granted pontifical recognition in 1997—there are now more effective laws to deal with lay offenders. Other changes could still be made in canon law concerning the dismissal of religious brothers and sisters and making sexual abuse an irregularity.

Bishops and religious superiors must implement the penal law. As well, bishops need to make particular law for their dioceses to implement safeguarding law and define "grooming" in their cultural context. Law cannot solve every problem, and there needs to be a change in culture and mentality in the Church so that clericalism and a sense of entitlement are removed from the life of the Church. Pope Francis said in promulgating the changes in Book VI, "Charity thus demands that the Church's pastors resort to the penal system whenever it is required, keeping in mind the three aims that make it necessary in the ecclesial community: the restoration of the demands of justice, the correction of the guilty party and the repair of scandals."[79] These criteria have been the key elements for the revision.

2

OVERVIEW OF RECENT PENAL LEGISLATION

INCLUSION OF CHANGES IN LAW SINCE 1983

Since the 1983 Code came into effect, many significant changes were made in penal law via other documents such as the apostolic letter *Sacramentorum Sanctitatis Tutela*, issued *motu proprio* on April 30, 2001.[1] Most of these changes have been incorporated into the revised Book VI of the Code of Canon Law and include raising the age for sexual abuse from under age fourteen to under age eighteen years; a 1988 law imposing penalties for recording confessions; penalties for the attempted ordination of a woman;[2] penalties for bishops failing to report or take sufficient measures against perpetrators of sexual abuse; and for clerics using child pornography.

CANON ON SEXUAL ABUSE

There was a canon concerning the sexual abuse of minors in the 1983 Code, in the section under "Offences against Special Obligations," that makes it an offense against the obligation to observe celibacy. Victims and the Australian Royal Commission recommended that, in the revised penal law, there should be a canon specifically relating to sexual abuse.[3] Pope Francis has responded to this recommendation with a new canon 1398 in the section of the Code appropriately entitled "Offences against Human Life, Dignity and Liberty":

> §1. A cleric is to be punished with deprivation of office and with other just penalties, not excluding, where the case calls for it, dismissal from the clerical state, if he:
> 1° commits an offence against the sixth commandment of the Decalogue with a minor or with a person who habitually has an imperfect use of reason or with one to whom the law recognises equal protection;

2° grooms or induces a minor or a person who habitually has an imperfect use of reason or one to whom the law recognises equal protection to expose himself or herself or to take part in pornographic exhibitions, whether real or simulated;

3° immorally acquires, retains, exhibits or distributes, in whatever manner and by whatever technology, pornographic images of minors or of persons who habitually have an imperfect use of reason.

§2. A member of an institute of consecrated life or of a society of apostolic life, or any one of the faithful who enjoys a dignity or performs an office or function in the Church, who commits an offence mentioned in §1 or in can. 1395 §3 is to be punished according to the provision of can. 1336 §§2–4, with the addition of other penalties according to the gravity of the offence.[4]

Pope Francis had used the term *sexual acts* in *Vos Estis Lux Mundi* rather than "delicts against the Sixth Commandment," which is used in *Sacramentorum Sanctitatis Tutela*. This change makes a significant difference to what crimes are encompassed by the legislation. The term *sexual acts* is in accord with secular legislation and the terminology of the United Nations. However, "delicts against the Sixth Commandment" is the traditional term in canon law and encompasses the intention to commit a crime. The revised Book VI returns to the use of the traditional term of "offence against the sixth commandment." This term is also used by the *Catechism of the Catholic Church*, sections 2351–56,[5] where it is made clear that these offenses include adultery, rape, and the accessing of pornography.

The meaning of "sexual acts with a minor or vulnerable adult" is clarified by the Dicastery of the Doctrine of the Faith in its "*Vademecum*: On Certain Points of Procedure in Treating Cases of Sexual Abuse of Minors Committed by Clerics":[6]

1. The delict in question includes every external offense against the sixth commandment of the Decalogue committed by a cleric with a minor (cf. canon 1395 §2 CIC; art. 6 §1, 1° SST).

2. The typology of the delict is quite broad; it can include, for example, sexual relations (consensual or non-consensual), physical contact for sexual gratification, exhibitionism, masturbation, the production of pornography, inducement to prostitution, conversations and/or propositions of a sexual nature, which can also occur through various means of communication.[7]

"Sexual abuse" includes "forcing someone, by violence or threat or through abuse of authority, to perform or submit to sexual acts." By including "abuse of authority" in this description, the cases of people such as Cardinal McCarrick in the United States are encompassed. Jurisprudence of the Dicastery for the Doctrine of the Faith will interpret exactly what this "abuse of authority" means in its decisions on individual cases.

Any ordained cleric or religious has significant spiritual authority over laypeople. If a cleric had a ministerial relationship with a person with whom he has sex, the cleric would be guilty of sexual abuse because he is abusing his authority. This would mean a sexual relationship between a bishop and a member of the faithful from his diocese; a priest and a parishioner; a priest-lecturer and a student; and a seminary staff member with a seminarian would all be crimes of sexual abuse.

PENALTIES FOR ABUSE BY RELIGIOUS BROTHERS AND SISTERS

The 1983 Code recognized that sexual abuse of a minor under age fourteen years by a religious brother or sister was a grave offense for which there was an administrative process outlined in canon 695 for dismissal from the religious institute:

> §1. A member must be dismissed for the offences mentioned in cann. 1395, 1397, and 1398, unless, for the offences mentioned in can. 1395 §§2–3, the Superior judges that dismissal is not absolutely necessary, and that sufficient provision has been made in some other way for the amendment of the member, the restoration of justice and the reparation of scandal.
> §2. In these cases, the major Superior is to collect the proofs concerning the facts and the imputability of the offence. The accusation and the proofs are then to be presented to the member, who shall be given the opportunity for defence. All the acts, signed by the major Superior and the notary are to be forwarded, together with the written and signed replies of the member, to the Supreme Moderator.

Very few religious brothers and sisters, however, were ever dismissed from religious institutes.

Canon 1398 §2 states that the sexual abuse of minors by religious brothers and sisters is a crime:

> A member of an institute of consecrated life or of a society of apostolic life, or any one of the faithful who enjoys a dignity or performs an office or function in the Church, who commits an offence mentioned in §1 or in canon 1395 §3 is to be punished according to the provision of canon 1336 §§2–4, with the addition of other penalties according to the gravity of the offence.[8]

This change corrects an anomaly in the 1983 Code where although sexual abuse by religious brothers and sisters was a grave offense that incurred dismissal from the religious institute, it was not made clear that it was also a crime in canon law.

GROOMING

A significant addition of canon 1398 §1, no. 2 to the penal law making grooming a crime:

Canon 1398 §1. A cleric is to be punished with deprivation of office and with other just penalties, not excluding, where the case calls for it, dismissal from the clerical state, if he:...
2° grooms or induces a minor or a person who habitually has an imperfect use of reason or one to whom the law recognises equal protection to expose himself or herself pornographically or to take part in pornographic exhibitions, whether real or simulated.

Grooming in the canon is stated in relation to pornography. However, grooming is not defined and what exactly it encompasses will be shown by the jurisprudence of the Dicastery for the Doctrine of the Faith or another canonical document.

In New Zealand and many other countries, one cannot photograph children or obtain children's phone numbers without parental consent. In our society, these actions are considered grooming because of how pedophiles operate using pictures of children's faces. It will be significant how these actions are interpreted at the Dicastery for the Doctrine of the Faith. People normally only recognize how an offender was grooming in hindsight, but bishops now have the capacity to take preventive measures, in particular laws to penalize clergy and lay church officials who carry out clearly recognized grooming practices, such as having people under age eighteen stay alone with them or spending significant time alone with them. Experience has demonstrated that guidelines on behavior are insufficient. There is a need for diocesan bishops to legislate safeguarding laws that have consequences if they are not observed.

VULNERABLE PEOPLE

In Article 1 of *Vos Estis Lux Mundi*, Pope Francis legislated that abuse of vulnerable people was a crime:

§1. These norms apply to reports regarding clerics or members of Institutes of Consecrated Life or Societies of Apostolic Life and concerning:
a) delicts against the sixth commandment of the Decalogue consisting of:
i. forcing someone, by violence or threat or through abuse of authority, to perform or submit to sexual acts;
ii. performing sexual acts with a minor or a vulnerable person.[9]

There is criticism that there is no mention of "vulnerable" in the revised penal law. Bishop Arrieta, the secretary for the revision process, said at the press conference after the promulgation of the changed penal law, that vulnerable people were encompassed by the phrase "one to whom the law recognizes equal protection" in canon 1398.[10] Bishop Arrieta also added that "vulnerable" is not accepted in many countries as a legal category of persons who should receive special protection.[11]

§1. A cleric is to be punished with deprivation of office and with other just penalties, not excluding, where the case calls for it, dismissal from the clerical state, if he:
1° commits an offence against the sixth commandment of the Decalogue with a minor or with a person who habitually has an imperfect use of reason or with one to whom the law recognises equal protection.[12]

Cardinal Gracias, who was involved in the drafting of the 2021 revisions in Book VI, acknowledges that the law will have to be improved over time:

> We have something new called vulnerable adults. This is added to the minors. We will need to define it. It refers to one who is mentally not strong. Would a professional superiority mean a vulnerable adult? How far can you go without exaggerating? We will have to study and analyse this law and improve it surely.[13]

A vulnerable person was defined in *Vos Estis Lux Mundi* as "any person in a state of infirmity, physical or mental deficiency, or deprivation of personal liberty which, in fact, even occasionally, limits their ability to understand or to want or otherwise resist the offence."[14]

Cases of vulnerable people are not within the competence of the Dicastery for the Doctrine of the Faith, as the *Vademecum* states:

> The revision of the Motu Proprio SST, promulgated on 21 May 2010, states that a person who habitually has the imperfect use of reason is to be considered equivalent to a minor (cf. art. 6 §1, 1° SST). With regard to the use of the term "vulnerable adult," elsewhere described as "any person in a state of infirmity, physical or mental deficiency, or deprivation of personal liberty which, in fact, even occasionally limits their ability to understand or to want or otherwise resist the offence" (cf. art. 1 §2, b VELM), it should be noted that this definition includes other situations than those pertaining to the competence of the CDF, which remains limited to minors under eighteen years of age and to those who "habitually have an imperfect use of reason." Other situations outside of these cases are handled by the competent Dicasteries (cf. art. 7 §1 VELM).[15]

This would mean that cases of allegations of clerics abusing vulnerable people would be handled either by the Dicastery for Evangelization of Peoples for mission countries or the Dicastery for Clergy. Allegations against religious brothers and sisters would be handled by the Dicastery for Institutes of Consecrated Life and Societies of Apostolic Life.

ABUSE OF AUTHORITY

The revised penal law reiterates that abuse of authority as a cleric is a crime. It recognizes that many so-called consenting adult relationships are not ones with equal consent and often vulnerable people are manipulated by people with positions of power and authority. In the revised Book VI, canon 1389 has become canon 1378:

§1. A person who, apart from the cases already foreseen by the law, abuses ecclesiastical power, office, or function, is to be punished according to the gravity of the act or the omission, not excluding by deprivation of the power or office, without prejudice to the obligation of repairing the harm.

§2. A person who, through culpable negligence, unlawfully and with harm to another or scandal, performs or omits an act of ecclesiastical power or office or function, is to be punished according to the provision of canon 1336 §§2–4, without prejudice to the obligation of repairing the harm.[16]

Abuse of authority includes culpable negligence and failing to act. The revised canon points directly to penalties that may be imposed on an offender and makes explicit mention of their obligation to repair the harm they have caused.[17] A penalty is not to be remitted until there has been reparation of harm:

> Remission must not be granted until, in the prudent judgement of the Ordinary, the offender has repaired any harm caused. The offender may be urged to make such reparation or restitution by one of the penalties mentioned in can. 1336 §§2–4; the same applies also when the offender is granted remission of a censure under can. 1358 §1. (c. 1361 §4)

This provision gives Church authorities real power to demand restitution or reparation for offenses causing harm to others. The ordinary must not remit a penalty before he prudently judges the offender has repaired any harm caused.

RIGHTS AND PROCEDURES

In the 1983 Code, canon 1395 did not mention abuse of authority. The revised canon 1395 has been changed significantly. Two new paragraphs have been added to canon 1395 and §3 explicitly addresses abuse of authority by clerics:

§1. A cleric living in concubinage, other than in the case mentioned in can. 1394, and a cleric who continues in some other external sin against the sixth commandment of the Decalogue which causes scandal, is to be punished with suspension. To this, other penalties can progressively be added if after a warning he persists in the offense, until eventually he can be dismissed from the clerical state.

§2. A cleric who has offended in other ways against the sixth commandment of the Decalogue, if the offense was committed in public, is to be punished with just penalties, not excluding dismissal from the clerical state if the case so warrants.

§3. A cleric who by force, threats or abuse of his authority commits an offense against the sixth commandment of the Decalogue or forces someone to perform or submit to sexual acts is to be punished with the same penalty as in §2.

Many so-called consenting adult relationships are not equal and there is a power imbalance. Canon 1395 §3 improves the penal law significantly and will make it easier to deal with clerics abusing their authority with vulnerable adults. There are many complaints from adult victims who believe that the priest abuser used his position and the authority of his office to take advantage of their vulnerability.

ABANDONING MINISTRY

Abandonment of one's ministry voluntarily and illegitimately is an additional crime included in canon 1392 of the revised Book VI:

> A cleric who voluntarily and unlawfully abandons the sacred ministry, for six months continuously, with the intention of withdrawing himself from the competent Church authority, is to be punished, according to the gravity of the offence, with suspension or additionally with the penalties established in can. 1336 §§2–4, and in the more serious cases may be dismissed from the clerical state.[18]

This crime is related to other provisions for clergy and religious abandoning ministry that had been made in earlier documents.[19]

FINANCIAL CRIMES

The addition of the new canon 1376 concerns financial crimes:

> §1. The following are to be punished with the penalties mentioned in canon 1336 §§2–4, without prejudice to the obligation of repairing the harm:
>
> 1° a person who steals ecclesiastical goods or prevents their proceeds from being received;
> 2° a person who without the prescribed consultation, consent, or permission, or without another requirement imposed by law for validity or for lawfulness, alienates ecclesiastical goods or carries out an act of administration over them.
>
> §2. The following are to be punished, not excluding by deprivation of office, without prejudice to the obligation of repairing the harm:
>
> 1° a person who through grave personal culpability commits the offense mentioned in § 1, n. 2;
> 2° a person who is found to have been otherwise gravely negligent in administering ecclesiastical goods.

This canon encompasses stealing, parish priests and bishops invalidly alienating Church property, or unlawfully carrying out extraordinary administration. Administrators, including lay church employees who are gravely negligent, can lose their office or position.

As can be seen in canon 1393, the law regarding financial crimes also applies to religious:

> A cleric or religious who, apart from the cases already foreseen by the law, commits an offence in a financial matter, or gravely violates the stipulations contained in canon 285 §4, is to be punished with the penalties mentioned

in canon 1336 §§2–4, without prejudice to the obligation of repairing the harm. (Canon 1393 §2)

PORNOGRAPHY

Pope Benedict XVI approved *in forma specifica* the "Revised Norms on Dealing with Clerical Sex Abuse of Minors and Other Grave Offenses"[20] published on July 15, 2010, and made the use of child pornography a crime:

> The acquisition, possession or distribution by a cleric of pornographic images of minors under the age of 14 for purposes of sexual gratification, whatever means or using whatever technology.[21]

While clergy sexting those under age eighteen or using child pornography has been a canonical crime for many years, there has been no canonical definition or description of pornography. Limiting the crime to abusing those under age fourteen years was far too restricted. People buying or using pornography are financing its manufacture and are cooperating[22] in the commission of the crime.

Pope Francis, in *Vos Estis Lux Mundi*, stated that child pornography means "any representation of a minor, regardless of the means used, involved in explicit sexual activities, whether real or simulated, and any representation of sexual organs of minors for primarily sexual purposes."[23]

In 2019, Pope Francis amended Article 6 §1, 2° of *SST*, which was replaced in its entirety by the following text, changing the age for pornography to include people under eighteen years:

> The acquisition, possession or distribution by a cleric of pornographic images of minors under the age of eighteen, for purposes of sexual gratification, by whatever means or using whatever technology.[24]

These provisions concerning pornography are included in the revised canon 1398:

> A cleric is to be punished with deprivation of office and with other just penalties, not excluding, where the case calls for it, dismissal from the clerical state, if he: 3° immorally acquires, retains, exhibits or distributes, in whatever manner and by whatever technology, pornographic images of minors or of persons who habitually have an imperfect use of reason.[25]

The wording of the canon ensures that it includes any use of pornography on social media.

In jurisprudence, a clear distinction is made between accidentally seeing pornography on the Internet and downloading or copying it. Accidentally seeing pornography is not a crime. However, if it is downloaded or copied in any way, a crime has been committed in canon law.

The Dicastery for the Doctrine of the Faith has pointed out in paragraphs 6 and 7 of its *Vademecum* that the law is not retroactive. Investigations of alleged offenses must be careful to establish when the action took place to establish if a delict or crime was committed:

6. SST has also introduced (cf. art. 6 §1, 2° SST) three new delicts involving minors, that is, the acquisition, possession (even temporary) or distribution by a cleric of pornographic images of minors under the age of fourteen (as of January 1, 2020, under the age of eighteen) for purposes of sexual gratification by whatever means or using whatever technology. From June 1 to December 31, 2019, the acquisition, possession, or distribution of pornographic material involving minors between fourteen and eighteen years of age by clerics or by members of Institutes of Consecrated Life or Societies of Apostolic Life are delicts for which other Dicasteries are competent (cf. arts. 1 and 7 VELM). From January 1, 2020, the CDF is competent for these delicts if committed by clerics.
7. It should be noted that these three delicts can be addressed canonically only after the date that SST took effect, namely, May 21, 2010. The production of pornography involving minors, on the other hand, falls under the typology of delict listed in nos. 1–4 of the present *Vademecum*, and therefore is also to be dealt with if it occurred prior to that date.

ABORTION

Procuring an abortion was a crime in the 1983 Code in canon 1398, which is now renumbered as canon 1397 §2.[26] It is not a crime reserved to the apostolic see and any priest is able to grant absolution for it.[27]

There has been an addition to canon 1388 in the revised penal law:

> A person who comes forward for sacred orders bound by some censure or irregularity which he voluntarily conceals is ipso facto suspended from the order received, apart from what is established in canon 1044, §2, no. 1. (c. 1388 §2)

This is a significant addition to penal law in some countries where the crime of abortion is very common. When a seminarian conceals an irregularity that he has incurred, the revised penal law provides for his automatic suspension if he is ordained.

STATEMENTS OPPOSING CHURCH TEACHING ON ABORTION

There is often publicity in the media about politicians who vote for liberalized abortion laws and at the same time claim they are sincere Catholics who are personally opposed to abortion. Pro-choice politicians are encompassed by canons 915[28] and 1369.[29] In 2004, then Cardinal Ratzinger advised that a pastor should meet with a Catholic politician voting for permissive abortion laws, instruct him about the Church's teaching, and inform him he is not to present himself for communion:

> When "these precautionary measures have not had their effect or in which they were not possible," and the person in question, with obstinate persistence,

still presents himself to receive the Holy Eucharist, "the minister of Holy Communion must refuse to distribute it" (cf. Pontifical Council for Legislative Texts Declaration "Holy Communion and Divorced, Civilly Remarried Catholics" [2000], nos. 3–4). This decision, properly speaking, is not a sanction or a penalty. Nor is the minister of Holy Communion passing judgement on the person's subjective guilt, but rather is reacting to the person's public unworthiness to receive Holy Communion due to an objective situation of sin.[30]

American bishops have sometimes stated that these politicians cannot receive communion.[31]

On May 7, 2021, Cardinal Ladaria, the prefect of the Congregation for the Doctrine of the Faith, wrote to Archbishop Gomez, the president of the Unites States Conference of Catholic Bishops about this matter.[32] Cardinal Ladaria advised the bishops should first dialogue among themselves to formulate a national policy on support for pro-choice legislation, and then there should be dialogue "between bishops and Catholic pro-choice politicians within their jurisdictions."[33]

Cardinal Ladaria stated that the Conference would have to discern "the best way forward for the Church in the United States to witness to the grave moral responsibility of Catholic public officials to protect human life at all stages."[34] If the bishops formulate a national policy, it should express a true consensus and "would best be framed within the broad context of worthiness for the reception of Holy Communion on the part of all the faithful, rather than only one category of Catholics."[35]

LAYPEOPLE AND LAY ORGANIZATIONS

Penal law is directed primarily at clerics and religious. There are still some serious issues regarding complaints against leaders of lay associations of the faithful such as the *Sodalitium Christianae Vitae* founded by Figari.

The Australian Royal Commission into Institutional Responses to Child Sexual Abuse[36] demonstrated that within the Catholic Church perpetrators of sexual abuse were 37 percent nonordained religious (32 percent were religious brothers and 5 percent were religious sisters); 30 percent were priests; and 29 percent were laypeople. Since a significant proportion of offenders are laypeople, there was a need for serious penalties for lay faithful who sexually abuse minors.

Young people would be exempted from the penalty for a variety of reasons outlined in canon 1323.[37] The penalty must be diminished if any of the circumstances exist as outlined by canon 1324.[38] In 2021, with the revised Book VI, lay church employees such as youth workers and institutional leaders who commit crimes of sexual abuse can be punished:

> A member of an institute of consecrated life or of a society of apostolic life, or any one of the faithful who enjoys a dignity or performs an office or function in the Church, who commits an offence

mentioned in §1 or in can. 1395 §3 is to be punished according to the provision of can. 1336 §§2–4, with the addition of other penalties according to the gravity of the offence. (c. 1398 §2)

Penalties could include loss of office, suspension, as well as requirements to repair harm.

CONCLUSION

The changes in penal law through the revised Book VI, *Sacramentorum Sanctitatis Tutela*, and the *motu proprio Vos Estis Lux Mundi* are gigantic improvements in penal law. There are more preventive and safeguarding measures in the law. Pope Francis has added a new clause in canon 1350 preventing a person found guilty being employed by the Church in future:

> If a person is truly in need because he has been dismissed from the clerical state, the Ordinary is to provide in the best way possible, but not by the conferral of an office, ministry or function. (c. 1350 §2)

There have been many scandals because former priests and religious have been employed in misguided charity and they have then abused others.

Canon 1339 of the revised penal law makes procedural requirements for the imposition of medicinal penalties and the use of precepts:

§1. When someone is in a proximate occasion of committing an offence or when, after an investigation, there is a serious suspicion that an offence has been committed, the Ordinary either personally or through another can give that person warning.

§2. In the case of behaviour which gives rise to scandal or serious disturbance of public order, the Ordinary can also correct the person, in a way appropriate to the particular conditions of the person and of what has been done.

§3. The fact that there has been a warning or a correction must always be proven, at least from some document to be kept in the secret archive of the curia.

§4. If on one or more occasions warnings or corrections have been made to someone to no effect, or if it is not possible to expect them to have any effect, the Ordinary is to issue a penal precept in which he sets out exactly what is to be done or avoided.

§5. If the gravity of the case so requires, and especially in a case where someone is in danger of relapsing into an offence, the Ordinary is also to subject the offender, over and above the penalties imposed according to the provision of the law or declared by sentence or decree, to a measure of vigilance determined by means of a singular decree.

The additional provisions in this revised canon 1339 emphasize the importance of ordinaries issuing written precepts to clerics continuing to offend against the sixth commandment. The recalcitrant cleric or religious[39] must understand clearly what behavior is to be avoided or what is to be done.

3

REMOVAL OF THE FACULTIES OF A PRIEST

A faculty is an authorization by an ecclesiastical authority, usually a bishop, enabling a priest to participate in the ecclesiastical power of teaching, sanctifying, or governing for the good of the faithful. Consequently, the priest has "the ability to act in a licit or juridically efficacious manner."[1] The grant of faculties is necessary because the priest would not be able to act without it, since some faculties are granted by law or are attached to certain offices such as the office of parish priest or chaplain.

IMPORTANCE OF FACULTIES TO MINISTER

Faculties are essential for many ecclesiastical celebrations that the faithful associate with the ministry of a priest. For example, a priest requires faculties to officiate at a wedding, to confirm and to celebrate the sacrament of penance validly in normal circumstances. However, when the recipient is in danger of death, faculties come from the law itself, enabling a priest lacking faculties to celebrate a sacrament.[2]

Usually, upon ordination priests in a diocese are granted habitual faculties for all cases that continue throughout their lives as priests.[3] These faculties include real power such as the delegated power to grant marriage dispensations for disparity of cult marriages. Other faculties involve authorization to act. For example, to confirm members of the faithful or to assist at weddings.[4]

The granting of faculties is a serious matter and bishops should not automatically grant them to priests.[5] Before a priest can minister in the diocese or functions publicly on behalf of the Church it is required that his suitability be established. Rodger Austin points out that before a priest is granted faculties to hear confessions, the suitability of the priest must be established:

By reason of his ordination to the priesthood, a priest is empowered to absolve sinners of their sins, but he requires authorisation from the bishop, that is being given the faculty, to act as the minister of the sacrament. Prior to granting a priest this faculty the bishop must determine that he is suitable to exercise this ministry of reconciliation.[6]

The grant of faculties should be in writing.[7] A priest without faculties is a little like a nonregistered professional such as a teacher who has the requisite degree but is not a member of the professional association.

DISTINCTION BETWEEN DIOCESAN AND RELIGIOUS PRIESTS RECEIVING OR LOSING FACULTIES

Distinctions must be made concerning receiving or losing faculties, between a diocesan priest incardinated in a diocese; a diocesan priest from another diocese working in the diocese; and a religious priest working in the diocese.

There is no obligation for a diocesan bishop to grant faculties to a priest from another diocese or a religious institute who has moved to the diocese. Nor is the diocesan bishop required to grant him incardination.

When someone is ordained, the law states that he is required to be suitable and useful for ministry.[8] If there is any doubt about his suitability or usefulness, then the person should not have been ordained.[9] Diocesan priests incardinated in a diocese should have faculties from their diocesan bishop. Although they do not have a specific right to ministry, there is an expectation in the law because they have been ordained, they will be able to minister.[10]

REASONS FOR WITHDRAWING FACULTIES OF PRIESTS

Before a religious priest or a priest from another diocese receives faculties in a diocese, there should have been an agreement between the priest, his religious institute/diocese, and the diocesan bishop to enable him to work in the diocese. The diocesan bishop must observe the terms of the agreement and for a just reason, the bishop could withdraw the faculties of the priest. The decree must give the reason(s) at least in summary form.[11] Depending on the wording of the agreement, a just reason could be the priest's services are no longer required in his diocese. If there is no agreement, then any reasonable motive would qualify as a just reason.

Removal of the faculties of an incardinated priest, however, would have to be for a grave reason.[12] An example would be a credible complaint that the priest was too inquisitive asking questions during a confession. Prior to any removal of faculties, there would have to be a preliminary investigation establishing the facts.[13] Merely saying the priest's services are no longer required is insufficient. If a bishop wishes to remove the faculties from a priest incardinated in his diocese, following a complaint against him, it would not merely be a decision after an administrative process. An example of a lawful administrative decision to withdraw faculties would be because a priest was developing dementia. The loss of faculties would be through no fault of the priest.

PROHIBITION TO EXERCISE PUBLIC MINISTRY OR ADMINISTRATIVE LEAVE

Administrative leave is not a canonical term and is not found in the 1983 Code. The term has been borrowed from secular society, where people such as police officers or government officials are put on leave without pay while being investigated for possible misconduct. It has come into common usage in the Church because of the sexual abuse crisis and is equivalent to a priest losing his faculties and his capacity to function publicly. It has been used "to mean that the cleric has been moved from his place of residence, and prohibited from the exercise of public ministry."[14] Following a preliminary investigation, canon 1722 states,

> The Ordinary can, after consulting the Promotor of Justice and summoning the accused person to appear, prohibit the accused from the exercise of the sacred ministry or of some ecclesiastical office and position, or impose or forbid residence in a certain place or territory, or even prohibit public participation in the blessed Eucharist.

Prohibition of "the exercise of sacred ministry" is not a penalty. A reason for these actions could be the prevention of scandal. However, these restrictions must be revoked if the reason for them no longer exists.

The Congregation for the Doctrine of the Faith in its "*Vademecum*: On Certain Points of Procedure in Treating Cases of Sexual Abuse of Minors Committed by Clerics" reinforces the use of the phrase "prohibit the accused from the exercise of the sacred ministry" rather than *administrative leave* or removal of faculties:

> It has been noted that the older terminology of *suspensio a divinis* is still frequently being used to refer to the prohibition of the exercise of ministry imposed on a cleric as a precautionary measure. It is best to avoid this term, and that of *suspensio ad cautelam*, since in the current legislation suspension is a penalty, and cannot yet be imposed at this stage. The provision would more properly be called, for example, *prohibition* from the exercise of the ministry.[15]

The *Essential Norms for Diocesan/ Eparchial Policies Dealing with Allegations of Sexual Abuse of Minors by Priests or Deacons* for the United States constitutes particular law for the dioceses, eparchies, clerical religious institutes, and societies of apostolic life of the United States. These norms were approved by the Apostolic See and state,

When an allegation of sexual abuse of a minor by a priest or deacon is received, a preliminary investigation in accordance with canon law will be initiated and conducted promptly and objectively (CIC, c. 1717; CCEO, c. 1468). During the investigation the accused enjoys the presumption of innocence, and all appropriate steps shall be taken to protect his reputation. The accused will be encouraged to retain the assistance of civil and canonical counsel and will be promptly notified of the results of the investigation. When there is sufficient evidence that sexual abuse of a minor has occurred, the Congregation of the Doctrine of the Faith shall be notified. The bishop/eparch shall then apply the precautionary measures mentioned in CIC, canon 1722, or CCEO, canon 1473—i.e., withdraw the accused from exercising the sacred ministry or any ecclesiastical office or function, impose or prohibit residence in a given place or territory, and prohibit public participation in the Most Holy Eucharist pending the outcome of the process.[16]

Canon 1722 specifically mentions "public participation in the blessed Eucharist." This would include concelebration. According to canons 904 and 906, a priest on "administrative leave" can celebrate the Eucharist "privately." Much would depend on what the ordinary (diocesan bishop, vicar general, or religious provincial) specified with his decree placing the priest on administrative leave. For example, the ordinary might specifically allow the celebration of the Eucharist with a religious community or with family members. The circumstances of being accused of sexual misconduct could constitute a "good and reasonable cause" requiring that the priest celebrate Mass alone.

Usually, key provisions of a "prohibition from the exercise of sacred ministry" are that the accused priest is not permitted to celebrate the Eucharist publicly or to administer the sacraments. Also, he is not to wear clerical dress or to present himself publicly as a priest. The imposition of administrative leave is not a penalty, and recourse does not have a suspensive effect.[17]

PROCESS FOR REMOVAL OF FACULTIES

Removal of faculties is an expiatory penalty outlined in canon 1336:

§1. Expiatory penalties can affect the offender either forever or for a determined or an indeterminate period. Apart from others that the law may perhaps establish, they are those enumerated in §§2–5...

§3. A prohibition:...
3° against performing all or some acts of the power of order...

§4. A deprivation:
1° of all or some offices, duties, ministries or functions, or only of certain functions attaching to offices or duties;
2° of the faculty of hearing confessions or of preaching.

Canon 1336 articulates that expiatory penalties[18] can affect an offender perpetually, for a determined period of time, or for an indeterminate period of time.

Permanent withdrawal of faculties or placing a priest on administrative leave[19] requires a process.[20] Any procedures used by a bishop must be in accord with canon law.[21] Giuseppe Di Mattia affirms that "the procedural provisions established to inflict penalties juridically and administratively must be observed in applying the penalties that deprive of the good indicated."[22]

First, there must be a preliminary investigation[23] to establish "the facts, circumstances, and imputability"[24] of the allegations. The Congregation for the Clergy found, in a Canadian case, that a bishop should carry out a preliminary investigation and follow the procedures in canons 1717–20 before withdrawing faculties or imposing any penalty.[25] Then the facts of the case and the imputability of the cleric will have been properly documented.[26] This documentation is important whether there is a judicial trial or an administrative process.

Following the preliminary investigation, the diocesan bishop must "ascertain that fraternal correction or rebuke or other means of pastoral solicitude cannot sufficiently repair the scandal, restore justice, reform the offender."[27]

If the diocesan bishop decides that these means cannot achieve all these ends, then there are two penal procedures that can be used:

(a) administrative
(b) judicial (see cc. 1720–31).

Theoretically, both processes are equally valid. In the first case, the bishop or superior acts hierarchically and issues a decree as provided for by canon 1720.[28] This might be when a priest is arrested by the police and charged with child sex crimes in a secular court.

In the judicial process, the judge(s) in a church court decrees the sentence after the Ordinary hands the case over to the tribunal to conduct a judicial trial.[29] In every case, if truth is in doubt, then in the interests of justice there should be a canonical trial. The diocesan bishop or ordinary can remove the faculties or prohibit the accused priest from the exercise of public ministry "to prevent scandals, to protect the freedom of witnesses, and to guard the course of justice."[30]

The criteria for whether a bishop proceeds administratively or judicially are contained in canon 1342:

§1. Whenever there are just reasons against the use of a judicial procedure, a penalty can be imposed or declared by means of an extrajudicial decree, observing canon 1720, especially in what concerns the right of defence and the moral certainty in the mind of the one issuing the decree, in accordance with the provision of can. 1608. Penal remedies and penances may in any case whatever be applied by a decree.

§2. Perpetual penalties cannot be imposed or declared by means of a decree; nor can penalties that the law or precept establishing them forbids to be applied by decree.

§3. What the law or decree says of a judge in regard to the imposition or declaration of a penalty in a trial is to be applied also to a superior who imposes or declares a penalty by an extrajudicial decree, unless it is otherwise clear, or unless there is question of provisions which concern only procedural matters.

Canon 1342 has a bias toward a judicial process. This is related to the right of the Christian faithful in canon 221 to "legitimately vindicate and defend the rights which they possess in the Church in the competent ecclesiastical forum according to the norm of law."[31]

The judicial process is always the preferred method for imposing penalties on an offender,[32] but canon 1342 §3 allows for extrajudicial processes. Bishops must understand that perpetual penalties cannot be imposed or declared by an administrative decree.[33] Penalties may prohibit the exercise of Holy Orders or some of its acts, but they cannot deprive a priest of the power of the sacrament of Holy Orders.[34]

CAPACITY OF PRIESTS TO FUNCTION WITHOUT FACULTIES

A priest without faculties can always celebrate the Eucharist privately because celebration of the Eucharist and priesthood are so essentially related.[35] Preaching is also a very important part of the ministry of a priest. Priests have faculties to preach from the law itself, but these faculties of a priest to preach can be restricted or removed by the competent authority for any just reason.[36]

Furthermore, a priest without faculties, lawfully and validly absolves penitents in danger of death, even if an approved priest is present.[37] Therefore, a priest on administrative leave could absolve validly and lawfully anyone in danger of death. However, a priest on administrative leave, without faculties could not validly absolve penitents in ordinary circumstances outside the danger of death. This is because canon 966 §1 requires, for validity, that a priest needs the faculty to absolve.[38]

When the ordinary removes faculties, he should do so in writing giving a reason(s) for his decree.[39] For example, the diocesan bishop may have given the priest a precept, requiring him to observe the restrictions on his ministry under threat of a penalty for failure to observe the restrictions. As a parallel, when a priest is guilty of a crime of sexual abuse, but is not dismissed from the clerical state, Norm 8, of the American Essential Norms states,

> If the penalty of dismissal from the clerical state has not been applied (e.g., for reasons of advanced age or infirmity), the offender ought to lead a life of prayer and penance. He will not be permitted to celebrate Mass publicly or to administer the sacraments. He is to be instructed not to wear clerical garb, or to present himself publicly as a priest.[40]

A priest can have recourse against a bishop who has removed his faculties. The priest remains unable to function publicly pending the outcome of the recourse *in devolutivo*.

A clerical religious who has been dismissed from his religious institute "may not exercise sacred orders until he finds a bishop who will, after a suitable probation, receive him into his diocese in accordance with canon 693, or who will at least allow him to exercise his sacred orders."[41] Such a religious priest without faculties should not celebrate the Eucharist, but if he does so, the celebration of the Eucharist would be valid.

Analysis of a Canadian Case of Removal of Faculties by the Signatura

On August 19, 2003, without a preliminary investigation, a bishop revoked a priest's faculties when he wrote in a letter,

> As of today, your faculties are herewith revoked. You can no longer celebrate Mass publicly nor hear confessions nor preach....You are not to invite people to attend your privately celebrated Masses and not to concelebrate Mass publicly.[42]

Then, on October 8, 2004, the bishop wrote to the priest permitting him to administer the sacrament of the anointing of the sick on an individual basis to family members, but only with the permission of the chancellor or the bishop himself.[43]

Later, the bishop claimed that he revoked the priest's faculties by an administrative act rather than by using a judicial process. The bishop maintained that the removal of faculties was not a penalty, and that he did not need to use the preliminary process of canon 1717ff. The bishop argued that no canon in the Latin Code gives a priest a right to ministry. The bishop claimed that prescription[44] applies in judicial cases, but not in administrative matters. The bishop said, "1) I did not impose a penalty...; 2) I used my administrative authority for the good of the diocese; 3) I did not want another court case implicating the Catholic Church; 4) Father Christopher was not suspended and is allowed to celebrate mass privately; 5) Father Christopher receives the same financial benefits as...a priest in active ministry."[45]

The priest appealed his case to the Congregation for the Clergy, who decided on October 28, 2005, that the bishop imposed an expiatory penalty depriving the priest of a faculty (see c. 1336 §1, 2°), without the required judicial process (see c. 1341) since a permanent penalty was imposed (see c. 1342 §2).

The bishop appealed the decision to the Signatura, who issued a sentence in which it accepted that a priest enjoys the faculty to preach everywhere unless this faculty has been restricted or removed or express permission is required by particular law. It acknowledged that the faculty to preach can be removed for any just reason.[46] Also, a bishop can revoke the faculty to hear confessions for a grave cause.[47] Both these faculties can be removed administratively and not for a penal reason. Similarly, the law concerning the minister of the anointing of the sick[48] mentions the presumed consent of the pastor entrusted to care for the sick member of the faithful. It is not a penalty for a bishop to restrict the priest anointing the sick.[49] As well, since an inactive priest requires delegation to officiate at a wedding (see cc. 1108 §1 and 1111), the bishop could set criteria for granting delegation and decide that the priest does not qualify to receive delegation.

The Signatura also agreed that the priest can always celebrate the Eucharist daily as recommended by canon 904 unless he is impeded by canon law (c. 900 §2). It recognized that the removal of faculties may be an administrative decision rather than an expiatory penalty. However, in the administrative process for the removal of a parish priest from a parish (cc. 1740–47), the motivating reason is the protection of the good of the faithful. On March 18, 2006, the Signatura accepted that a diocesan bishop could use an administrative decree to restrict a priest from publicly celebrating the Eucharist because of his imprudence with young people.[50]

However, the Signatura pointed out in this case the bishop had removed permanently the faculties of a priest primarily to avoid a civil lawsuit, rather than for canonical reasons "to prevent scandals, to protect the freedom of witnesses, and to guard the course of justice."[51] The Signatura said bishops cannot remove the faculties of a priest for extraneous reasons such as avoiding civil lawsuits. It noted there was no preliminary investigation. The bishop "entirely neglected an examination about Fr. Christopher's imputability, the suitability of conducting a judicial process and observing prescription. He did not initiate a previous investigation or observe the penal procedure mentioned in canon 1720."[52]

The Signatura accepted that the bishop had not made a perpetual decision in this case, but a decision for an indeterminate time while the cause endures. The Signatura quoted *coram* Fagiolo, June 11, 1993: "A prohibition to exercise power…can affect an offender as an expiatory penalty (cf. canon 1336 §1 3°); however, apart from a delict, it can be imposed as a mere disciplinary precept for a just and proportionate cause, while the cause endures. A perpetual prohibition to exercise power, however…cannot easily be considered a mere disciplinary precept."[53] The bishop did not make his decision based on right motivation, and he did not follow correct procedures.

Analysis of Australian Cases

An Australian archbishop removed the faculties of three priests using the same process and similar reasons in each case. In one case, the archbishop decreed on July 17, 1998,

> that his pastoral office required of him to protect the unity of the people of God and to build up the Body of Christ. Therefore, "Remedial considerations arising from that responsibility lead me to derogate from the normal diocesan custom and withdraw as from this date [17 July 1998] your faculty to celebrate the Eucharist publicly, to hear confessions and to preach….These remedies will remain in force for such time as is necessary for the public good of the Church."[54]

The priest requested that the archbishop revoke his decree because "no motives were expressed in his decree and that a basis for the removal of my faculties had not been canonically proven."[55] The archbishop did not revoke the decree. The priest proposed recourse against the decree to the Congregation for the Clergy seeking the restoration of full faculties of the archdiocese. The Congregation found that the archbishop had employed a commissioner using a mixture of canonical and civil procedures giving canons 1717 and 1722 as the basis for an investigation and decision. The Congregation found the archbishop violated canons 221, 51, 39, 1717, and 483 §2.

The Congregation considered that the archbishop had applied a perpetual penalty using canon 1722 without a clear canonical administrative or judicial process. There was no indication that the Promotor of Justice was involved in the process as canon 1722 requires. The Congregation considered the procedures used were confused and not in accord with canon law, and in particular canon 221. Furthermore, the accusations kept changing and were already extinguished by prescription. The priest's good reputation was tarnished by the archdiocese circulating information contrary to the prescripts of canons 1717 §2 and 220.

On August 23, 2001, the Congregation declared that the decree of the archbishop removing the faculties of the priest on July 17, 1998, was "null and void and without juridical effect," because of serious flaws in procedure.

In a second case, the Congregation was critical of the procedural irregularities in the local process that ignored prescription. The Congregation concluded that the decree of the ordinary dated September 3, 1998, lacked a basis both in law and in fact. The Congregation pointed out that, according to canon 51, a decree is to be "issued in writing, with the reasons at least summarily expressed, if it is a decision."[56]

In a third Australian case, an archbishop had stated in his decree that the criteria of proof to be applied were the "balance of probabilities" and "unacceptable risk." The Congregation found that these criteria were foreign to canon law and its processes, from which no dispensation is possible.[57] The standard of proof in ecclesiastical cases is moral certainty.[58] Judith Hahn explains:

> Considering moral certitude in comparison with other standards of proof, it has become apparent that there are broad overlaps between the ecclesiastical and the secular approaches to finding the truth in jurisprudence. This is not surprising as many standards come from the same root, as James Whitman elucidated with regard to the origins of the beyond a reasonable doubt standard. Moral certitude and beyond a reasonable doubt not only have common roots but also function as equivalents. It is possible to reformulate moral certitude by using beyond a reasonable doubt terminology, and vice versa.[59]

CONCLUSION

Although priests do not have a right to an office in the Latin Code, the law presumes from the fact that the priests were ordained that they should be able to minister and have faculties to function publicly. When it is necessary to remove the faculties of a priest, it cannot be done arbitrarily, and the bishop must follow correct canonical procedures. For example, if a priest has developed a mental problem, such as dementia, a bishop can remove his faculties by an administrative act. If a bishop wishes to "prohibit the exercise of sacred ministry" to remove his faculties because of a complaint of abuse, the bishop must respect the rights of the priest to a good reputation and due process involving the Promotor of Justice and carrying out a proper preliminary investigation. The imputability of the priest must be established. The standard of proof is to be that of moral certainty.[60] A bishop should never try to "short-circuit the law,"[61] or remove faculties for noncanonical reasons such as avoiding lawsuits. A proper preliminary investigation should establish the facts and then correct procedures must be followed using an administrative or judicial process. The bishop in his decree removing the faculties of a priest or "prohibiting the exercise of sacred ministry" must give valid canonical reasons. He cannot be like Caiaphas (see John 11:50) and simply claim that he is acting for the good of the Church.

4

SUSPENDING PRIESTS

"Removal of faculties" or "prohibition from the public exercise of sacred ministry" stops a priest from functioning publicly. However, if a bishop wants to stop a priest functioning both publicly and privately,[1] he must suspend that priest. "Suspension is a censure…by means of which they are forbidden fully or partially to exercise the power of order, the power of governance or of office (canon 1333 §1) or of all of those simultaneously (canon 1334 §2) and in some cases, the right to receive any goods with economic value."[2] The word "suspension" comes from the Latin *suspendere*, meaning "to hang, to shelve, to put in cold storage." It is one of the most common penalties that can be imposed on a priest.

Suspension can also now be used as a penalty for a layperson "who enjoys a dignity or performs an office or function in the Church, who commits an offence mentioned in canon 1398 §1 or in canon 1395 §3."[3] The laity could be either employed or be voluntary workers.

HISTORICAL DEVELOPMENT OF THE PENALTY

In the early Church when priests or deacons were prohibited from functioning, no clear distinctions were made between the penalties of suspension, interdict, and excommunication. The word *excommunication* included suspension.[4] Nevertheless, key aspects of today's understanding of "suspension" existed in the early Church. Gradually a distinction was made between suspension and other penalties. The holding of an office and holy orders were closely connected.[5] The penalty of deposition took away one's office completely, while the penalty of suspension deprived a cleric of rights or functions associated with an office. The Council of Ancyra in 314 seemed to distinguish between a cleric being dismissed from the clerical state and a cleric being suspended. When priests had been found guilty of idolatry, they remained clerics but could not function as priests.[6] Hefele states that priests guilty of idolatry "may neither sacrifice or preach nor fulfil any priestly office."[7]

Clerics could have restrictions imposed restricting the exercise of their ministry. Eligius Rainer refers to the penalty of *communio peregrine*.[8] An example was Armentarius, who was illegitimately consecrated a bishop in 438. In 439, the Council of Riez declared the ordination void and then allowed Armentarius restricted faculties.[9] There is no doubt that suspension existed in the third and fourth centuries, although there is no specific terminology. Saint Cyprian (200–258) wrote to Bishop Rogation advising him to suspend a deacon who had rebelled against his bishop.[10] Saint Cyprian seemed to use the word *abstinere* as a synonym for *suspendere*. The Third Synod of Carthage (398) decreed that as a penalty, clerics could be deprived of their stipend.[11]

Suspension as a medicinal penalty[12] began in the sixth century.[13] Prior to the sixth century all penalties were expiatory[14] to reestablish Church order and repair the scandal caused by a crime. The *Novellae of Justinian* (535) stated that for some offenses clerics were unable to function for a year, and in other cases, they could not function for three years.[15] Medicinal penalties grew out of the expiatory penalties because clerical offenders, without reforming, could simply exercise their office again after serving out the term of their suspension. To remedy this, the Church instituted medicinal penalties that remained in force until the offender had repented and had given an assurance that the offense would not happen again. The Council of Epaon in Burgundy (517) decreed that a bishop who had committed a crime had to suspend himself from receiving the Eucharist for three months, while a priest could not receive the Eucharist for two months for the same offense.[16] It also legislated that if a cleric stole from other priests or the Church, he was to be suspended from communion.[17]

The rights of suspended clerics became more clearly recognized because the Council of Narbonne (589) legislated that suspended clerics were not to lose their income unless they were suspended for more than a year.[18] The Council of Lerida (524) stated that if a cleric was warned twice and did not amend his actions, he was to be deprived of his office until he reformed.[19] A significant development was the suspension of a cleric, or the prohibition of a cleric to exercise certain rights or functions to prevent more scandal during an investigation into his behavior.[20] The first example was from the Council of Lérida (524). Gratian[21] cited the law that prescribed that if a priest had lost his reputation among his people and the bishop could not obtain proof, then the priest was to be suspended until he had atoned for what he had done wrong. Popes, including Gregory the Great,[22] wrote to Bishop Januarius of Caralis in 600, implementing this law of suspension. Around this time, suspensions were also divided into those that were *ferendae sententiae* (imposed) and those that were *latae sententiae* (automatic) penalties. *Latae sententiae* penalties were first instituted by the Thirteenth

Council of Toledo in 683. Canon 11 of this council states that those who harbored fugitive clerics were excommunicated for as long as they harbored them.[23]

THE TWELFTH CENTURY TO THE COUNCIL OF TRENT

In the first few centuries of the Church, someone could not be ordained unless they had already received some office. The Council of Chalcedon (451) had forbidden the ordination of unattached clerics, that is, those without a title to support them.[24] Consequently, penalties inflicted on problem priests also affected the offices they had been received. However, problems continued because some clergy were itinerant and were not accountable to any bishop. Therefore, the Third Lateran Council (1179) decreed,

> If a bishop ordains someone as a deacon or priest without a definite title from which he may draw the necessities of life, let the bishop provide him with what he needs until he shall assign him the suitable wages of clerical service in some church, unless it happens that the person ordained is in such a position that he can find the support of life from his own or family inheritance.[25]

The ordaining bishop was required to ensure that the candidate for ordination had a guaranteed income when he was ordained. If the ordained cleric did not have a benefice or other means of support, the bishop had to provide for the cleric himself.

This was an incentive to make bishops observe the law. This requirement of a "means of support" contributed to the development of canon law because the requirement implicitly separated the reception of the sacrament of orders from holding an office. Consequently, there was now a clearer distinction between the power of orders and the power of holding an office (jurisdiction). Clerics could now be punished with a suspension from an office, a suspension from holy orders, a suspension from a benefice, or from all three of them. Pope Innocent III clarified the nature of penalties and developed clearer distinctions between censures. He decreed that suspension, interdict, and excommunication should all be considered censures.[26]

THE COUNCIL OF TRENT TO THE 1917 CODE OF CANON LAW

The Council of Trent did not change the nature of the penalty of suspension and confirmed the previous law concerning suspensions such as clerics living in concubinage were to be suspended.[27] The Council added a new suspension for administering tonsure to those who were not the subjects of the prelate.[28] As well, the Council of Trent did enable a bishop, with knowledge of an occult crime, to prevent the perpetrator being promoted to higher orders. The bishop could also prevent someone from exercising orders if he learned that an occult crime had been committed.[29] Pope Pius IX confirmed the suspensions that had been introduced by the Council of Trent.[30] Seven other *latae sententiae* penalties reserved to the Roman pontiff were added,[31] including a penalty of suspension for bishops and abbots administering benefices or other acts of office without the correct apostolic letters.

In 1884, the Sacred Congregation for the Propagation of the Faith issued an Instruction for bishops possessing confidential information concerning occult crimes of a priest that merit his suspension.[32] This document gave a full explanation of the law concerning suspension and formed the basis for the law on suspension included in the 1917 Code.

1917 CODE OF CANON LAW

There were eight canons concerning suspension in the 1917 Code (cc. 2278–85). A suspension is described in canon 2278:

§1. Suspension is a censure by which a cleric is prohibited from office or benefice or both.

§2. The effects of suspension can be separated; but, unless otherwise provided, suspension generally imposed includes all the effects that are enumerated in the canons of this article; otherwise, suspension from office or from benefice contains only the effects specified in either.[33]

The following canon (c. 2279) then explained the effects of general or partial suspension:

§1. Simple suspension from office, with no limitations being added, forbids every act, whether of the power of orders and jurisdiction, or even merely of administration, of the involved office, except for the administration of the goods of one's own benefice.

§2 Suspension

1° From jurisdiction generally forbids every act of jurisdictional power in both fora, whether ordinary or delegated;

2° From divine things [restricts one] from every act of the power of orders, whether one has obtained it from ordination or through privilege;

3° From orders [restricts one] from every act of the power of orders received from ordination;

4° From sacred orders [restricts one] from every act of the power of orders received from sacred ordination;

5° From the exercise of a certain and definite order [restricts one] from every act of the designated order; one suspended is also prohibited from conferring that order and from receiving a higher order and from exercising one received after suspension;

6° From the conferral of a certain and definite order [restricts one] from conferring that order, but not from conferring an inferior or superior one;

7° From a certain and definite ministry, for example, hearing confessions, or office, for example, one with the care of souls [restricts one] from every act of that ministry or office;
8° From pontifical orders [restricts one] from every act of the power of episcopal orders;
9° From pontificals [restricts one] from the exercise of pontifical acts according to the norm of Canon 337 §2.

One effect of the introduction of the 1917 Code was that all general penal legislation not contained in the 1917 Code was no longer binding. However, seven new suspensions had been included in the 1917 Code.[34]

REVISION OF THE 1917 CODE OF CANON LAW

After Vatican II, the 1967 Synod of Bishops enunciated ten principles for the revision of the Code of Canon Law.[35] Principle 2 stated that the Code would "incorporate all such norms as are necessary for making clear the provisions of the internal forum in so far as the salvation of souls demands."[36] Principle 9 stated, "It is generally agreed that penal laws be *ferendae sententiae*, inflicted only *in foro externo*, and remitted likewise only *in foro externo*. As for penal laws *latae sententiae*, while the abolition of all of these has been proposed by not a few canonists, we suggest that they be reduced to the smallest possible number and concern only the gravest of crimes."[37] The Commission for the Revision of the Code voted to keep some *latae sententiae* penalties to punish occult crimes and safeguard the supreme goal of the Church to save souls.[38]

The 1917 Code contained eight canons concerning suspension, which could be either a medicinal or an expiatory penalty. The 1973 schema reduced to three the canons concerning suspension as a medicinal penalty. There were sixteen *latae sententiae* suspensions in the 1917 Code.[39] The 1973 Schema in canon 28 preferred that suspension be inflicted by a judicial procedure unless there were grave reasons preventing this.[40] Some wanted only a judicial process to be used but the Commission decided that, since the administrative procedure was quick and practical, it should be retained.[41]

THE 1983 CODE OF CANON LAW

Suspension in the 1983 Code is only a medicinal penalty and is no longer an expiatory penalty. They wanted to emphasize that suspension was aimed at reforming the offender. The 1983 Code has four types of suspensions:

1. Total or partial suspension of orders;
2. Total or partial suspension of governance;
3. Total or partial suspension of office;[42]
4. Total suspension, which includes suspension of orders, governance, and office.[43]

These are spelled out in detail in canon 1333:

§1. Suspension prohibits:

1° all or some of the acts of the power of order;
2° all or some of the acts of the power of governance;
3° the exercise of all or some of the rights or functions attaching to an office.

§2. In a law or a precept it may be prescribed that, after a judgement or decree that imposes or declares the penalty, a suspended person cannot validly perform acts of governance.

§3. The prohibition never affects:

1° any offices or power of governance that are not within the control of the superior who establishes the penalty;
2° a right of residence that the offender may have by virtue of office;
3° the right to administer goods that may belong to an office held by the person suspended, if the penalty is *latae sententiae*.

§4. A suspension prohibiting the receipt of benefits, stipends, pensions, or other such things, carries with it the obligation of restitution of whatever has been unlawfully received, even though this was in good faith.

The suspension of a cleric totally or partially restricts his ability to function liturgically or in ecclesiastical governance but does not mean the cleric has lost his office or place of residence. If the cleric has received a *latae sententiae* penalty, he can still administer the goods associated with his office, for example, parish property if he is the parish priest. Normally, a suspension is a general suspension unless it is specified that the suspension is limited to certain acts. For example, a bishop ordaining a cleric without dimissorial letters would not be able to ordain again for another year.[44] A suspension can forbid all or some of the acts of the power of the sacrament of orders, including celebrating the Eucharist, anointing of the sick, and the sacrament of penance. If a suspended priest celebrated the Eucharist, it would be valid but illicit. A partial decree of suspension should make mention of the withdrawal of the faculty to officiate at weddings because the priest is an official witness of the Church, and the couple bestow the sacrament on themselves. The validity of any marriage could be in doubt.

Latae Sententiae Penalties

It was recognized that automatic or *latae sententiae*[45] penalties are necessary to provide immediate punishment for serious crimes, as well as to deal with secret crimes.[46] Canon 1314 states that penalties are normally to be *ferendae sententiae*[47] (imposed by an ordinary or a tribunal), but can be *latae sententiae* if the law or precept determines this.[48] There are six *latae sententiae* suspensions in the 1983 Code:

1. Physically attacking a bishop[49]
2. a deacon attempting to celebrate the Eucharist[50]
3. Simulating absolution in the sacrament of penance,[51] e.g., a deacon or a priest without the faculty

4. Falsely accusing a confessor of solicitation the Coetus for the Commission was concerned to protect the priest
5. Unauthorized ordination, canon 1383
6. Cleric attempting to marry, canon 1394 §1

Ferendae Sententiae Suspensions

There are three possible *ferendae sententiae* (imposed) suspensions in the 1983 Code:
1. Simoniacal celebration of the sacraments[52]
2. Solicitation[53]
3. Sexual Misconduct in an ongoing manner[54]

A bishop could also suspend a cleric for other offenses:

> Besides the cases prescribed in this or in other laws, the external violation of divine or canon law can be punished, and with a just penalty, only when the special gravity of the violation requires it and necessity demands that scandals be prevented or repaired. (c. 1399)

There is a legal principle: "There is no crime and no penalty unless there is an already established penal law."[55] Canon 1399 appears to contradict this but was allowed by the Code Commission in 1977 to protect the Church's mission and the salvation of souls when there is harm to persons and the Church or serious scandal has occurred or is likely to occur.[56]

Suspension of a Priest

Suspending a priest is a last resort in canon law.[57] Canon 1347 requires that an offender must be warned to withdraw from contumacy or contempt for the authority of the Church.[58] The warning should be recorded in a document kept in the secret archives.[59] The warning is necessary for *ferendae sententiae* penalties because although the law is broken the priest might not be in contumacy.

The offender could be in ignorance or have acted without realizing the seriousness of what he was doing. In the 2021 changes, new paragraphs were added to canon 1339 clarifying the procedures to impose the medicinal penalty of suspension.[60] For *latae sententiae* penalties, the law contains the warning that ignorance is no excuse for clerics.[61] During the process for the revision of the Code of Canon Law, there was a request for more penalties for specific crimes, and these were increased to thirty-six penalties in the 1980 schema. "Grave cause" in the 1973 Schema was replaced with "just cause" in the 1980 schema making it easier to use the administrative process. An ordinary can suspend a priest using an extrajudicial decree; canon 1342 §1 and canon 1720[62] require the ordinary to "hear" the person upon whom he proposes to impose the penalty. There must always be a preliminary investigation (cc. 1717–20)[63] and due process in any penal case. The penal trial is the preferred process to impose a suspension.[64] It has the objects of repairing scandal, restoring justice, and reforming the offender.[65] In an Australian penal case, the Congregation for Clergy found that the archbishop violated canons 221, 51, 39, 1717, and 483 §2 by using civil procedures.[66] This Congregation also pointed out in a Canadian case that a bishop should carry out a preliminary investigation and follow the procedures in canons 1717–20 before withdrawing faculties, or imposing any penalty.[67] This means that the facts of the case and the imputability of the cleric have been properly documented.[68] This documentation is important whether there is a penal trial or an administrative process. Since a suspension is a medicinal penalty, it cannot be imposed for a specified period, but it can only apply "for as long as the scandal continues in the community," or "until the priest ceases the affair."[69]

Effects of Suspension

Suspension does not prevent reception of the sacraments. A suspended priest can receive the sacraments provided he is not in grave sin. When a cleric is suspended with a *latae sententiae* penalty that has not been declared, any acts contrary to the suspension are valid but illicit. However, when the suspension *latae sententiae* or *ferendae sententiae* is declared, the law may establish that acts of governance contrary to the suspension are invalid. If a suspended priest officiated at a wedding, it is always invalid.[70] However, if the suspension of the cleric has not been declared,[71] the cleric may celebrate a sacrament, administer a sacramental, and issue an act of governance for any just reason.

Even when another priest is available who is not suspended, the suspended priest can celebrate the sacraments at the request of the faithful for any just reason. This reason could be simply for the spiritual benefit of the member of the faithful. Because the supreme law of the Church is the salvation of souls (c. 1752), the faithful have a right to the sacraments and the cleric has an obligation to celebrate them.[72] Also, the cleric has no obligation to dishonor himself and say that he is suspended.[73] When a member of the faithful is in danger of death, the suspended cleric can and must celebrate the sacraments for the person whether the suspension is a declared *latae sententiae* or a *ferendae sententiae* suspension.[74]

Authority to Remove the Penalty of Suspension

To have a suspension removed, the suspended person must have withdrawn from contumacy, that is, a "rebellious inclination against authority and discipline."[75] Once the person has withdrawn from contumacy, the suspension must be remitted and remission cannot be refused.[76] "Withdrawal from contumacy" includes repentance for committing the crime and reparation for damages or the promise to make reparations.[77] Canon 1354 §3 allows for the Apostolic See to reserve penalties to itself and these reservations are to be interpreted strictly.[78]

Nonreserved Suspensions

Those suspensions not reserved to the Apostolic See, according to canon 1355 §1,[79] can be remitted by the ordinary[80] who initiated the trial, the ordinary where the offender lives, the ordinary of the territory where the offense took place, or any bishop in sacramental confession. Remission is normally made in writing,[81] unless it needs to be public to protect the reputation of the offender or to repair scandal.

Any ordinary and any confessor under specific circumstances can usually remit the penalty of suspension even when it has been declared.[82] All who can dispense from a law including a penalty and all who can exempt one from a precept giving a penalty can remit the penalty.[83]

Conclusion

Unfortunately, penalties such as suspension are necessary in the Church. Priests do not always, in Saint Paul's words, lead a "life worthy of their vocation" (Eph 4:1). There was once little distinction made between expiatory and medicinal penalties, but careful distinctions are now made between them. For some offenses, expiatory penalties, such as dismissal from the clerical state, are primarily motivated to repair scandal and remedy the damage done to the Church by the offender.

Suspension is a medicinal penalty with the primary aim to reform the offending priest. The suspension is imposed after the priest has been warned and when all other actions such as fraternal correction have failed. There are just the two canons—1333 and 1334—dealing with suspension in the 1983 Code. Once the suspension has been imposed, it can have other benefits of repairing the scandal, and reducing the harm to the Church community. The specific details of the suspension are determined by the precept that the priest was given or by the decree that imposed the suspension. Suspensions continue until they are remitted by a competent ordinary, or in specific circumstances, a priest in the sacrament of penance. A suspension that prohibits the celebration of a sacrament is suspended when a member of the faithful is in danger of death and wishes to receive a sacrament. Also, a member of the faithful can receive a sacrament from a priest suspended by a *latae sententiae* (automatic) suspension that has not been declared, provided the member of the faithful is in good faith when he or she requests the sacrament. Any suspended priest *latae sententiae* retains the right to use the dwelling associated with the office that he holds.

5

THE EFFECTS OF EXCOMMUNICATION

The penalty of excommunication has often been discussed in the media. In 2014, for example, Pope Francis stated that members of the mafia were excommunicated: "Those who follow this evil path in life, such as members of the mafia, are not in communion with God: they are excommunicated."[1] Pope Francis, here, was using "excommunicated" in a nontechnical sense. There has been no process and he was indicating the mafia was cutting off itself from the Church by its sinful conduct. Sexual abuse does much more harm to people and the Church, so for most Catholics the sexual abuse of a minor merits a penalty of excommunication.

In 1988, Archbishop Marcel Lefebvre was excommunicated along with four bishops he ordained without a pontifical mandate.[2] Pope Benedict XVI stated that "they were excommunicated because they had received episcopal ordination without a papal mandate,"[3] thereby incurring an automatic or *latae sententiae* excommunication. The excommunication was lifted in 2009.[4] The most common offense incurring the penalty of excommunication is the crime of abortion.[5] It also affects the collaborators of any abortion.[6] Sister Margaret McBride, RSM, was a member of an ethics committee that approved an abortion at a Catholic hospital in Phoenix. She was excommunicated on May 19, 2010, but the excommunication was later lifted on December 8, 2011, when she repented.[7] Sometimes excommunications occur for other offenses. Father Greg Reynolds of Melbourne was excommunicated on May 31, 2013, because he continued celebrating the Eucharist when not permitted to do so and advocated the ordination of women and same-sex marriage.[8]

SCRIPTURAL BASIS

Jesus Christ conferred on his Church the right to excommunicate members of the faithful for persevering in grave sin:

If another member of the church sins against you, go and point out the fault when the two of you are alone. If the member listens to you, you have regained that one. But if you are not listened to, take one or two others along with you, so that every word may be confirmed by the evidence of two or three witnesses. If the member refuses to listen to them, tell it to the church; and if the offender refuses to listen even to the church, let such a one be to you as a Gentile and a tax-collector. Truly I tell you, whatever you bind on earth will be bound in heaven, and whatever you loose on earth will be loosed in heaven. (Matt 18:15–18)

This text presents a procedure for the correction of Christians when required. First, there is a reprimand aimed at reforming the offender. If they do not reform, the community issues an official rebuke. If they refuse to listen to the community, they are to be treated as tax collectors. The community is then relieved of its responsibility toward sinners because they have shown that they have obstinately persisted in a grave fault. Saint Paul heard of a notorious case of sexual immorality in the Corinthian community. Incest was illegal in Roman law, but Saint Paul exhorted the Corinthian church to use its own judicial discipline and excommunicate the incestuous man:[9]

Sexual Immorality Defiles the Church

It is actually reported that there is sexual immorality among you, and of a kind that is not found even among pagans; for a man is living with his father's wife. And you are arrogant! Should you not rather have mourned, so that he who has done this would have been removed from among you? For though absent in body, I am present in spirit; and as if present I have already pronounced judgement in the name of the Lord Jesus on the man who has done such a thing. When you are assembled, and my spirit is present with the power of our Lord Jesus, you are to hand this man over to Satan for the destruction of the flesh, so that his spirit may be saved on the day of the Lord. (1 Cor 5:1–5)

The community had been negligent, had overlooked, and had tacitly condoned the crime. The sin was both an offense to God and the Church. The presence of a grave sinner raised questions about the authenticity of the community's conversion and the credibility of the Church. Such laxity was to their discredit. Saint Paul angrily invites the community to adopt a position in the name of the Lord. "Handing him over to Satan" has an educative value.

This capital sin requires expulsion from the community so the obstinate sinner can find the grace of conversion, and the purity of the community can be protected (see 2 Cor 2:6). Saint Paul told the Thessalonians, "Take note of those who do not obey what we say in this letter; have nothing to do with them, so that they may be ashamed. Do not regard them as enemies, but warn them as believers" (2 Thess 3:14–15). Titus was told "after a first and second admonition, to have nothing more to do with those who cause divisions" (Titus 3:10). Saint

Paul intended to exclude grave, public sinners from the Christian community. He tells Timothy that "among them are Hymenaeus and Alexander, whom I have turned over to Satan, so that they may learn not to blaspheme" (1 Tim 1:20). The expression "to turn over to Satan" at the very least designates a form of excommunication for Hymenaeus and Alexander. An excommunication is a generic concept of separation of the offender from the community. Since they have been excluded from the Christian community, in effect they belong to the kingdom of Satan.

PENAL DISCIPLINE IN THE FIRST CENTURIES

It has been a constant doctrine of the Church that a person in a state of grave sin should abstain from receiving communion. Saint Cyprian was angry with those who violated the body and blood of Christ before receiving penance.[10] Many early documents demonstrate penal discipline: the *Didache*; Clement of Rome wrote to the Corinthians reprimanding sinners;[11] the Shepherd of Hermas alluded to this practice of giving reprimands;[12] Irenaeus of Lyon (late second century), in *Adversus Haereses*, gave the example of Gnostic Cerdon, who was separated from the community and became a penitent.[13]

PENITENTIAL SYSTEM OF PUBLIC PENANCE

From the fourth century, there was an organized, penitential discipline for grave sinners (e.g., murderers, adulterers). Grave sinners confessed their sins to the bishop or someone delegated by him. The bishop then assigned the sinners to the order of penitents and imposed a penance to be performed over a significant period. Sinners demonstrated their desire for conversion by penances, including pilgrimages, fasting, and caring for the needy. Penitents wore penitential garments and were dismissed after the Liturgy of the Word at the Eucharist as catechumens were. At the conclusion of their time of penance, penitents were readmitted to the community in a liturgical ceremony.

The Council of Elvira (304) was the first council to use the term *anathema*.[14] *Anathema* literally means "set apart," or cut off. Generally, it was associated with heresy. The use of the word *anathema* signified the seriousness of an offense and expressed the judgment of God. It is possibly a traditional formula for expulsion from the community and represents the beginning of a system of penal law. Gradually the Church developed more sanctions and procedures. The Edict of Milan (313) stated that a bishop could relegate a sinner into the Order of Penitents known as the *conversi*. The Council of Nicaea (325) declared *anathema* all those who denied the divinity of Christ.[15] Those who had lapsed from the faith without persecution were to spend twelve years as public penitents before they might be readmitted to the sacraments—and then, of course, only if a sincere conversion was demonstrated by perseverance in a reformed life:

Concerning those who have fallen without compulsion, without the spoiling of their property, without danger or the like, as happened during the tyranny of Licinius, the Synod declares that, though they have deserved no clemency, they shall be dealt with mercifully. As many as were communicants, if they heartily repent, shall pass three years among the hearers; for seven years they shall be prostrators; and for two years they shall communicate with the people in prayers, but without oblation.[16]

Penitential discipline was very strict in the early Church. Saints like Augustine delayed receiving baptism till later in life and the sacrament of penance was only received once in a lifetime. In fact, most Christians delayed receiving penance until they were in danger of death.[17] Becoming a monk became a substitute for public penance and gradually in the monasteries a system of private penance developed.

GROWTH OF PENALTIES

In the early Church, before private confession prevailed, penitents formed a special order like catechumens. The system of the order of penitents had dealt effectively with grave sinners who impacted on the Christian community. With the gradual demise of the penitential system, there was an increasing need for the Church community to impose penalties for grave offenses. Penalties were developed so a cleric[18] who was prohibited from functioning as a priest could not attend the Eucharist and was separated from the communion of the faithful for a time.[19] Armentarius, for example, was illegitimately consecrated a bishop in 438. The Council of Riez, in 439, declared the ordination void and then allowed Armentarius restricted faculties.[20]

Gratian

Around 1140, Gratian compiled a collection of canonical decisions known as the *Decretum*. Gratian included rulings on "excommunication" in his collection because it was a very general term used during the first millennium of Christianity. Gratian distinguished two kinds of excommunication: (1) the excommunication that forbade access to the sacraments; and (2) the excommunication that separated one from the Body of Christ that is the Church. An example of the latter more serious excommunication was that of Engeltrude:

> Know that Engeltrude is not only under ban of excommunication, which separates her from the society of the brethren, but under anathema which separates from the Body of Christ which is the Church.[21]

Over time, however, the distinction between the two types of excommunication became blurred. *Latae sententiae* penalties began in the fourth century and increased in their use so that they were frequently used in the eleventh and twelfth centuries. Pope Innocent IV criticized the excessive use of *latae sententiae* penalties at the Council of Lyons in 1245.[22] With the privatization of penitential discipline came an increase in the number of public excommunications for grave sinners.

During the twelfth century, there was an increasing distinction made between the internal forum (e.g., sacrament of penance) that was private and the external forum (e.g., criminal action) that was public. After the twelfth century, offenders had to be warned before being excommunicated. The Third Lateran Council (1179) decreed "that prelates should not pass sentence of suspension or excommunication without a previous canonical warning, unless the fault is such that by its nature it incurs the penalty of excommunication."[23] Pope Innocent III declared that excommunication was always to be considered a censure and therefore warning was always required before the penalty of excommunication was imposed.[24] Any person who repented and repaired the harm for what they had done had to be forgiven. Different degrees of exclusion from the Church were developed. In 1418, Pope Martin V in the constitution *Ad Vitanda* distinguished between *tolerati* and *vitandi*.[25] The *tolerati* received a minor excommunication and, while they could not receive communion, they could attend Mass. Those who were excommunicated with the major excommunication, *vitandi*, were named and could not attend Mass.

The Council of Trent

The Council of Trent considered the penalty of excommunication to be useful for the Church to maintain its values, but warned against its excessive use:

> Although the sword of excommunication is the chief instrument of church discipline and of great effect in keeping the people to their duty, yet it is to be wielded with great reserve and caution, since experience teaches that if it is inflicted rashly or for trivial reasons, it is despised rather than feared and breeds disorder rather than salvation. Wherefore the excommunications imposed after repeated warnings to produce a disclosure (as it is called), or lost or alienated property, are never to be decreed except by a bishop, and then on no ordinary matter and only after such a case, which arouses his special concern, has been examined with great care and thoroughness; nor should he be persuaded to use excommunication by the authority of any secular person.[26]

Although the council warned against the excessive use of *latae sententiae* penalties like excommunication, ironically, their number increased.[27] Three hundred years later, on October 12, 1869, the apostolic constitution *Apostolicae Sedis* reformed and reduced the number of *latae sententiae* penalties.[28]

THE 1917 CODE

The 1917 Code defined excommunication:

> §1. Excommunication is a censure by which one is excluded from the communion of the faithful with the effects that are enumerated in the canons that

follow and that cannot be separated. §2. Moreover, it is called anathema especially when it is inflicted with the formalities that are described in the Roman Pontifical. (c. 2257)

Note that excommunication is also called "anathema" in paragraph 2—a term often used in Council documents—especially when it is inflicted using the rite in the Roman Pontifical. Excommunicated persons were divided into those with the more serious excommunication who were banned or to be avoided (*vitandi*) and those to be tolerated (*tolerati*). Most excommunicated people were the latter, *tolerati*.

Vitandi and *Tolerati*

In the 1917 Code, *vitandi* were named and declared to have received the major excommunication by the Holy See through a public announcement, and the decree or sentence expressly stated that they were to be avoided. *Vitandi* had committed more serious crimes.[29] One who assaulted the pope was, by that action, *vitandus* and did not have to be named.[30] Those with a major excommunication were to be avoided in both Church and civil matters and this was to pressure the person to reform. Excommunicated people lacked the right to participate in worship.[31]

Excommunicated persons (*tolerati*) did not have to be ejected from the celebration, but *vitandi* were to be ejected or the celebration was to be stopped, provided it did not cause grave inconvenience.[32] Excommunicated people could not receive the sacraments. If there had been a declaratory or condemnatory sentence, the excommunicated person could not receive sacramentals such as the ashes on Ash Wednesday, and they could not receive an ecclesiastical burial.[33] Excommunicated people could not celebrate or administer sacraments or sacramentals[34] but canon 2261 §2 allowed a member of the faithful to request a sacrament or sacramental from an excommunicated priest for any just reason. This would include for their spiritual good, and the excommunicated priest could celebrate or administer it. However, if the excommunicated priest was *vitandus*, a person could ask for sacramental absolution and be anointed only in danger of death.[35] The excommunicated person was forbidden to carry out administrative acts, or to enjoy the fruit of privileges previously granted to him.[36] If he was a parish priest, he was not to administer parish goods. If he did so, the acts were valid but illicit. However, if there had been a condemnatory or declaratory sentence, these administrative acts would be invalid.[37] An excommunicated person, after a condemnatory or declaratory sentence was deprived of the fruits of an office, benefice, or pension. One who was a *vitandus* was also deprived of the office, pension, or position itself that they held in the church.[38] Nor could they obtain an office or position or be promoted to orders.[39] Altogether, the 1917 Code contained forty *latae sententiae* excommunications,[40] sixteen *latae sententiae* suspensions,[41] and four *latae sententiae* interdicts.[42]

The Revision of the 1917 Code

In 1967, the Synod of Bishops enunciated ten principles for the revision of the Code of Canon Law.[43] Principle 2 stated that the Code would "incorporate all such norms as are necessary for making clear the provisions of the internal forum in so far as the salvation of souls demands."[44] Principle 9 stated that "it is generally agreed that penal laws be *ferendae sententiae*, inflicted only *in foro externo*, and remitted likewise only *in foro externo*."[45] Principle 3 stated,

> The juridic ordering of the Church, with the laws and precepts, rights and duties, which flow from it, must be in accord with the supernatural end or purpose of the Church....Nor should the Code easily establish laws...that would impose ecclesiastical punishments upon members of the Church, unless the reason for such punishment or censure be a matter of grave importance and the punishment be necessary for the public good and Church discipline.[46]

As for penal laws *latae sententiae*, while the abolition of all of these has been proposed by not a few canonists, we suggest that they be reduced to the smallest possible number and concern only the gravest of crimes.[47] The Commission for the Revision of the Code voted to keep some *latae sententiae* penalties in order to punish occult crimes that had to be punished to safeguard the supreme goal of the Church to save souls.[48]

THE 1983 CODE

Unlike the 1917 Code, the 1983 Code of Canon Law did not give a definition of "excommunication" but left its meaning to doctrine and jurisprudence according to the principles[49] for the revision of the Code.[50] Furthermore, after the 2021 revision of Book VI, canon 1331 of the 1983 Code simplified the effects of an excommunication:

§1. An excommunicated person is prohibited:
 1° from celebrating the sacrifice of the Eucharist and the other sacraments;
 2° from receiving the sacraments;
 3° from administering sacramentals and from celebrating the other ceremonies of liturgical worship;
 4° from taking an active part in the celebrations listed above;
 5° from exercising any ecclesiastical offices, duties, ministries or functions;
 6° from performing acts of governance.

§2. If a *ferendae sententiae* excommunication has been imposed or a *latae sententiae* excommunication declared, the offender:
 1° proposing to act in defiance of the provision of §1 nn. 1–4 is to be removed, or else the liturgical action is to be suspended, unless there is a grave reason to the contrary;

2° invalidly exercises any acts of governance which, in accordance with §1 n. 6, are unlawful;
3° is prohibited from benefiting from privileges already granted;
4° does not acquire any remuneration held in virtue of a merely ecclesiastical title;
5° is legally incapable of acquiring offices, duties, ministries, functions, rights, privileges or honorific titles.

Imposition of Excommunication

There is a *regula iuris* (rule of law) *odiosa restringenda, favorabilia amplianda*, meaning "it is fitting that odious things be restricted, and favorable ones are extended."[51] "Penal laws always limit rights, and in this sense are 'odious.'"[52] Consequently, the imposition of a penalty is a last resort (c. 1341). Canon 18 specified that "laws which prescribe a penalty, or restrict the free exercise of rights, or contain an exception to the law, are to be interpreted strictly."

A strict interpretation uses the narrowest interpretation of the words describing the conditions for the penalty. However, an authentic interpretation[53] by the legislator has the force of law and is not covered by canon 18. Therefore, the killing of a fetus by any method incurs the excommunication outlined in canon 1397 §2 (previously c. 1398).[54] Traditionally, the crime of abortion was considered by many to apply only to physically removing a child from the womb by surgery. This did not consider the developments in modern medicine. On January 19, 1988, and with papal approval *in forma specifica*, the Pontifical Council for the Interpretation of Legislative texts replied to a question:

Q. Whether abortion, mentioned in canon 1398, is to be understood only as the ejection of an immature foetus, or also of the killing of the same foetus in whatever way or at whatever time from the moment of conception it may be procured?

R. Negative to the first part; affirmative to the second.[55]

This reply extended the crime of abortion to include abortion by any means. Because the procuring of an abortion is not a crime reserved to the Apostolic See, the local ordinary, that is, the diocesan bishop or the vicar general, has the authority to act according to canon 1341.[56] Although canon 1397 §2 states that the penalty for actually procuring an abortion is a *latae sententiae* (automatic) excommunication, this does not mean that the penalty is received like an instant fine for speeding in one's car when caught by a speed camera. There needs to be a process to establish that the canonical penalty has been received. The penalty needs to be declared in some sense, and it is not enough to write an article in a diocesan newspaper saying that any Catholic woman who has had an abortion is now excommunicated. It must be established that the circumstances mentioned in canons 1323 and 1324 do not apply in a particular case.[57]

The ordinary, if it is an administrative process, or the tribunal, if it is a judicial process, must examine the factors to establish that the circumstances, including that the woman was at least sixteen years old, and so on. Juan Arias points out that "the *latae sententiae* penalty may be applied only when the offence has been fully consummated; consequently, as indicated in 1324 it is not incurred when an extenuating circumstance is present."[58] Moral theologians have traditionally used the principle of "double effect" to deal with difficult moral cases. The principle of double effect note that "it is morally allowable to perform an act that has a bad effect under the following conditions:

1. The act to be done must be good in itself or at least indifferent...
2. The good intended must not be obtained by means of the evil effect...
3. The evil effect must not be intended for itself but only permitted...
4. There must be a proportionately grave reason for permitting the evil effect."[59]

A case where this principle might be applied is when a pregnant mother has a cancerous womb. An indirect abortion in an individual case might occur whereby the only workable treatment is surgery that results in the death of the child as an unavoidable byproduct. These cases are entirely different from cases where the aim is to terminate the pregnancy. Medicinal penalties aim to reform the offender. An offender must be given an opportunity to reform and must be warned first.[60] No one is to be punished for an offense "unless it is gravely imputable by reason of malice or of culpability."[61]

A warning makes this clear to the sinner. "Penalties are to be imposed only for the more grave offences"[62] when the person deliberately violated the law with grave imputability.[63] The excommunication can be imposed by a judicial sentence or by an administrative decree declaring the *latae sententiae* penalty.[64]

Latae Sententiae Excommunication

A *latae sententiae* excommunication is imposed by the law itself. Edward Peters explains: "For the valid declaration of a censure incurred automatically, no independent warning is required, nor, for the valid imposition of a censure threatened under penal precept, is an independent warning required."[65] For example, for a priest soliciting a penitent,[66] the law provides the warning; the penalty is incurred by the mere commission of the offense. The declared excommunicated person cannot be appointed validly to any office or use any privileges. The excommunicated person still has a right to support according to canon 1350,[67] and has an obligation to be restored to full communion.[68]

However, ignorance is no excuse for clergy and religious. The criminal act must be completed. An unsuccessful attempt to commit a crime does not incur a *latae sententiae* penalty, but only a completed crime.[69]

Effects of Excommunication

The effect of an excommunication depends on which excommunication has been incurred:

1. Undeclared *latae sententiae* excommunication.
2. Declared *latae sententiae* or *ferendae sententiae* excommunication.

Undeclared *Latae Sententiae*

When the person has been excommunicated with an undeclared *latae sententiae* excommunication, the penalty will not be publicly known. The crime is not notorious, if it is not publicly known.[70] The excommunicated person, including a lay celebrant, is forbidden to exercise ministry by celebrating the Eucharist or performing any other public worship such as weddings or funerals. In danger of death, the excommunicated cleric can and must provide the last rites and grant absolution in the sacrament of penance.[71] When an excommunicated priest is asked for a sacrament by any member of the faithful for a just reason, he can celebrate the sacrament to avoid embarrassing himself or revealing that he has been excommunicated.[72]

This is to protect the offender's reputation and to avoid giving grave scandal to the community.[73] The excommunicated person can come to Mass, but may not receive the Eucharist or other sacraments, but can receive sacramentals, including the ashes on Ash Wednesday. The excommunicated person cannot exercise any official function, ministry, or ecclesiastical office in the Church.[74] "Ministry" includes an extraordinary minister of the Eucharist or an excommunicated priest taking communion to the sick. "Function" means any activity with a spiritual purpose that has a public dimension.[75] An act of governance is any act of judicial, executive, or legislative power, for example, a parish priest administering the goods of a parish.

Declared *Ferendae* or *Latae Sententiae* Excommunications

There are four aspects to note when an excommunication is declared:

1. The offense has a public character.
2. The offense is legally notorious.
3. The offender must observe all the effects in the external forum.
4. The penal effects are aggravated by the declaration.[76]

When a person has a declared excommunication, the consequences are more severe: If possible, the offender must be removed from public worship. Furthermore, the offender invalidly exercises the power of governance and is forbidden to benefit from privileges already received. If an excommunicated priest with a declared excommunication officiates at a marriage,[77] the marriage will be invalid.

Specific Crimes with the Penalty of *Latae Sententiae* Excommunication

In the 1983 Code, there are seven *latae sententiae* excommunications:

1. Apostasy heresy and schism[78]
2. Profanation of the sacred species[79]

3. Solicitation or other crime in celebrating or receiving a sacrament[80]
4. Consecration of a bishop without pontifical mandate[81]
5. Violation of seal of confession[82]
6. Violence against pope[83]
7. Abortion[84]

Removal of the Penalty of Excommunication

Censures must be remitted when the offender has repented[85] and either made or promised to make reparation.[86] Penalties are normally to be remitted in the external forum by someone holding the appropriate executive power of governance:[87] If the Holy See reserves remission of the penalty to itself, only the Holy See is competent to remove the penalty. The 1983 Code contains five automatic excommunications: (1) desecration of the Eucharist (c. 1382); (2) violence against the pope (c. 1370); absolution of an accomplice or other sacramental crimes (c. 1384); consecration of a bishop without papal mandate (c. 1387); and seal of confession (c. 1386).

When the excommunication is declared but not reserved, consultation with the ordinary[88] who imposed it is required for the lawful remission of the penalty,[89] but it is not a requirement for validity.[90] An excommunication that has not been declared and is not reserved can be remitted by a bishop in the course of sacramental confession or by an ordinary in whose territory the offense was committed, or for his subjects or for those present in his territory.[91] Similarly, if someone incurs an excommunication from a *latae sententiae* penal precept, remission is given by an ordinary for his subjects or for those present in his territory.[92] The ordinary carrying out the remission consults with the ordinary who imposed the penal precept for lawfulness (liceity), and not for the validity of the remission.[93]

Remission in the Internal Forum

Remission of a penalty in the internal forum is exceptional because remission is normally in the external forum.[94] Canon 980 states that "if the confessor is in no doubt about the penitent's disposition and the penitent asks for absolution, it is not to be denied or deferred."[95] Excommunication can be remitted in the internal forum:

1. All bishops during sacramental confession 1355 §2, no. 3 when the offenses are not reserved to the Holy See. This provision was an innovation introduced after the 1980 schema and the reasons for this are unclear.[96]
2. The Canon Penitentiary[97] can grant absolution in the sacramental forum for all nondeclared and nonreserved *latae sententiae* censures such as excommunication.[98]
3. Any priest in the circumstances of danger of death,[99] with or without faculties. But if the penalty is reserved to the Holy See, the excommunicated person who recovers must have recourse directly [to the Holy See] or through the priest.[100]

4. Chaplains in prisons, hospitals, and at sea,[101] can absolve nondeclared, not reserved *latae sententiae* excommunications without prejudice to canon 976.
5. Confessors[102] can remit nondeclared *latae sententiae* excommunications if it is difficult for the person to remain under penalty.

If the penalty is reserved to the Holy See, the penitent is obliged to take recourse personally or through the confessor within one month of receiving absolution.[103] The excommunicated person needs to repair scandal and damage.[104] If the person does not make recourse, then the penalty is reincurred in the opinion of Borras and Armstrong.[105] Since penalties should be remitted in the external forum, recourse is required if someone recovers from being in danger of death.[106] If the excommunication has been declared, recourse is still required in danger of death cases.

Excommunications reserved to the Holy See can be remitted by any priest in danger of death situations, or when it is difficult for the sinner to remain in the state of grave sin.[107] When the penalty is reserved to the Holy See, recourse to the Holy See is always required if absolution was granted because it was hard for the person to remain in that state. If recourse is gravely inconvenient for more than a month, then this ecclesiastical law does not oblige.[108] An example would be if this happened during a COVID-19 lockdown when the borders of many countries were closed, and normal communication was impossible.

CONCLUSION

Contrary to popular belief, the excommunicated person remains a member of the Church. An analogy is a player in a sports team, who after a warning and a yellow card, commits another bookable offense and is red carded.

The player is still a member of the team but cannot play. "Excommunication"[109] means that the excommunicated person cannot celebrate or receive any sacraments. The excommunicated person does not stop being a Catholic and is not expelled from the Church. "Excommunication is not so much an exclusion from the Church, as from the goods of the Church."[110] The person is still bound by all the laws of the Church, including going to Mass on Sunday. If the excommunication is a declared *ferendae sententiae* or *latae sententiae* penalty, the excommunicated person is not to be allowed to participate actively in the Eucharist or in any public worship.[111] In practice, it is extremely rare for a layperson to receive an excommunication, especially a declared one. Therefore, in nearly every case, any priest can deal with the excommunicated person in the sacrament of penance.

An excommunicated priest is not to celebrate any sacraments, exercise any function, or carry out any work as an office holder such as a parish priest. An excommunicated priest could celebrate the Eucharist validly, but it would be a highly illicit action. The excommunicated priest is not deprived of any offices or ministries, but he may not exercise these ministries or place acts of governance. The excommunicated priest still has a right to the necessary means of support, but this does not mean a full salary or include vehicle expenses, since he cannot perform official ministry.[112] In the rare case of a priest with a declared excommunication or suspension, any marriages[113] he officiated at and any acts of governance he attempted would be invalid.

6

PRECEPTS FOR CLERGY AND RELIGIOUS

There is a great deal of disillusionment with clerical sexual abuse and leaders in the Church failing to deal with sexual abuse, leading to some disillusioned clergy who behave badly. Occasionally, we see cases of recalcitrant priests and religious whom the religious superior or bishop summon to rebuke verbally or counsel to behave correctly.

The recalcitrant priest or religious may respond by making a verbal commitment to change their behavior only to continue the same pattern. Usually, the behavior in these cases is not a crime in canon law, but it can cause scandal. Sometimes there may be a suspicion that crimes are committed, but they cannot be proven with moral certainty. These unsatisfactory situations often persist for many years. Occasionally, observers note the recalcitrant priest or religious seems to have lost their vocation or their heart is not in the priesthood or religious life. Eventually, a diocesan bishop or religious superior finally decides to take concrete action against the priest or religious and then discovers that because there were no proper written warnings or precepts given in the past, they are unable to act decisively, and they must begin at step one and give a warning or a precept in writing.

CHURCH CULTURE TODAY

There is a huge gap between bishops and their priests, as well as between clergy and laity, concerning their acceptance of canon law and the teaching of the Church associated with the problems of recalcitrant clergy and religious.[1] A 2005 survey of Catholics in the United States showed that 42 percent of Catholics in America thought everyone should decide for themselves whether to remarry after a divorce. Only 13 percent thought that the teaching of the Church on contraception was significant. Almost half of the

Catholics surveyed thought that a decision about abortion was a matter for an individual's personal choice; 46 percent considered the morality of being in homosexual partnerships to be a matter of personal opinion; 47 percent considered nonmarital sexual intercourse as a private matter.[2] These percentages will almost certainly be worse now with the prolonged sexual abuse crisis in the Church. There is probably not much difference between these figures and the reality in many Western countries, including Australia and New Zealand. Judith Hahn summarizes the situation:

> For members of the Church raised in modern societies, however, respect for the law is ultimately connected with the norms being based on arguments and reasons. In this regard, the findings of the sociological study "American Catholics Today" are especially interesting, as the researchers concluded: "The followers obey the teachings if they believe that the teachings are legitimate, justified, and true to the will of God as they understand that will. If the followers doubt the claims for whatever reason, including their own consciences, they feel free to follow their own consciences as having supremacy over obedience."[3]

This attitude to Church authority is reinforced by the sexual abuse crisis and some priests and laity observing the treatment of abusers and victims. Personal respect for a bishop or religious leader is a significant aspect as to how much actual authority he holds. Most people used to obey the bishop out of respect for his office. Some people now question the credibility of bishops and superiors of religious institutes because they financially support and treat abusers better than they treat victims. Others question why they should take the sexual morality teaching of the Church seriously when some priests seem to do whatever they like with impunity. These people think that the clergy don't take the law seriously, so why should they? Pope John Paul II was conscious of the impact of the example of priests and, in 1979, in his first Holy Thursday letter to priests, he said,

> The commitment to married fidelity, which derives from the sacrament of Matrimony, creates similar obligations in its own sphere; this married commitment sometimes becomes a source of similar trials and experiences for husbands and wives, who also have a way of proving the value of their love in these "trials by fire." Love, in fact, in all its dimensions, is not only a call but also a duty. Finally, we should add that our brothers and sisters joined by the marriage bond *have the right to expect from us*, Priests and Pastors, good example and the *witness of fidelity to one's vocation until death*, a fidelity to the vocation that we choose through the sacrament of Orders just as they choose it through the sacrament of Matrimony.[4]

In these insightful words, Pope John Paul II saw that priests who did not keep their commitment to celibacy greatly impacted on lay faithful struggling to be faithful to their commitments.

PRECEPTS

The essential content of a precept is the requirement to do or not to do an action. The principal function of the precept is to urge the observance of the law. Precepts specify the individual(s), the situations, and circumstances encompassed by the law. Evidence is necessary before a precept is issued. It "immediately binds the behavior of the faithful affected by it, imposing an obligation on them."[5] The penal precept should have a determined penalty, so that the offender is protected from arbitrary impositions of penalties by a superior. Clergy and laity need to have a clear understanding of what is expected of them. That is why job descriptions are very important so that expectations are spelled out in writing, ensuring that people are aware of them.

History of the Process to Impose a Precept

Pope Leo I (440–61) taught that penalties were a last resort and encouraged bishops to try to correct offenders by exhortation and kindness before imposing penalties "since often kindness towards those to be corrected is more effective than severity, exhortation more than threat, charity more than command."[6] However, experience taught that some offenders exploited excuses to escape penalties and those in authority had to be alert to this.[7]

The Sacred Congregation for Bishops and Regulars issued an instruction on June 11, 1880, outlining the procedure to be followed when people continued to ignore warnings. The procedure involved the ordinary issuing a precept in which he declared what was to be done or not done, as well as including the threat of an ecclesiastical penalty if the precept was transgressed.[8] Three years later on October 18, 1883, the Sacred Congregation for the Propagation of the Faith issued an instruction so that people, after warnings and precepts had been issued, were to be threatened with penalties if they did not reform.[9] The Sacred Congregation for the Propagation of the Faith issued an instruction, *Cum Magnopere*, for the United States. It was very similar to the instruction issued on June 11, 1980. *Cum Magnopere* prescribed the procedures to be followed before preventive measures or penalties were imposed.

A person had to receive three canonical warnings and at least one canonical admonition in a serious case. Then a precept could be imposed: "This command must state clearly and distinctly, (a) what the delinquent should do or avoid, (b) and what specific punishment he will incur, in case he disobeys the injunction.[10]...If a prelate, without first giving the canonical warnings, imposed the precept, and subsequently ordered the trial for the violation of the precept, the whole procedure will be invalid."[11] For validity, the precept had to be in writing, read, or communicated to the delinquent in person by the chancellor or secretary of the episcopal curia in the presence of the vicar general or of two proper witnesses. If the precept was not in writing, a written record was to be made by the chancellor and signed by all present.[12] The precept could be sent to the delinquent by registered mail as well. A canonical trial could not begin until the delinquent had been given a warning and a precept. This procedure of *Cum Magnopere* was reflected in canon 2310 of the 1917 Code:

> Admonition or formal; correction having been applied without effect or, if there seems no hope that an effect will come of it, a precept should be given, in which there is accurately indicated what the one prevented must do or avoid, with a statement of the penalty in case of transgression.[13]

LAWS, GUIDELINES, AND POLICIES

A fundamental problem that has been exposed by the sexual abuse crisis is the absence of detailed laws or the gaps in existing legislation concerning grooming, and so on. There are approximately 1.3 billion members of the Catholic Church in many countries all over the world and from hundreds of ethnic and cultural backgrounds. Obviously, civil laws concerning privacy, safeguarding, and financial matters will vary enormously from one country to another. It is impossible to have detailed universal law on all these matters encompassing the needs of the faithful in every culture and country, and therefore particular law is very important.

Protocols for the handling of sexual abuse complaints are often not legislated as particular law for several reasons. Sometimes, major superiors of religious institutes and diocesan bishops want the protocol documents to be merely policies or guidelines. This allows them to handle complaints on a case-by-case basis and make an exception for a particular accused cleric, or even not report the complaint to an office for professional standards. Finally, if there are only guidelines in place, a bishop or major superior of a religious institute can easily disregard the recommendation. Guidelines are not law and are open to more flexible interpretations. It is essential that protocol documents have the status of particular law to prevent flexible interpretations and processes. All particular laws must be in accord with universal law.[14] If there is particular law legislated by the bishops conference, it requires the review of the Holy See.[15] However, if each diocesan bishop legislates a protocol document as particular law for his diocese, it is particular law for the whole country without the prior review of the Holy See.

Article 2 of *Vos Estis Lux Mundi* on the reception of reports and data protection requires all episcopal conferences to have protocols for dealing with complaints of sexual abuse:

> §1. Taking into account the provisions that may be adopted by the respective Episcopal Conferences, by the Synods of the Bishops of the Patriarchal Churches and the Major Archiepiscopal Churches, or by the Councils of Hierarchs of the Metropolitan Churches *sui iuris*, the Dioceses or the Eparchies,

individually or together, must establish within a year from the entry into force of these norms, one or more public, stable and easily accessible systems for submission of reports, even through the institution of a specific ecclesiastical office. The Dioceses and the Eparchies shall inform the Pontifical Representative of the establishment of the systems referred to in this paragraph.[16]

Most dioceses in Western countries have also introduced child protection and safeguarding norms or guidelines. These include prohibitions on photographing children without parental permission or obtaining the phone numbers of children without parental consent. If these prohibitions, however, are only norms or guidelines, then there is insufficient legal obligation to observe them.

Also, there are few sanctions for their nonobservance unless the action violates civil child protection laws. Particular law is also required for financial management and prevention of theft.[17] Many dioceses have financial norms and procedures such as having payments approved with two signatures on invoices or statements. One signature is to be the parish priest's signature and the other is often that of a member of the parish finance committee. Clergy and religious engaged in misconduct can easily disregard or dismiss guidelines or policies as being optional and not applying to them and they can rationalize their behavior. Therefore, key elements of financial norms and procedures need to be made particular law in the diocese so that priests can be held to account.

Written Laws and Guidelines

Today, most countries require that official actions of leaders and officials be in writing. Similarly, canon 37 also requires this. An administrative act that concerns the external forum is to be effected in writing likewise, if it requires an executor, the act of execution is to be in writing. Canon 37 states that an act concerning external forum matters is to be in writing, and if an executor of the law is required to apply the law, then the record of the execution of the law must also be in writing.

The person who applied the law must make a written record of his application of the law and this may need to be communicated to interested parties such as victims. However, putting the act in writing is not required for the validity of the act.[18] Obviously, there is less room for misunderstandings and miscommunication when an act is recorded in writing. Consequently, the code of canon law requires a written record for the confirmation of an election (c. 179); loss of an office by reason of expiry of a predetermined time or reaching an age limit (c. 186); the transfer to another office (c. 190); the decree of removal from office (c. 193); letters of incardination and excardination (c. 268 §1); the consent of the diocesan bishop to establish an association in a diocese (c. 312 §2); the granting of faculties to a priest (c. 973). When there are acts emanating from the curia of the diocese, they must be signed by the ordinary[19] to be valid:

Acts of the curia which of their nature are designed to have a juridical effect must, as a requirement for validity, be signed by the Ordinary from whom they emanate. They must also be signed by the chancellor of the curia or a notary. The chancellor is bound to notify the Moderator of the curia about these acts. (c. 474)

This canon notes the double signature system of the ordinary and the chancellor both signing the document. The signature of the chancellor ensures the authenticity of the act. Canon 1339 notes that penal remedies are to be recorded in writing:

§1. When someone is in a proximate occasion of committing an offence or when, after an investigation, there is a serious suspicion that an offence has been committed, the ordinary either personally or through another can give that person warning.

§2. In the case of behavior that gives rise to scandal or serious disturbance of public order, the ordinary can also correct the person, in a way appropriate to the particular conditions of the person and of what has been done.

§3. The fact that there has been a warning or a correction must always be proven, at least from some document to be kept in the secret archive of the curia.

§4. If on one or more occasions warnings or corrections have been made to someone to no effect, or if it is not possible to expect them to have any effect, the ordinary is to issue a penal precept in which he sets out exactly what is to be done or avoided.

§5. If the gravity of the case so requires, and especially in a case where someone is in danger of relapsing into an offence, the ordinary is also to subject the offender, over and above the penalties imposed according to the provision of the law or declared by sentence or decree, to a measure of vigilance determined by means of a singular decree.

Note that the additional paragraphs 4 and 5 as part of the 2021 changes in canon law ensure that the offender knows exactly what is to be done or to be avoided. The ordinary is to exercise vigilance over the offender, which may mean implementing a safety plan. Penal remedies are measures normally used to prevent a person committing a crime, but they are not a punishment or a penalty for committing a crime.[20] The remedies may be warnings[21] to direct a person to change their behavior and avoid an occasion of committing an offense or to correct someone who has done something wrong. Penal remedies relate to actions in the external forum and therefore should be in writing to prove what happened and what action was taken by the ordinary.[22]

PENAL LAWS AND PRECEPTS

Laws are concerned with the common good, and both universal and particular laws are distinct from precepts. Universal laws have general application to any member of the faithful anywhere in the world. Particular laws, legislated by a diocesan bishop for his diocese or an episcopal conference for their territory, are laws enacted for the faithful of a specific diocese or territory. They do not bind the entire Church[23] because they are limited by personal criteria such as the territory in which members of the faithful live. A precept in the modern usage of the word is not understood as a law.[24]

The word *precept* comes from the Latin *praecipere* meaning "to command." In its proper sense, a precept is not a law, but an obligation imposed on an individual person or persons to do or omit some behavior by a competent ecclesiastical superior. Canon 49 of the 1983 Code defines the term *precept* as "a decree by which an obligation is directly and lawfully imposed on a specific person or persons to do or omit something, especially in order to urge the observance of a law." In other words, it is an order commanding a person to observe what is already a legal requirement.[25] It is not just an exhortation or admonition. Michiels points out that precepts "should only be made if warnings have proved fruitless."[26] When a cleric is warned by the diocesan bishop or ordinary, the warning is usually in the form of a precept.

Therefore, a precept given by a competent superior is "a decree that orders someone to do, or to refrain from doing, something. A precept can be used as a specific application of a general law or to deal with a unique, one-time situation."[27] A precept is usually issued by an ordinary when Church teaching, discipline, or law is not being observed. When a precept is issued with the threat of a penalty, it is then called a penal precept. In one sense, the penal precept is a warning to the person violating the law so that the person will comply to avoid the penalty. Precepts must be issued by an ordinary[28] who is competent to issue them, namely, "one who possesses executive power within the limits of that person's competence"[29] on those subject to them.[30] A penal precept applies to an individual or a group of individuals.[31] The precept applies the law in more detail: for example, forbidding a cleric to go to a gay bar or to visit a woman's house.

Essential Elements of Precepts

A precept is by its nature specific. Evidence of misconduct is necessary before a precept is issued so that both the requirement and the obligation are clear. The precept "immediately binds the behavior of the faithful affected by it, imposing an obligation on them."[32] The penal precept should have a determined penalty, so that the offender is protected from arbitrary impositions of penalties by a superior.

The ordinary must be careful that an injustice is not perpetrated when a penalty is imposed on someone. In particular, the ordinary is to be mindful of the requirement of "a strict interpretation" of the meaning of words in a precept when penalties are threatened or inflicted.[33] No one is to be punished for violating a precept if they are not gravely imputable.[34] Furthermore, there may be circumstances that affect someone's imputability for disobeying a precept.³⁵ The ordinary must obtain the necessary proof and information, as well as consult with those who could be affected by any precept.³⁶ The exercise of authority must be fair and balanced. The rights of the faithful need to be protected before a penalty is imposed, otherwise, the infliction of the penalty could be the subject of recourse.³⁷ For example, an accused cleric could appeal a decision to the Dicastery of the Doctrine of the Faith or the Apostolic Signatura. A precept must include justifying reasons at least in summary form.³⁸ This would include the legal basis for the precept, the facts of the case and the reasons that led to this decision, and the issuing of the precept. The precept affects only those matters that are determined by the precept.³⁹ Also, the precept only applies to the individual or the individuals specified in the precept. It cannot be applied to other people doing the same thing, so another precept must be issued to other recalcitrants.

Communication of the Precept or Law

All acts in the external forum are to be in writing to ensure juridical certainty.⁴⁰ The written precept does not come into effect until it is communicated to the person or persons concerned.⁴¹ A precept is valid from the moment its contents are conveyed to the addressee. If it is not in writing, then it cannot be notified with certainty. The addressee must be certain about what is commanded.

The precept may also be the subject of recourse⁴² by the addressee, which is another reason for the precept to be in writing. In most cases, the legislator wants the addressee to have the text of the precept. There is a presumption that the precept is in writing so that it is to be at least read to the person.⁴³ Only very grave reasons are to prevent the handing over of the text. It could be communicated orally, for example, if there is a genuine fear that the person to whom the precept is addressed might hand it over to the news media and cause scandal and embarrassment to the Church.⁴⁴ If the precept is not to be handed over to the addressee, then there is to be a written record signed by the ordinary and the two witnesses proving that it has been issued.⁴⁵ In these circumstances, the precept is deemed to have been made known to the person if it is read to the person to whom it is directed in the presence of two witnesses and a notary. It is not specified exactly who must read the precept, but regardless of who it is, there is still a requirement to have an additional two people as witnesses. The fact that the precept was issued is to be documented and signed by the person who read the precept and the two witnesses. When a precept is issued to someone without the contents being put in writing, the obligation to observe the precept expires upon the expiry of the authority who issued it.⁴⁶ Therefore, if a diocesan bishop forbids one of his priests to allow a particular woman to stay at the presbytery and does not put the precept in writing, then this precept expires when the bishop dies.

Stephen Doktorczyk proposes "ten commandments" concerning precepts and implementing canon 1371, no. 2 when the precept is disobeyed:

1. Thou shalt be sure to issue a written warning before proceeding penally;
2. Thou shalt warn only those people subject to you and for matters over which you are competent;
3. Thou shalt clearly and concisely set out expectations in a command, prohibition, or warning and schedule follow-up meetings with the person to ensure that the precept is understood and is being respected;
4. Thou shalt be as consistent as possible in applying this canon;
5. Thou shalt keep in mind that the penalty/punishment should fit the crime;
6. Thou shalt act with concern for the *salus animarum*;
7. Thou shalt be proactive in your *munus* of governance;
8. Thou shalt be obedient to the legitimate commands of your hierarchical superiors, including the Apostolic See;
9. Thou shalt normally undertake a penal process before imposing penalties upon one accused of a delict (cf. cc. 1341; 1342; 1718 par 1).
10. Thou shalt attempt to employ conciliatory methods when possible.[47]

Clergy have successfully taken recourse against penal actions by bishops and religious ordinaries, so superiors would be wise to observe carefully all the procedural and penal laws.

Doktorczyk provides the following as an example of specificity in a precept:

Further criticism of the bishop, whether during a homily or any other occasion that provides an audience to the priest, will be interpreted as persistent disobedience (cf. c. 1371 §2) and may result in the eventual imposition of a just penalty, not excluding removal from your office as pastor (c. 1336), or other consequences, including removal of your faculties to preach (c. 764).[48]

This example ordering a priest not to publicly criticize the bishop, covers the priest doing this in the homily, as well as encompassing any other situation. The consequences of disobeying the precept are clear and unequivocal.

Receipt of Laws

A fundamental aspect of making clergy accountable is to ensure that each cleric receives particular laws and has them explained to him. Each priest needs to sign a declaration that he has received a copy of the particular law and that he understands the law, whether it be financial law or safeguarding and sexual abuse law. This prevents accused priests escaping punishment or sanction in the future by simply saying "I never received a copy of that law," or "I did not know or understand I was not allowed to do that."

Warnings

If the penalty for an offense is a medicinal penalty such as suspension, then the cleric must be warned before he receives the penalty of suspension for a repeat offense.[49] Most importantly, if there is no warning given, the cleric cannot be considered to be persistently disobedient under canons 1339[50] and 1371. The diocesan bishop is implicitly giving a warning to the cleric when he gives him a precept. If the text of the warning is not recorded in writing, it will be difficult to prove whether it was ever given. A religious superior is required by canon 697 to give at least two warnings before proceeding to dismiss a religious for offenses in canon 696 such as neglect of the obligations of consecrated life:

> In the cases mentioned in canon 696, if the major Superior, after consulting his or her council, judges that the process of dismissal should be commenced:
>
> 1° the major Superior is to collect or complete the proofs;
> 2° the major Superior is to warn the member in writing, or before two witnesses, with an explicit caution that dismissal will follow unless the member reforms. The reasons for dismissal are to be clearly expressed and the member is to be given every opportunity for defence. If the warning has no effect, another warning is to be given after an interval of at least fifteen days. The preference always is that the member of the religious institute is given written warnings, but allowance is made for the warnings to be given verbally before two witnesses and then recorded in writing. (c. 697)

Penalties as a Result of Precepts

If a precept has not resulted in improving the behavior of a cleric, then a penalty should be imposed. An ecclesiastical penalty is the privation of some good and is inflicted by the legitimate authority for the correction of an offender or the punishment of a crime. Offenders are not to receive a penalty unless they have violated a law in the external forum and this action is imputable by reason of malice or negligence.[51] *Dolus* or malice is understood to mean a "deliberate violation of a penal law or precept."[52]

The essence of *malice* "is the positive will to act against the law, humanly and freely, whatever the reasons may be that lead to violating the law or precept, provided that freedom continues during the act."[53] *Negligence* is "the omission of due diligence including ignorance, and even inadvertence and error."[54] "Before a person can be accused of an offence the person must be a proper subject of penal action."[55] There should always be a preliminary investigation (cc. 1717–20) before any precept or penalty is given. This requirement and the procedures involved are spelled out in detail in the *Vademecum* of the Dicastery for the Doctrine of the Faith promulgated on June 5, 2022.[56] While canon 1342 §1 allows for an extrajudicial decree by a bishop, the law requires the ordinary to "hear" the person upon whom he proposes to impose the penalty.[57] Therefore, there must always be some due process involved in any penal case. Offenses such as sexual abuse of minors[58] incur an expiatory penalty and so a priest can be dismissed from the clerical state without a warning and a religious brother or sister can be dismissed from the religious institute without a warning.[59]

CONCLUSION

Apart from legislation, there are other good employment and personnel practices such as performance reviews. Each year there needs to be a performance review for clergy and diocesan employees. The review could be incorporated into the process for clergy changes. A performance review helps to keep job descriptions and expectations updated. It can easily happen that a person's workload or responsibilities evolve and develop over time.

Circumstances change and other people can impinge on an individual's role. Many of these things can affect how a person carries out their duties and responsibilities, and a performance review gives both parties an opportunity to deal with this. Accountability and transparency are important in all areas of life today, and society rightly expects accountability and transparency in the Church. For clergy, knowledge of canon law is professional knowledge that the Church can reasonably expect them to know. Similarly, accountants can be expected to know financial regulations. Consequently, after there is an external violation of the law or a precept, it is presumed that the offender is imputable,[60] and if he is a cleric, he cannot use the excuse of ignorance.

Before an ordinary imposes penalties, he must have considered all pastoral means available to him.[61] Jesus taught this approach for dealing with wrongdoers (see Matt 18:15–17). Correction of an offender is most important for the Church that wants all members of the faithful to live according to the teaching and example of Jesus Christ. Therefore, in dealing with clergy or religious engaged in crimes or misconduct, put precepts and warnings in writing.

7

ABSOLVING AN ACCOMPLICE IN A SIN AGAINST THE SIXTH COMMANDMENT

Accomplice normally means being a co-operator or participator in another's sin. People can obviously cooperate in a wide variety of sins. Canon 1329 §2 specifies that "in the case of a *latae sententiae* penalty attached to an offence, accomplices, even though not mentioned in the law or precept, incur the same penalty if, without their assistance, the crime would not have been committed."[1] With regard to the sacrament of penance, *accomplice* refers specifically to the person sinning with a priest in a sin against the sixth commandment. Because there is such obvious potential to bring the sacrament into disrepute and abuse it, there are specific provisions in canon law to prevent this abuse of both the sacrament and the penitent.

With sexual abuse and misconduct cases today, a priest in a "consenting adult relationship" could invalidly attempt to grant absolution to an accomplice in a sin against the sixth commandment. It does not matter whether the accomplice is a man or a woman, or what age the person is. The absolution of an accomplice is a crime reserved to the Dicastery for the Doctrine of the Faith,[2] and the priest/confessor can be dismissed from the clerical state as a result.

HISTORY OF LEGISLATION ON ABSOLVING ACCOMPLICES

In 1215, the Fourth Lateran Council had legislated that the faithful were to confess once a year to their parish priest:

All the faithful of either sex…should individually confess all their sins in a faithful manner to their own priest at least once a year….If any persons wishes, for good reasons, to confess their sins to another priest lest them first ask and obtain the permission of their own priest; for otherwise the other priest will not have the power to absolve or bind them.[3]

This law required the penitent to confess their sins at least once a year. It also required the penitent to seek permission from his/her parish priest in order that another priest would be competent to hear their confession and grant them absolution. This was obviously a complication for any case in which an accomplice of a priest needed absolution for a sin against the sixth commandment.

Saint Thomas Aquinas (1224–74) taught that "a priest should not hear the confession of the woman accomplice with whom he had sinned, but ought to remit the penitent to another priest. If the priest denied permission or recourse to a superior, at that time on account of the danger, then that is disgraceful."[4] From the seventeenth century, there are some records of priests having absolved accomplices in sins against the sixth commandment. The first case of absolving an accomplice is found in the archives of the Holy Office in 1658.[5] At that time, it was made clear in a circular letter to all bishops that confessors lacked jurisdiction in the case of a priest absolving his accomplice.[6] In another case in 1665, it was noted that if the soliciting priest could absolve the accomplice it would be a way of avoiding being denounced for solicitation.[7] In 1679, in a third case of solicitation, the Sacred Congregation for the Council forbade a confessor under threat of a grave penalty from hearing the confession of an accomplice.[8]

The most comprehensive and significant legislation regarding a priest absolving an accomplice in a sexual sin comes from Pope Benedict XIV in his apostolic constitution *Sacramentum Poenitentiae*, on June 1, 1741,[9] which was the first general law that forbade the absolution of one's accomplice in a sexual sin. The pope reserved the absolution of the priest who absolved an accomplice to himself. He did this to stop the sacrament of penance being abused, to avoid the dangers of penitents being seduced, and to prevent confessors relapsing into the same sin again. Absolving an accomplice in a sexual sin is of course highly improper and unprofessional. Furthermore, the priest does act as a judge in the sacrament of penance. Canons 888 §1[10] of the 1917 Code and 978 of the 1983 Code reminded priests:

> In hearing confessions, the priest is to remember that he is equally a judge and a physician and has been established by God as a minister of divine justice and mercy, so that he has regard for the divine honor and the salvation of souls.

Effectively by absolving the accomplice, the priest is making a judgment about his own case. The priest is acting in the person of Christ and is supposed to be leading penitents to follow the teaching and example of Jesus Christ. Obviously, he cannot do this if he has sinned with the penitent. A confessor who has committed external sins against the sixth commandment cannot validly absolve his accomplice from such sins. Canon 884 of the 1917 Code stated,

> The absolution of an accomplice in a sin of turpitude is invalid, except in danger of death; even in case of danger of death, outside of a case of necessity, it is illicit on the part of the confessor according to the norm of the apostolic constitutions, specifically the constitution of Benedict XIV *Sacramentum Poenitentiae* of 1 June 1741.

The apostolic constitution of Pope Benedict XIV was document III in the appendix to the 1917 Code. There was a distinction made between a penitent in good health and a case of the penitent being in danger of death. "Danger of death" also included mobilized soldiers.[11] "Turpitude" means "a corrupt or depraved or degenerate act or practice";[12] but in this context, it means the granting of absolution of a sin that one was complicit in and personally involved in. However, the 1917 Code omitted reference to "dares or presumes," which meant that ignorance of the law or the penalty attached did not excuse the priest from receiving the censure. Woywod-Smith taught that ignorance, caused by grave and culpable negligence in acquiring sufficient knowledge, does excuse from the penalty.[13]

Except in danger of death, the absolution of an accomplice is always invalid and illicit. To be both valid and lawful under the 1917 Code, two conditions had to be met: (a) no other priest was present or available; and (b) another priest could not be called without danger of grave infamy or public scandal.[14] Furthermore, the excommunication would not be incurred if the penitent in danger of death refused to confess to anyone else.[15] For the crime of complicity or to be truly an accomplice, Palazzini explains:

> The following conditions must be present: a) the act committed must be a mortal sin, both materially and formally; b) it must be a grave sin for both i.e. the sinful action must involve formal complicity, which is clearly present not only when both partners actively and willingly engage in the impure action, but also when one of the participants, though remaining passive, manifests consent by failure to offer proper or sufficient resistance; c) the sin must be an external act against the sixth commandment, for only an external sin admits of complicity; d) the sin must be certain; e) the sin must be one not yet directly remitted.[16]

If the confessor absolved or pretended to absolve his accomplice in a sin of impurity, the confessor incurred an automatic excommunication reserved to the Apostolic See according to canon 2367 §1 of the 1917 code.[17] The canon makes a distinction between a penitent being in danger of death and a case of necessity. Canon 884 of the 1917 Code stated that it was unlawful for a priest to absolve an accomplice in danger of death of a sin of complicity if it was not necessary to do so.

If the penitent was in danger of death, it was valid for the priest accomplice to grant absolution if there was no other priest available; or if there was one and there was grave danger of infamy and scandal arising; or if the penitent refused to have the other priest hear the confession. If the penitent had not yet received absolution for the sexual sin with the priest, and this priest accomplice persuaded the penitent to confess other sins without mentioning the sexual sin, the priest accomplice still incurred the penalty of excommunication.[18] The priest also incurred the excommunication if he encouraged the penitent directly or indirectly to omit mention of the sexual sin, and then the priest granted absolution.[19] The sexual sin must certainly have been committed, and be external and grave for both parties unless the confessor has, prior to committing the sin, convinced the penitent to believe it was not a grave sin.[20]

The canon makes a clear distinction between the cases of a priest pretending to absolve an accomplice of a sin of complicity, and the case where the penitent, with the encouragement of the priest accomplice, seeks absolution without mentioning the sin of complicity. The Holy Office was asked

> whether the persons of whom there is question in canon 2367 §2, as *indirectly inducing* (an accomplice not to confess to them the sin of complicity) include also a confessor who, either in confession or out of it, has persuaded a person that, in acts of impurity to be committed by them together, there is no sin at all, or at least no grave sin, and in consequence has absolved or pretended to absolve the person, when he or she afterward made a sacramental confession to him, only of other sins than the sin of complicity.

Reply. In the affirmative, *facto verbo cum Sanctissimo*. His Holiness, Pius XI, deigned to approve and confirm this reply by his supreme authority, and ordered that it be published.[21]

Prior to this interpretation from the Holy Office, the common opinion was that the crime of complicity did not occur when the priest persuaded the penitent that it was not a sin or at least not a grave sin that they committed between them.[22] Because it goes beyond the concept of complicity, Vermeersch commented that "the complicity with the priest included a person of either sex, conscious of committing a grave sin in the external forum. If the penitent thought that it was a venial sin or no sin, then the sin of complicity in the strict sense did not occur." De Paolis also points out how this interpretation was contrary to the common opinion of authors.[23] Cappello taught that the addition changed the ancient teaching since it declared a true extension or a new law with the added words.[24]

A priest "who dares or presumes to absolve the accomplice" was excommunicated. Also, the priest who had absolved his accomplice and is under excommunication cannot be absolved from the sin of absolving his accomplice without a special faculty.[25] However, those priests having absolved an accomplice can, when they are in danger of death, be absolved by another priest even if their penalty is most especially reserved to the apostolic see.[26] The 1917 Code allowed any confessor in the sacramental forum to absolve a priest if it was hard on him to remain in a state of grave sin, or if there was a grave danger of scandal or infamy:

> §1. In more urgent cases, namely if the automatic censure cannot be observed exteriorly without grave danger of scandal or infamy, or if it is hard on the penitent to remain in a state of grave sin for the time necessary for the competent Superior to provide, then any confessor in the sacramental forum can absolve from these, no matter how reserved, [and he will enjoin] the burden of having recourse, under pain of reincidence, within a month at [most] by letter and through the confessor, if this can be done without grave inconvenience, withholding the name, to the S. Penitentiary or to a Bishop or other Superior endowed with the faculty [of absolving], and stands by his mandates. (c. 2254)

When the priest who had absolved his accomplice receives absolution under these latter circumstances, he was required to have recourse to the Sacred Penitentiary within one month or he relapsed under the penalty of excommunication.

REVISION OF THE 1917 CODE

The Commission for the Revision of the Code of Canon Law after Vatican II drew up ten principles to guide its drafting of the new code. These principles were approved by the 1967 Synod of Bishops. Principle 9 stated, "Penalties are sometimes necessary, but they are to be imposed in the external forum and after judgment; those imposed by the law itself are to be reduced to a minimum."[27]

The application of this principle led to the reduction of canons in the book on penal law from 220 canons in the 1917 Code to 89 canons in the 1983 Code. The number of penalties for specific crimes reduced from 101 in the 1917 Code to just 35 in the 1983 Code. These changes impacted on the penalties concerning abuses of the sacrament of penance such as absolving an accomplice. The 1973 Schema, the draft canon concerning the offense of absolving an accomplice included the broader understanding of the crime as in the Holy Office Interpretation in 1934. Canon 55 §1, no. 2 of the schema stated that "the penalty of interdict is automatically incurred, or if it is a priest, he is suspended and is unable to validly grant sacramental absolution whether he imparts it or pretends to do so."[28] Some consultors also wanted the canon to include accomplices in other grave sins, but this was rejected by the Commission for the Revision of the Code.[29] The legislator did not seem to want to include the severity of the old legislation and was possibly influenced by limiting the number of penal offenses and penalties. Chiapetta states that bishops are included in this by the word *sacerdos*.[30] Nigro argues that bishops were not included by the word *sacerdos*,[31] but with the changes that have occurred in the 1983 Code, it is clear *sacerdos* includes bishops and priests.[32]

1983 Code

Canon 977 of the 1983 Code stated that "the absolution of an accomplice in a sin against the sixth commandment of the Decalogue is invalid except in danger of death." The penalty for a priest absolving an accomplice was an excommunication reserved to the Apostolic See according to canon 1384 §1 [2021, 1384]. "A priest who acts against the prescript of canon 977 incurs a *latae sententiae* excommunication reserved to the Apostolic See." De Paolis describes the crime in his commentary:

> The sin of complicity occurs when two or more persons, whether or not of the same sex, each conscious of the gravity of the sin, consents to an external sin— also grave in the external dimension— that is in itself libidinous [lustful].[33]

It does not matter when the sexual sin took place, including before the priest was ordained.[34] The law itself deprives the priest of the faculty to grant absolution. However, once an accomplice has received absolution for the sin against the sixth commandment, the penitent can then validly and lawfully confess more recent sins to the priest with whom the penitent was an accomplice.[35]

The canon does not make any mention of the availability of other confessors at this time, but simply provides for the priest/accomplice to validly absolve the penitent in danger of death. It does not matter whether the penitent[36] knows that the absolution is invalid. The priest should know from his professional knowledge as a priest when the absolution is invalid or not.[37] The rationale for the law is to promote respect for the sacrament, the common ecclesiastical good, as well as the spiritual good of both the priest and penitent. Absolving one's accomplice undermines the sacrament of penance being for one's salvation and conversion. If one could in ordinary circumstances absolve one's accomplice in a sin against the sixth commandment, effectively this would be tacit approval for the priest and penitent to commit more sexual sins together in the future.

Loza notes that this canon is a "'iure' revocation of the penitential faculty of said priest, over this penitent, and with respect to this sin."[38] Also Loza points out that "the sin must be serious and external: in word or in deed; committed at any time: even before the priest received sacred ordination."[39] There had been a decree of the Sacred Penitentiary to this effect on January 22, 1879.[40] The phrase "reserved to the Apostolic See" (*Sedi Apostolicae reservatum*) was added by Pope John Paul II during his final review of the draft canons of the Code. This addition was to the text of what was canon 1378 §1 of the 1982 draft.[41] A penitent, committing a sin against the sixth commandment with the priest, could not only confess their other sins to the priest/accomplice, and receive absolution.

Canon 988 §1 states that such an absolution by the priest/accomplice is an invalid absolution for all sins because the absolution is indivisible, and a penitent must make an integral confession.[42] However, the priest would not incur the penalty if he did not recognize the accomplice, or if he was doubtful that it was the accomplice in a confession behind a screen. Nor would the priest incur the penalty if he heard the confession of the accomplice but then refused to grant absolution.[43]

Because the description of the crime of absolving an accomplice was relatively restricted in the 1983 Code, the crime did not encompass the case of a priest pretending to absolve a penitent or simulating the sacrament of penance. These crimes are encompassed by canons 1384 and 1379.[44] The crime of absolving an accomplice only occurs when a priest absolves an accomplice confessing the sin of complicity. De Paolis concludes:

> The offence of absolving an accomplice now only occurs when the absolution is given to an accomplice who confesses the sin of complicity. There is no longer anything about pretending to absolve, nor absolving a penitent who has been directly or indirectly induced into confessing the sin of complicity.[45]

ABSOLUTION IN DANGER OF DEATH

According to canon 976, when a penitent is in danger of death, the penitent can receive absolution from the priest/accomplice validly and lawfully:

> Even though a priest lacks the faculty to hear confessions, he absolves validly and licitly any penitents whatsoever in danger of death from any censures and sins, even if an approved priest is present.

When any penitent is in danger of death it is obligatory for any priest, including a priest/accomplice, a suspended priest or a priest dispensed from the obligations of priesthood, to hear the confession and grant absolution. Canon 986 §2 states that "in urgent necessity, any confessor is obliged to hear the confessions of the Christian faithful, and in danger of death, any priest is so obliged." Canon 991 also clarifies the right of each member of the faithful so that "every member of the Christian faithful is free to confess sins to a legitimately approved confessor of his or her choice, even to one of another rite."

GRAVIORA DELICTA

On April 30, 2001, Pope John Paul II promulgated norms concerning the more grave crimes reserved to the Congregation for the Doctrine of the Faith,[46] and Pope Benedict XVI ordered the promulgation of revised norms on May 21, 2010.[47] Included among the grave crimes was the absolution of an accomplice in a sin against the sixth commandment of the Decalogue:

> The more grave delicts against the sanctity of the Sacrament of Penance reserved to the Congregation for the Doctrine of the Faith are: 1° the absolution of an accomplice in a sin against the sixth commandment of the Decalogue, mentioned in canon 1378 §I [Book VI, 2021 c. 1384] of the Code of Canon Law, and in canon 1457 of the Code of Canons of the Eastern Churches. (Pope John Paul II, *Sacramentorum sanctitatis tutela*, Article 4 §1)[48]

Conclusion

The law concerning a priest absolving an accomplice is very clear. Except in danger of death, a priest who has sinned against the sixth commandment with another person cannot absolve that person in the sacrament of penance. Whether or not the priest is aware of the law on this matter, if he absolves an accomplice, he incurs a *latae sententiae* excommunication reserved to the Dicastery for the Doctrine of the Faith. Any absolution granted by the priest is invalid. The only exception would be if the accomplice was in danger of death. If a priest claims he was ignorant of the law, or that he thought it only applied to acts of sexual intercourse, ignorance is not an excuse. This knowledge is professional knowledge that a priest should have. Delegates and Sexual Abuse Committees investigating so-called consenting adult relationships need to be aware that when a priest absolves his accomplice in a sin against the sixth commandment, they are dealing with a grave crime in canon law as well as a grave sin.

8

SOLICITATION IN THE SACRAMENT OF PENANCE

TRADITIONAL UNDERSTANDING OF SOLICITATION

The Dicastery for the Doctrine of the Faith in its Glossary of Terms on the Vatican website describes *solicitation*:

> Solicitation: in penal law, an invitation to another to commit a sin. Specifically, as a delict, it involves the suggestion or invitation of a priest in the context of the sacrament of penance to a penitent to commit a sin against the Sixth Commandment with the priest.[1]

This is the traditional and strict interpretation of the meaning of the term. After Pope John Paul II issued the motu proprio *Sacramentorum Sanctitatis Tutela*, a set of "Substantive Norms" were issued by the Congregation for the Doctrine of the Faith in *Epistula ad totius Catholicae Ecclesiae Episcopos*.[2] The crime of solicitation was included in article 4 of the "Substantive Norms," hereinafter referred to as *Gravia Delicta*:

> Article. 4 §1. The more grave delicts against the sanctity of the Sacrament of Penance reserved to the Congregation for the Doctrine of the Faith are....
> 4° the solicitation to a sin against the sixth commandment of the Decalogue in the act, on the occasion, or under the pretext of confession, as mentioned in canon 1387 [Book VI, 2021 c. 1385] of the Code of Canon Law, and in canon 1458 of the Code of Canons of the Eastern Churches, if it is directed to sinning with the confessor himself.[3]

Significantly the crime of solicitation referred to in *Graviora Delicta* is only a reserved crime when the confessor seeks to have the penitent sin against the sixth commandment with the confessor himself.[4] Other crimes of solicitation, when a priest encourages a penitent to sin against the sixth commandment alone or with a third party, are not reserved to the Congregation for the Doctrine of the Faith, but come under the jurisdiction of the local ordinary.

FIRST LEGISLATION ON SOLICITATION

The first legislation concerning the crime of solicitation was issued by the Council of Treves in 1227 in canon 8: "Likewise, priests should be on guard against taking away their dignity, so we prohibit them from soliciting any person in confession by actions and words and we excommunicate any [priest] doing this."[5] The Council decreed that a priest who solicited a women penitent be deposed and excommunicated.[6] Pope Pius IV (1559–65) was clearly concerned about instances of this crime. He gave jurisdiction for this delict to the Inquisition in Spain when he issued the constitution *Cum Sicut Insuper*, on April 16, 1561.[7] Pope Gregory XV (1621–23) then enacted legislation making this law applicable throughout the world with the constitution *Universi* of August 30, 1622.[8]

To do everything to eliminate soliciting priests, Pope Gregory XV also decreed that penitents who were victims of solicitation had the strict obligation to denounce soliciting confessors.[9] Then, in 1741, Pope Benedict XIV promulgated comprehensive legislation in the Apostolic Constitution *Sacramentorum Poenitentiae*.[10] The legislation provided more detailed law on solicitation, including a specific procedure to try to get to the truth of the matter concerning the alleged solicitation, while at the same time respecting the seal of confession and the dignity of the sacrament. There was strict confidentiality in the process and the credibility of the accused and the accuser were both considered. *Sacramentum Poenitentiae* was an appendix to the 1917 Code of Canon Law and gave the Supreme Sacred Congregation of the Roman and Universal Inquisition the responsibility of safeguarding the sanctity of the sacrament of penance.[11]

THE 1917 CODE

Because solicitation was considered a most serious crime, canon 2368 §1 of the 1917 Code stated,

> Whoever commits the crime of solicitation mentioned in canon 904 is suspended from the celebration of Mass and from hearing sacramental confessions and even, for the gravity of the delict, is declared incapable of receiving them, is deprived of all benefices, dignities, active and passive voice, and is for all of these declared incapables, and in more serious cases is also subject to degradation.

Crimen Sollicitationis (1922)

In 1922, specific norms were issued in "On the Method of Proceeding in Cases of Solicitation" (*Crimen Sollicitationis*). This Instruction was approved *in forma specifica* by Pope Pius XI and signed by Cardinal Merry del Val, the cardinal secretary of the Holy Office. Although the document was printed by Vatican Press, it was not promulgated in the normal way in the *Acta Apostolicae Sedis*. The Holy Office was given competence to deal with cases administratively or in a judicial process.[12] *Crimen Sollicitationis* gave detailed instructions to bishops on how to deal with the crime of solicitation.[13]

Crimen Sollicitationis (1962)

In 1962, the Holy Office reissued *Crimen Sollicitationis*[14] with minor changes to the 1922 text to include religious priests. Pope John XXIII approved the revised document, with Cardinal Ottaviani acting as Secretary of the Holy Office and signing it. The contents of *Crimen Sollicitationis* are explained in an article by Nicholas Cafardi:

> One thing the document established was that the Holy Office had jurisdiction over these crimes, and was, in this document, telling local bishops how to handle them. More than anything, the instruction is a dry statement of the rules of criminal procedure that apply when a priest has been accused of solicitation.[15]

Abbo and Hannan specify that:

> the delict consists in soliciting any penitent whatever to the commission of grave sin against purity[16] even on the pretext of confession, whether it is done by word, sign or touch, or by sinful conversation, or by missives to be read even after departure from the place where they were given. The resistance of the penitent is immaterial; so also the fact that a third person is solicited through the penitent as agent. Indeed, the delict is committed even by wrong advice as to the sinfulness of evil thoughts. Moreover, if the external action is performed by the confessor, specific malice is presumed [canon 2200 §2], except in the case of conversation in regard to which the malice must be apparent from the circumstances. The delict is committed by the confessor even if the initiative came from the penitent. On the other hand, the consent of the penitent is not a relevant element in the delict; it is committed even if the penitent is unaware that solicitation was attempted.[17]

The new edition of *Crimen Sollicitationis* in 1962 aimed to cover cases of religious priests.[18] However, in the latter half of the twentieth century, the canonical norms were not often followed by bishops or major Superiors of religious institutes.[19] Between 1993 and 1998 only twelve judicial trials were conducted in the United States of America. Only six of these trials had been completed by the end of 1998.[20] The canonical approach was rarely implemented. Instead, a therapeutic approach consisting of counselling and treatment was usually taken, and offending clergy were not removed from ministry and not dismissed from the clerical state.

THE 1983 CODE

Canon 1385 of the 1983 Code addresses solicitation:

> A priest who in confession, or on the occasion or under the pretext of confession, solicits a penitent to commit a sin against the sixth commandment of the Decalogue, is to be punished, according to the gravity of the offence, with suspension, prohibitions and deprivations; in the more serious cases he is to be dismissed from the clerical state.

There is a difference between this canon and canon 904 of the 1917 Code, which obliged the solicited penitent to denounce the priest. Under the 1917 Code, if the penitent failed to denounce the soliciting priest, then the penitent received an automatic excommunication under canon 2368.[21] The 1983 Code neither requires the penitent to denounce the soliciting priest, nor requires another confessor to advise the solicited penitent to denounce the soliciting priest.[22]

MEANING OF *SOLICITATION*

While the Congregation of the Doctrine of the Faith defines the grave crime of solicitation reserved to the Congregation, in fact, solicitation is a much broader concept. In fact, solicitation is a much broader concept. Igino Tarocchi defines the crime of solicitation as "any act by which a confessor in the sacrament of penance either induces a penitent to sin seriously against chastity or accepts the inducements of a penitent against chastity (1917 canon 904)."[23]

Solicitation can be either active or passive. Therefore, solicitation leads another to commit sinful acts by using explicit words, advice, promises, signs, actions, or any other method that reveals the intention of the solicitor to solicit. McKeever points out that "the solicitation is connected with the Sacrament of Penance if it takes place either in the confession, or immediately before or after the confession, or on the occasion or pretext of confession, or in a confessional or some other place designated for confession or chosen with the pretence of hearing a confession."[24] McAreavy points out that "the offence consists of the action of the priest: it is not necessary that the penitent accede to the suggestions made; consequently, even if nothing further occurs, the offence has been committed and the priest is liable to the penalty."[25]

Edward Peters gives a much more extensive understanding of solicitation again:

> The image of solicitation that springs to mind here is...that of a priest and... female penitent....But neither the text of Canon 1387 (2021 c. 1385) (specifically the phrase, "solicits a penitent to sin against the sixth commandment of the Decalogue") nor the tradition behind the modern canon construes the crime of solicitation that narrowly.[26]

Consequently, Peters quotes a range of modern commentaries on the Code of Canon Law, demonstrating that solicitation covers a wide range of sexual sins apart from what the average person in the pew might consider to be solicitation:

First, the canonical crime of solicitation is not limited to cases wherein a confessor's bad advice given is only toward a penitent's sexual misconduct with the priest himself. John Martin, commenting on Canon 1387 in the British-Irish canonical commentary *Letter & Spirit* (1985) at 799, observes: "The offence is committed whether the priest encourages the penitent to sin either with the priest himself or with any third party." Thomas Green, writing in the 2000 *CLSA New Commentary* (at 1591), agrees: "The delict might also be verified if the solicited sexual activity involves the penitent and a third party, not necessarily the priest and the penitent." And Leon del Amo in the 2004 *Code of Canon Law Annotated* (at 1077), notes: "The offense consists in soliciting the penitent to sin against the sixth commandment, either with the person soliciting or with a third party." No commentator on the 1983 Code disputes the understanding of solicitation in Canon 1387 as embracing not only a confessor's advice toward sexual sin between the penitent and the confessor himself, but also between the penitent and a third party. But to see clearly how a confessor's giving a penitent objectively immoral advice, even if such advice is directed toward the solitary acts of the penitent alone, can also constitute a form of solicitation, a review of canonical commentary on the crime of solicitation under the earlier, 1917 Code, is helpful.[27]

The commentators are consistent in their understanding of solicitation, and how it is a much broader crime than what most people think. Many canonists understand that "it consists in the confessor approving a behavior of the penitent that is contrary to the sixth commandment."[28] It is certainly a much broader crime than the particular form of solicitation that is a grave crime reserved to the Dicastery for the Doctrine of the Faith. But since penal laws are "subject to a strict interpretation,"[29] there is more precision required to a description of the crime of solicitation than "bad advice." Some forms of what could be described as "bad advice" are, in fact, crimes of solicitation encompassed by canon 1387. However, they would not be grave crimes reserved to the Congregation of the Doctrine of the Faith. Many priests are unaware of the breadth of what is encompassed by the crime of solicitation.

Time and Place of Solicitation

In analyzing the crime of solicitation, Green points out the timing of the crime is understood broadly so that "the delict could happen during the sacramental celebration, immediately before or after it, or in a setting in which the penitent could reasonably expect the hearing of his or her confession."[30] The crime does not have to be only between the sign of the cross at the beginning of the sacramental celebration and the end of the words of absolution. Therefore, for example, if a priest hears a penitent's confession and grants the person absolution, then immediately afterwards kisses the person, it constitutes solicitation.

Obligation to Denounce a Priest Soliciting before 1983

The Church imposed on the penitent who was solicited the most serious obligation to denounce the soliciting priest within one month. Naturally, most people would have been unaware of this obligation. Therefore, the most likely scenario would have been that a priest would have to advise them of their obligation under penalty of excommunication. Canon 904 of the 1917 Code stated,

> In accord with the norm of the apostolic constitutions and specifically the constitution of [Pope] Benedict XIV *Sacramentum Poenitentiae* of 1 June 1741, a penitent must within one month denounce to the local Ordinary or to the Sacred Congregation of the Holy Office a priest [accused] of the delict of solicitation in confession; the confessor, must, under grave obligation of his conscience, advise the penitent of this duty.

The serious obligation to denounce to the proper authority, local Ordinary or the Holy Office, any confessor guilty of solicitation in the confessional is clear. The Church wants to stop such a priest from functioning. If a solicited penitent reports the abuse and then does not follow through with giving evidence against the priest, the Church could use the threat of a penalty to get the evidence to have the offending priest convicted and removed from ministry. The solicited penitent who failed to denounce the soliciting confessor within one month was also subject to the penalty of excommunication. Canon 2368 §2 of the 1917 Code stated,

> But the faithful who knowingly omit to denounce him by whom they were solicited within one month against the prescription of Canon 904 incur automatic excommunication reserved to no one and shall not be absolved until after satisfying the obligation or seriously promising to satisfy it.

The Church's intention was to have the offender stopped and prevent possible future abuses. The denunciation of soliciting confessors also upholds the dignity of the sacrament and helps to save souls. Therefore, the Congregation for the Holy Office legislated to compel penitents who had been solicited to reveal the fact that a priest had attempted to solicit them.

Prior to 1983, the victim of solicitation, who disregarded the obligation to denounce the soliciting priest, could only be absolved when the obligation to denounce was fulfilled, or the penitent had promised to fulfil that obligation.[31]

The instruction *Crimen Sollicitationis* stated,

> The crime of solicitation is ordinarily committed in the absence of any witnesses; consequently, lest it remain almost always hidden and unpunished with inestimable detriment to souls, it has been necessary to compel the one person usually aware of the crime, namely the penitent solicited, to reveal it *by a denunciation* imposed by positive law. Therefore:
>
> "In accordance with the Apostolic Constitutions and specifically the

Constitution of Benedict XIV *Sacramentum Poenitentiae* of 1 June 1741, the penitent must denounce a priest guilty of the crime of solicitation in confession to the local Ordinary or to the Sacred Congregation of the Holy Office within one month; and the confessor must, by an obligation gravely binding in conscience, warn the penitent of this duty." (c. 904)[32]

In fact, any member of the faithful, not just the solicited penitent, must denounce the soliciting priest:

> Moreover, in the light of Canon 1935, any member of the faithful can always denounce a crime of solicitation of which he or she has certain knowledge; indeed, there is an urgent duty to make such a denunciation whenever one is compelled to do so by the natural law itself, on account of danger to faith or religion, or some other impending public evil.[33]

Consequently, if a solicited penitent fails to denounce the soliciting priest within one month, the penitent incurs a *latae sententiae* excommunication:

> "A member of the faithful who, in violation of the (aforementioned) prescription of Canon 904, knowingly disregards the obligation to denounce within a month the person by whom he or she was solicited, incurs an excommunication *latae sententiae* reserved to no one, which is not to be lifted until he or she has satisfied the obligation, or has promised seriously to do so" (Can. 2368 §2).[34]

While the penalty of excommunication is not reserved to anyone, the solicited penitent must at least promise to denounce the soliciting priest to have the penalty removed.

FALSE DENUNCIATION OF A PRIEST SOLICITING

Now, false denunciations are possible. With the large amount of money involved in settling claims of sexual abuse against all members of society, there is potential for false claims to be made. If a penitent falsely accuses a priest out of bitterness, twisted interpretations or other motives, the penitent, guilty of the false denunciation, incurs an excommunication especially reserved to the Holy See. Because of the seal of confession,[35] and the circumstances of confession with the priest and penitent being alone, it is very difficult for a priest to prove his innocence. He cannot reveal the content of a confession to defend himself. All he can do is deny the accusation, admit it, or remain silent. It is for this very reason that there have been special legislation and procedures for dealing with the crime of solicitation such as *Crimen Sollicitationis*.[36]

Under the 1917 Code, the false accuser could not be absolved, even in danger of death, without a prior retraction of the false denunciation.[37] The 1983 Code legislated for false accusations of solicitation, whereby the penitent who confesses this crime is not to be absolved unless the penitent retracts the false denunciation and is prepared to repair any damages to

PENAL LAW IN ACTION

the reputation and the good name of the priest:

> Whoever confesses to have denounced falsely an innocent confessor to ecclesiastical authority concerning the crime of solicitation to sin against the sixth commandment of the Decalogue is not to be absolved unless the person has first formally retracted the false denunciation and is prepared to repair damages if there are any. (c. 982)

Furthermore, canon 1390 of the 1983 Code has a specific penalty for a person who makes a false denunciation:

> §1. A person who falsely denounces a confessor of the offense mentioned in canon 1385 to an ecclesiastical superior incurs a *latae sententiae* interdict and, if a cleric, he incurs also a suspension.
> §2. A person who calumniously denounces some other offense to an ecclesiastical superior, or otherwise unlawfully injures the good name of another, is to be punished according to the provision of can. 1336 §§2–4, to which moreover a censure may be added.
> §3. The calumniator must also be compelled to make appropriate amends.

The penalties for a person making a false denunciation and the conditions for the false accuser receiving absolution aim to restore the good reputation of priest. Woestman cautions superiors about the reality of false accusations:

> Ecclesiastical superiors must be most cautious in receiving such denunciations. There is the obligation both of protecting the faithful and of not unjustly accusing or punishing an innocent priest who has been accused without foundation by a malicious or psychologically disturbed individual. Obviously in the face of an accusation it may be very difficult, if not impossible, for the accused priest to defend himself. It may well be just his word against that of the accuser. Besides that, he is bound by the seal of confession.[38]

This is wise advice, and in these kinds of cases the credibility of the accuser as well as the accused always needs to be considered.

Questions Concerning the Accused and the Accuser during an Investigation

Often the name of the accuser cannot be revealed and great care must be taken not to violate the seal of confession. Linus Neli suggests questions that may require modification:

> Did you ever hear or see anything concerning the accused and the accuser? If so, what did you see or hear? Followed by When? Where? Why? On what occasion? From whom did you hear it? How did you come to know of this information? Was anybody else there? State what you know concerning the life and character of the accuser? Give examples. State what you know concerning the life and character of the accused? Give examples. How would you assess the reputation and credibility of the accuser? How would you

assess the reputation and credibility of the accused?[39]

SACRAMENTORUM SANCTITATIS TUTELA (2001)

Pope John Paul II promulgated the norms for "Grave Crimes" reserved to the Congregation for the Doctrine of the Faith on May 18, 2001.[40] These norms were revised by Pope Benedict XVI, and the Congregation for the Doctrine of the Faith released "Revised Norms on Dealing with Clerical Sex Abuse of Minors and Other Grave Offenses"[41] on July 15, 2010. The new norms had been approved *in forma specifica* by Pope Benedict XVI on May 21, 2010.[42] Charles Scicluna explains when a delict concerns the sacrament of penance:

> Article 3 of the *motu proprio* envisages four (4) delicts against the sanctity of the Sacrament of Penance…2. the solicitation to sin against the Sixth Commandment (Art. 3, no. 2 canon 1387 CIC [Book VI, 2021 c. 1385]; can. 1458 CCEO). It is important to note that the *motu proprio* limits the *delictum gravius* to solicitation which is directed to sinning with the confessor himself ("*quae ad peccandum cum ipso confessario dirigitur*"), while the classic definition of *sollicitatio* in the Code includes also the solicitation to sin against the Sixth Commandment with a third person. The jurisprudence concerning this delict has evolved substantially, in part because in the 1917 Code an obligation existed, under pain of excommunication, to denounce the soliciting confessor. Solicitation also includes the explicit encouragement to commit impure acts. Some cases of abusive behaviour show that some priests have used the Sacrament of Penance to identify their victims and to make their first contact with them. This behaviour could easily be included under *sollicitatio inchoata* in which the confessor begins an apparently innocent conversation leading to a meeting with the penitent outside of confession where sexual or indecent behaviour occurs.

Therefore, Scicluna specifies distinct delicts under the term "solicitation":

> The confessor seeking to have the penitent sin sexually with him. The confessor seeking the penitent to sin with a third person. The confessor encouraging the penitent to commit impure acts. The confessor using the Sacrament of Penance to make the first contact with potential victims ("grooming").[43]

DISMISSAL FROM THE CLERICAL STATE BY PAPAL DECREE

The Revised Norms include the faculty to dispense from a canonical, penal trial in the most serious of cases, including solicitation, so that the offending cleric can be dismissed from the clerical state by administrative process rather than a penal or judicial trial:

> The faculty to dispense from a judicial trial and therefore to proceed *per decretum extra iudicium*. In these cases

the Congregation for the Doctrine of the Faith, after a careful examination of the facts, decides on a case-by-case basis when to authorize an extrajudicial (administrative) process at the request of the ordinary or local hierarch or ex officio (in any of these cases the imposition of a perpetual, expiatory penalty requires the mandate of the Congregation for the Doctrine of the Faith) (Art. 21 §2 n. 1).[44]

The norms remind all that a perpetual expiatory penalty requires the mandate of the Dicastery for the Doctrine of the Faith. An ordinary deciding to permanently remove a cleric from active ministry should first seek from the Dicastery a mandate or authorization to do this. The Dicastery provides the faculty to present extremely grave cases to the Holy Father:

> The faculty to present cases directly to the Holy Father for *dimissio e statu clericali* or *depositio, una cum dispensatione a lege caelibatus*; to proceed in this manner, in addition to the extreme gravity of the particular case, the commission of the delict in question must be manifest and the right to a proper defence of the accused must be guaranteed (Art. 21 §2 no. 2).[45]

The case must be an extremely case, and the accused priest must still have the right to give evidence and to defend himself.

CONCLUSION

Because of the seriousness of the crime of solicitation, the Church rightly reserves the crime to the Dicastery for the Doctrine of the Faith when the priest suggests or invites the penitent within the context of the sacrament of penance to commit a sin against the sixth commandment with the priest himself at any time. The initiative to commit the sin must come from the priest and not from the penitent.[46] The delict for a priest consists in the act, on the occasion, or under the pretext of confession, to solicit a penitent to sin against the sixth commandment, either with the priest himself or with someone else.

To commit the crime, the forbidden conduct must happen in any manner between the beginning and end of the confession. The phrase "on the occasion" means the soliciting behavior took place before or after the confession, while "under the pretext" means the priest used the sacrament of penance only for the purpose of committing the sin.[47] "Confession" means the act by which the penitent intended to receive sacramental absolution. The crime is committed even if the penitent does not agree to commit the sin (see c. 1328 §1).[48] In dealing with these cases, the tribunal cannot reveal the name of the accuser to the accused priest or his advocate unless the accuser expressly consents to this. The judges must ascertain the credibility of the accuser while upholding the seal of confession.[49] The crime of solicitation is much broader than the crime reserved to the Dicastery for the Doctrine of the Faith. Although not reserved to the Dicastery, other crimes of solicitation include a priest encouraging or leading a person to commit sexual sins with a third party or alone by themselves. Therefore, a priest in confession encouraging a person to continue living with a partner or maintaining that there was nothing wrong with masturbation, would incur the crime of solicitation. The crime also includes a priest "grooming" or seeking potential sexual partners while celebrating the sacrament of penance.

9

VIETNAMESE AND CHINESE COMMUNISM IN CANON LAW

HISTORY OF COMMUNISM

Communism or Marxist socialism has its origin with Karl Marx (1818–83), who in 1848 with Friedrich Engels wrote the *Communist Manifesto*,[1] a summary document about socialism. Marx believed that property and its accompanying institutions were the cause of the exploitation of workers.

In 1916–17, Vladimir Lenin led the revolution against the oppression of the tsars using the communist theories of Marx and implementing them in Russia. Lenin is the architect of modern communism. In January 1918, Lenin disestablished the Orthodox Church in Russia and silenced the clergy, and in 1919, invited people to attend an international congress in Moscow to develop communism. Lenin died in 1924 and was replaced by Joseph Stalin. By 1927, Stalin had consolidated his power in Russia.

He died in 1953, and in 1956, the process of de-Stalinization began. Since communism is based on a materialist philosophy, it is fundamentally opposed to religion and the supernatural. The Sixth World Congress of the Communist International was held in 1928 at which it adopted a Programme:

> One of the most important tasks of the Cultural Revolution affecting the wide masses, is the task of systematically and unswervingly combating religion—the opium of the people.[2]

This is demonstrated in the fierce religious persecutions in Russia between 1917 and 1939. The 1928 Programme also stated that "the ultimate aim of the Communist International is to replace world capitalist economy by a world system of Communism."[3] It also predicted that Communist society "will bury forever all mysticism, religion, prejudice and superstition and will give a powerful impetus to the development of all-conquering scientific knowledge."[4] The aim was a classless, Godless society, and by 1935, communist parties existed in thirty-five countries.

Lenin believed that communists had to be flexible and pragmatic in their approach:

> The strictest loyalty to the idea of Communism must be combined with the ability to make all the necessary practical compromises, to "tack," to make agreements, zigzag, retreats, and so on.[5]

The Programme stated,

> Each Communist party must take into account the concrete internal and external situation, the correlation of class forces, the degree of stability and strength of the bourgeoisie, the degree of preparedness of the proletariat.... The party determines its slogans and methods of struggle in accordance with these circumstances.[6]

Father A. Michel, a priest who experienced communism under Lenin, said that communists attempt to destroy the unity of the Church:

> 1) Above all by breaking the unity with Rome, by preventing contact of the hierarchy and faithful with this centre of the Catholic Church. At the same time by skillful propaganda must be undermined the respect and affection of the clergy and faithful toward the Holy Father;
> 2) By breaking up the unity of the bishops among themselves,
> 3) By breaking up the unity between bishops and priests,
> 4) By breaking up the unity of the priests among themselves,
> 5) By breaking up the unity of the clergy and the faithful.[7]

Michel claimed that a tactic was to invite the clergy to get involved in social programs and thereby reducing their spiritual work. He also noted that communists have strong propaganda machines for attacking the status quo both economically and politically. Richard Murphy pointed out a common communist tactic has been the formation of "national" Catholic churches to separate the Church from the pope in a particular country.[8] Similarly, the Oriental Churches were targeted to become nationalized and tools of the state. These attempts were most obvious in Hungary, Romania, and Czechoslovakia.

VARIETIES OF COMMUNISM

Murphy explained that the term *communist* should be understood as embracing three categories of people: those who profess communism; those who join the Communist Party; and those who show favor to the movement.[9] There are a wide range of communist ideas and practices. Abortion is promoted by most governments in the world, but it is promoted most vehemently in communist countries. The Communist Party has had members in some Western countries for decades, for example, Italy. Since the so-called fall of communism in Eastern Europe in 1989, the strongholds of communism have been China and Vietnam.

China

Originally China was divided into Confucians and those classified as religious such as Buddhists and Taoists. Now the division is normally seen as being between *xinyesu* or "believers in Jesus" and the *info* or "believers in Buddha" (really all those holding other religious ideas).[10]

The first Catholic missionary to China was the Italian Franciscan Giovanni da Montecorvino, OFM, in 1294. He was the first bishop in the Beijing area. However, in 1368, during the Yuan Dynasty, Christianity was forbidden. Matteo Ricci, SJ (1552–1610) began the Jesuit mission toward the end of the Ming Dynasty (1368–1644), and successfully evangelized in China. His most famous book was *Tianzhu shiyi*, or the "True Meaning of the Lord of Heaven."[11] From the beginning of the Christian missionary activity in China, the early missionaries tried to foster Chinese leadership.

The first Chinese bishop, Gregory Luo Wenzao, OP, was consecrated in 1685. However, it was another 250 years before there was another Chinese bishop. On October 28, 1926, Pope Pius XI consecrated the first six Chinese bishops of modern times in St. Peter's Basilica.[12] He consecrated the bishops because European bishops in China had refused to consecrate them. It seems French bishops especially, followed the French government policies in China and were opposed to Chinese leadership.[13] There were other divisions in the Chinese Catholic Church before 1949. These sometimes resulted because of the work of religious orders from different countries with different spiritual traditions causing different affiliations among the people.[14] Many Chinese people link Christianity to colonialism, and there is still some anti-Western ill-feeling in China today.

Chinese Christians were heavily persecuted during the Maoist era of 1949–77. The Communist Party closed all churches and pagodas between 1966 and 1979,[15] but from 1976, China began to open economically, and a controlled number of church buildings were allowed to reopen. Recently, there has been a concentrated movement of people to the cities. However, people often still retain their identity partly from the original place of origin of their family and the religious practices there. In the cities, many new sects have arisen with the urban migration. They have a variety of beliefs, including the "Eastern Lightning" Sect founded in Heilongjiang Province in the 1990s around the female reincarnation of Jesus.[16] The Chinese constitution now allows for the existence of Protestant and Catholic churches. After the Cultural Revolution under Mao, Christians were divided into those who belong to registered churches or nonregistered churches.

The nonregistered church included the underground church for Catholics and numerous house churches for Protestants.

While Catholic churches are allowed, China has a policy of having bishops selected by the government. On July 6, 2012, in Harbin, Yue Fusheng was ordained a bishop without the mandate of the pope. The five ordaining bishops were then excommunicated automatically. They were Bishops Fang Xinyao of Linyi, Pei Junmin of Liaoning, Meng Qinglu of Hothot in Inner Mongolia, Wang Renlei of Xuzhou, and Yang Yonggiang of Zhoucun.[17] The five bishops were in union with Rome until that point.[18] In 2010 and 2011, three other illicit ordinations were forced by the National Church, known as "The Chinese Patriotic Catholic Association." These ordinations created confusion and divisions among Chinese Catholics. Beijing's department for administering religious affairs has dismissed the opposition of the Vatican to these episcopal consecrations as "barbarous and irrational."[19] However, if a bishop repented after taking place in an illegal ordination, the Holy See lifted the automatic excommunication imposed for participating in an ordination of a bishop without the mandate of the pope. Many Chinese officials see religion as something that must be controlled and managed, and so there is a power struggle in China between the Chinese authorities and the Catholic Church. Between 2013 and the end of 2015, more than 1700 crosses have been taken down from Catholic and Protestant churches and buildings in Zhejiang Province.[20] The removal of crosses began with crosses on Protestant buildings, along with some Protestant church leaders and a Catholic lawyer being arrested.[21]

In February 2016, the party made clear its latest strategy to control religions. Buddhist monks are to be given certificates detailing their secular names, religious names, national ID numbers, and their faith number. Christianity, however, is flourishing in China. There were an estimated 58 million Protestants and 9 million Catholics in 2010.[22] Yang Fenggang, director of the Centre on Religion and Chinese Society at Purdue University, has predicted that the Chinese Christian population will be the largest in the world by 2030, and reach 257 million by 2032.[23] The Chinese population is expected to peak at 1.4 billion in 2030, making Christians 16 percent of the Chinese population at that time.

Vietnam

Vietnam is very different from China. First, the Church is much stronger there than it is in China. Economically, Vietnam is not a communist model. The *Guardian* newspaper reported,

> Vietnam is one of the last remaining communist countries in the world, with a party membership of 4.5 million out of its 93 million people. But like its ideological ally China, the government believes in a quasi-free market economy alongside strictly controlled politics and society.[24]

Commentators agree that Vietnam has made significant economic advances in recent years.[25] After 1975, Vietnam had to import two hundred thousand tons of rice each year, but now, it exports rice. Aid from Russia was 40 percent of the state budget in 1981 but is now nonexistent. Another major economic change was in 1987, when Vietnam became a market economy, and in 1995, it joined the Association of South-East Asian Nations (ASEAN). A trade agreement was signed with the United States in 1999, and it joined the World Trade Organization in 2007.

Like China, Vietnam meets the material needs of its people now with a heavily regulated market economy while still building socialism. About half the biggest firms are state owned. Lenin once said, "Electricity plus soviets equals socialism."[26] Bill Hayton argues that Vietnam is a fundamentally socialist country even though there have been market reforms.[27] However, incomes are still low, and factory workers receive an annual salary of about US $3000.[28] Vietnam has a party membership of 4.5 million.[29] Significantly, there are about 9 million, or twice as many Catholics as there are members of the party.

CHURCH TEACHING CONCERNING COMMUNISM

In 1846, two years before the *Communist Manifesto* was published, Pope Pius IX in the encyclical *Qui Pluribus* described communism:

> Totally contrary to even the natural law itself, and which, once accepted, would utterly destroy personal rights, private property, and rights of ownership of all, and even human society itself.[30]

The *Communist Manifesto* attacked the bourgeoisie family, which it considered to be founded on capital and private gain. In 1864, in another encyclical, *Quanta Cura*, Pius IX condemned communism for attacking the family:

> Not content with removing religion from public society, they wish to banish it also from private families. For, teaching and professing the most fatal error of "Communism and Socialism," they assert that "domestic society or the family derives the whole principle of its existence from the civil law alone; and, consequently, that on civil law."[31]

On December 8, 1864, Pope Pius IX issued the *Syllabus of Errors*, which was attached to the encyclical *Quanta cura*. The *Syllabus* listed ten major errors in society. Fourth on the list was communism and socialism. Pope Leo XIII, on December 8, 1878, issued the encyclical *Quod Apostolici*, criticizing communism. Then on April 20, 1884, in the encyclical *Humanum Genus*, Pope Leo XIII critiqued communism and the Masons.[32]

THE 1917 CODE

Heretics, schismatics, and apostates were excommunicated by canon 2314:

§1. All apostates from the Christian faith and each and every heretic or schismatic incur by that fact excommunication.

§2. Unless they [all apostates, heretics, and schismatics] respect warnings, they are deprived of benefice, dignity, pension, office, or other duty that they have in the Church, they are declared infamous, and [if] clerics, with the warning being repeated, [they] are deposed [*sic*].³³

Canon 1325 §2 defines *apostasy* as a total rejection of the Christian faith.³⁴ Under the 1917 Code, when a person joined an organization such as a Masonic sect, they incurred excommunication. Canon 2335 stated, Those giving their name to masonic sects or other associations of this sort that machinate against the Church or legitimate civil powers contract by that fact excommunication simply reserved to the Apostolic See. If a cleric joined an organization such as a masonic lodge, canon 2336 applied:

§1. If a cleric commits the delict mentioned in canons 2334 and 2335, besides the penalties established in those referenced canons, he can be struck with penal suspension or with privation of benefices, offices, dignities, pensions, and responsibilities, if by chance he has any in the Church; religious likewise [suffer] the loss of office, of active and passive voice, and other penalties according to the norms of the constitutions.

§2. Moreover, clerics and religious giving their names to masonic sects and other similar associations must be denounced to the Sacred Congregation of the Holy Office.

In 1924, Pope Pius XI (1922–39) attacked communism in an allocution.³⁵ Then, in 1930, he directed that the Leonine prayers after Mass be for the Church in Russia. The following year, he issued the encyclical *Quadragesimo Anno*.³⁶ In it he attacked communism for its hostility to God and the Church.

In 1931, Pope Pius XI, promulgated the encyclical *Acerba Animi* in which he promoted education of the young against communist propaganda.³⁷ Eventually, in 1937, Pope Pius XI devoted the whole of his encyclical *Divini Redemptoris* to communism. He was very critical of communism and its propaganda:

> Venerable Brethren, take the greatest precaution that the Faithful avoid these snares. Since Communism is intrinsically evil whoever wants to save Christianity and civilization from destruction must refrain from aiding it in the prosecution of any project whatever.³⁸

In the elections of 1948, Italy was in danger of becoming a communist country. Pope Pius XII warned the bishops and the Christian voters about this reality. In response, the vice president of the Communist Party in Italy claimed that communists respected all religions.³⁹

Decree of the Holy Office (1949)

On July 1, 1949, the Sacred Congregation of the Holy Office issued a decree answering the following questions concerning communism:

1. Whether it is licit to join the Communist party or to favor it.
2. Whether it is licit to publish, propagate, or read books, periodicals, daily papers, or sheets that promote the doctrine or action of communists, or to write to them.
3. Whether the faithful who knowingly and freely do the acts mentioned in 1 and 2 can be admitted to the sacraments.
4. Whether the faithful who profess the materialistic and anti-Christian doctrine of communists, and especially those who defend or propagate it, incur *ipso facto* as apostates from the Catholic faith the excommunication specially reserved to the Holy See.

The Eminent and Most Reverend Fathers who are in charge of the safeguarding of faith and morals, after hearing the opinions of the Reverend Consultors, in the Plenary session of Tuesday (instead of Wednesday) June 28 1949, decided to reply:

1. In the negative: for Communism is materialistic and anti-Christian; and the leaders of the Communists, even though they sometimes verbally profess that they are not attacking religion, in fact nevertheless by doctrine and action show themselves to be enemies of God and of the true religion and the Church of Christ.
2. In the negative, for they are forbidden *ipso iure* (cf. canon 1399 of the Code of Canon Law).
3. In the negative, according to the ordinary principles governing the refusal of the sacraments to those who are not properly disposed.
4. In the affirmative.[40]

Next, the Holy Office issued a Declaration concerning celebration of the marriage of communists:

> It has been asked whether the exclusion of communists from the use of the Sacraments, prescribed by the Decree of the Holy Office of 1 July 1949, implies also exclusion from the celebration of marriage; and if not, whether the marriages of communists are governed by the provisions of canons 1060–1061.
>
> On this matter the Holy Office declares: In view of the peculiar nature of the Sacrament of Matrimony, whose ministers are the contracting parties themselves and in which the priest acts as a witness *ex officio*, the priest can assist at the marriages of communists according to canons 1065 and 1066.
>
> But in the marriages of the persons referred to in no. 4 of the aforesaid Decree, the provisions of canons 1061, 1102 and 1109 §3 are to be observed. Given from the Holy Office, 11 August 1949.[41]

Then, in 1950, the Holy Office issued a *Monitum* concerning children involved in communist associations:

> Some associations have been set up, under the pressure and leadership, as everyone knows, of the Communist party, which have for their purpose to imbue boys and girls with principles

and training which are materialistic and contrary to Christian morality and faith.

The faithful are therefore warned that such associations, whatever be the name under which they disguise themselves, are subject to the sanctions mentioned in the Decree of the Holy Office issued on 1st of July 1949.

1. Hence parents or those who stand in their place, who contrary to canon 1372 §2 and the above-mentioned Decree of the Holy Office, turn their children over to the aforesaid associations to be trained, cannot be admitted to the reception of the sacraments.
2. Those who teach boys and girls what is contrary to faith and to Christian morals incur an excommunication specially reserved to the Holy See.
3. The boys and girls themselves, as long as they have been part of these associations, cannot be admitted to the Sacraments. Given at Rome, from the Holy Office, 28 July 1950.[42]

To incur penalties, one must join the Communist Party externally, deliberately, and voluntarily.[43] In 1959, before Vatican II, Richard Murphy gave two examples:

By way of example, two men, A and B are members of the Communist party in a country where membership itself is not considered as an external manifestation of accepting the Communist doctrine. A has entirely abandoned the faith and has become a devoted party man. He gives lectures on Communism and writes articles for the Communist Press. He is active in all the Party's activities, and freely contributes his time and money to defend and propagate Communism. A falls under canon 2314 §1.

B, the other party member, is far from being a devout Catholic, but occasionally he does fulfil his religious obligations. However, he is occasionally seen at party meetings; he pays his dues and subscribes to the Party paper. He has not been heard to praise the efforts of the Communist leaders and the work the Party is doing. Nor is he loathe to associate with the leading Communists. In short, he has not performed actions which in themselves clearly amount to a profession of Communism. Hence in view of the considerations above, B would not fall under canon 2314. Nevertheless, his actions, associating with heretics, praising their methods and objectives, giving them material support have traditionally been considered as aiding in the propagation of heresy. Therefore, canon 2315 can be applied to B. This canon provides that the proper authority should warn such an individual to remove the causes of suspicion. (Canon 2307) If the warning proves fruitless, the suspected person must be forbidden to perform any ecclesiastical legal acts, according to canon 2256. If he is a cleric, he must be suspended *a divinis*, after a second warning has been left unheeded. If within six months the person has not removed the suspicion, he must be regarded as a heretic and subject to the penalties of canon 2314.

Because of the nature of circumstantial evidence upon which suspicions[44] are based, no hard and fast rule can be set down to distinguish violent suspicion from vehement suspicion. Each case must be examined and judged in the light of the circumstances of time and place, keeping in mind that violent suspicion is equivalent to moral certitude.[45]

To incur the penalty of excommunication, under the 1917 Code, the person had both to gravely violate the law and act in defiance of the law, that is, with contumacy. Ignorance, force, and fear would be excusing causes preventing the reception of the penalty. Furthermore, Murphy notes,

> Determining the basic canonico-juridical status of a person who merely joins the Communist Party has never been an easy task. The question was even discussed in pre-Code days. Nor can it be said that the Decree of the Holy Office issued in 1949 has settled the question.[46]

Most significantly, the response of the Holy Office in 1949 did not say that those who join the Communist Party are excommunicated. However, the 1949 Decree of the Holy Office did forbid Catholics from joining the Communist Party.

Some argue that communism is not a secret society like the Masons and so merely joining does not incur the penalty.[47] Richard Murphy points out that authors such as Prummer, Cappello, and Wernz-Vidal do not agree.[48] These authors argue that acting against the Church is sufficient to incur the penalty. Richard Murphy does admit, however, that "generally speaking, it does not seem that joining the Communist party is an intrinsically evil act, or one that involves a denial of the faith."[49] In 1934, the Pontifical Commission for the Authentic Interpretation of the Code of Canon Law answered this question:

> Whether according to the Code of Canon Law persons who belong or have belonged to an atheistic sect are to be considered as regards all legal effects, even those which concern sacred ordination and marriage, the same as persons who belong or have belonged to a non-Catholic sect.

The reply was in the affirmative.[50]

Because the philosophy of communism is atheistic, it does not mean that communism is an atheistic sect of the type envisioned by the Reply. Maroto says that to be an atheistic sect would require that the organization profess atheism as its principal foundation.[51] Lenin clearly expounded the communist stance on religion:

> The unity of that genuinely revolutionary struggle of the oppressed class to set up a heaven on earth is more important to us than a unity in proletarian opinion about the imaginary paradise in the sky. That is why we do not declare, and must not declare in our Programme that we are atheists: that is why we do not forbid and must not forbid proletarians who still cling to the remnants of old prejudices to come into closer contact

with our Party....We must not allow the forces waging a genuinely revolutionary economic and political struggle to be broken up for the sake of opinions and dramas that are of third-rate importance, which are rapidly losing all political significance, and which are being steadily relegated to the rubbish heap by the normal course of economic development.[52]

Favoring the Communist Movement

According to the 1917 Code, it was not a crime to favor a group such as the Masons:

> Those giving their name to masonic sects or other associations of this sort that machinate against the Church or legitimate civil powers contract by that fact excommunication simply reserved to the Apostolic See. (c. 2335)

F. X. Wernz pointed out that those who favored apostates under the constitution *Apostolicae Sedis*[53] were excommunicated.[54] Coronata presents a traditional explanation of "favor."[55] One can assist by sins of omission or sins of commission. Sins of omission include those in office failing to stop the spread of heretical doctrines. Sins of commission include praising heretics, excusing them, or giving them advice in their work.

Education of Youth in Communist Groups

The Communist Party often set up Front Organizations for the education of youth. In 1950, the *Monitum* of the Holy Office warned that its sanctions applied to all these organizations regardless of their names. Neither the parents nor the children involved in these organizations could receive the sacraments. Those who teach the children incur an automatic excommunication specially reserved to the Holy See. In 1949, the Holy Office had also stated that it was forbidden to read or publish communist books or magazines. Those who do so are not able to receive the sacraments. Canon 2318 §1 imposed an automatic excommunication on those who published books promoting the doctrines of heretics, schismatics, or apostates.[56]

Therefore, under the 1917 Code, Catholics who professed communism were considered apostates and excommunicated. They could not receive the Eucharist, be ordained, nor enter a religious novitiate, but they could marry in the Catholic Church. A person could only be refused ecclesiastical burial if that person's membership in the Communist Party was notorious. If a person favored the Communist Party, they were to be deprived of the sacraments.

Selling Communist Literature

A problem arose in Italy, in 1949, after the Decree of the Holy Office. In some countries such as Italy, newsagents were bound by union regulations to carry all registered publications. Cardinal Ruffini, archbishop of Palermo, asked the Holy Office about the situation of these news agents who could have their licenses revoked. The Holy Office responded that if news agents were coerced by their union, then material cooperation could be tolerated, and they could sell communist literature.[57]

Masonic Comparison

Frederick Condon explains what happens when a (Catholic) candidate joins a Masonic Lodge and the implications:

> He presents himself at a Masonic Lodge. He then strips himself of all articles, including crucifix and wedding ring, in preparation for the ceremony. He identifies himself as one who has spent his whole life (including his Christian formation and baptism) in ignorance and who now seeks the wisdom of Masonry, by which he intends to order his life hereafter. He affirms, under oath, both the freedom and sincerity of his actions. He undergoes a quasi-baptism. He passes an oral examination on Masonic teaching to demonstrate his total understanding of what he is doing and saying. This is a deliberate, external rejection of several fundamental teachings of the Catholic faith including: the salvific and necessary character of his baptism; the divine institution of the Church and her role as the recipient and interpreter of revelation; the sufficiency and necessity of the Christian faith for salvation. The denial of any one of these can be said to constitute an act of heresy. While the candidate may arrive at the Lodge door in genuine confusion or ignorance regarding the enduring canonical prohibition of joining a Masonic lodge qua society, he is nevertheless responsible for his words and actions in the course of the ritual of enrolment, in which he actively participates and attests to his understanding, and by which he rejects various teachings of the Catholic faith.[58]

After Vatican II, many wondered if the Catholic Church had become more tolerant toward Freemasons. So, in 1974, Cardinal Seper, prefect of the Congregation for the Doctrine of the Faith, wrote to some episcopal conferences with a restrictive interpretation for the application of a penalty:

> The opinion of those who hold that the aforesaid canon 2335 refers only to Catholics who enrol in associations which actually plot against the Church may be safely taught and applied.[59]

Consequently, a Catholic who joined the Freemasons was excommunicated only if the policies and actions of the Freemasons in his area are known to be hostile to the Church.

However, the status of Masons was again clarified in 1983, when Cardinal Ratzinger, Prefect of the Congregation for the Doctrine of the Faith with the specific approval of Pope John Paul II, issued a *Declaration on Masonic Associations*, continuing the Church's condemnation of Freemasonry:

> The faithful who enrol in Masonic associations are in a state of grave sin and may not receive Holy Communion...the Church's negative judgment in regard to Masonic association(s) remains unchanged since their principles have always been considered

irreconcilable with the doctrine of the Church and therefore membership in them remains forbidden.[60]

THE 1983 CODE

Sometimes, penalties are threatened in particular law for membership in an organization on the basis that the organization plots against the Church.[61] Canon 1374 distinguishes between an "interdict" for someone "who promotes or directs" the organization and "a just penalty" for "membership." Some dioceses in Vietnam maintain that the penalty of excommunication applies for membership of the "party." In some dioceses, Catholics can marry party members, while in other dioceses, Catholics are considered to be excommunicated if they marry members of the party. Penalties are supposed to be consistent across a territory.[62] It is confusing and problematic for Catholics to cross a diocesan boundary and no longer be excommunicated. Like many political parties in the world, the Communist Party does not accept the existence of God and it promotes abortion. Despite the issues, the Vatican has appointed its first diplomatic representative to the Vietnamese government formed by the party.[63] Since 2011, the Vietnamese government has accepted a "non-resident representative" of the Vatican, which implies some diplomatic recognition. Also, since 1996, the agreed process for appointment of bishops has involved the Vatican proposing a list of three names to the Vietnamese government which then chooses the one to be the bishop.[64] Becoming a member in the party does not involve taking an oath, but simply requires a person to have their name on a party list. To become a school principal or to have some other jobs, it is necessary to be a member of the party. All Catholic children go to state schools administered by party members. Since all Catholic children go to these schools, having a Catholic member of the party as a school principal is not a major issue. Canon 1318 stipulates,

> *Latae sententiae* penalties are not to be established, except perhaps for some outstanding and malicious offences which may be either more grave by reason of scandal or such that they cannot be effectively punished by *ferendae sententiae* penalties; censures, however, especially excommunication, are not to be established, except with the greatest moderation, and only for offences of special gravity.

Catholics should not be members of the party, but whether membership warrants excommunication is questionable. It is highly unlikely there has ever been a valid process to apply the penalty of excommunication in Vietnam.[65] All the faithful have the right to have their case heard before a competent ecclesiastical forum.[66] In all penal cases, the accused can ask to have the case heard before a tribunal. In fact, canon 1425 §1 states,

> The following cases are reserved to a collegiate tribunal of three judges: 2° penal cases: a) concerning delicts which can entail the penalty of dismissal from the clerical state; b) concerning the

imposition or declaration of an excommunication.

While canon 1342 §1 allows for an extrajudicial decree by a bishop,[67] canon 1342 §1 requires the ordinary to observe the right of defense and to "hear" the person upon whom he proposes to impose the penalty.[68] Therefore, there must always be due process in any penal case. There should always be a preliminary investigation (cc. 1717–20) before any penalty is imposed, or a precept is given.

Canon 1374 deals with a person joining an organization that plots against the Church and simplifying the norm of law in canon 2335 of the 1917 Code. Canon 1374 states,

> A person who joins an association which plots against the Church is to be punished with a just penalty; however, a person who promotes or directs an association of this kind is to be punished with an interdict.

Canon 1374 was added during the process for the revision of the Code at the request of the Congregation for the Doctrine of the Faith. Clerics and religious do not have to be denounced to the Holy Office. The canon distinguishes between simple membership, which incurs a just penalty, and holding an office or promoting the organization that incurs the penalty of an interdict. Both penalties are preceptive and indeterminate and are encompassed by canons 1344 and 1349. Whether the Communist Party plots against the Church in terms of this canon could be hard to prove.

Canon 1344 allows the judge to defer the imposition of the penalty "unless there is an urgent need to repair scandal":

> Even though the law may use obligatory words, the judge may, according to his own conscience and prudence:
> 1° defer the imposition of the penalty to a more opportune time, if it is foreseen that greater evils may arise from a too hasty punishment of the offender, unless there is an urgent need to repair scandal;
> 2° abstain from imposing the penalty or substitute a milder penalty or a penance, if the offender has repented, as well as having repaired any scandal and harm caused, or if the offender has been or foreseeably will be sufficiently punished by the civil authority;
> 3° may suspend the obligation of observing an expiatory penalty, if the person is a first-offender after a hitherto blameless life, and there is no urgent need to repair scandal; this is, however, to be done in such a way that if the person again commits an offence within a time laid down by the judge, then that person must pay the penalty for both offences, unless in the meanwhile the time for prescription of a penal action in respect of the former offence has expired.

The addition of the clause about repairing scandal is part of the general approach in the 2021 revision of Book VI to make the imposition of penalties obligatory.[69] Penalties must be proportionate to the scandal caused and the gravity of the harm.

> If a penalty is indeterminate, and if the law does not provide otherwise, the judge in determining the penalties is to choose those which are proportionate to the scandal caused and the gravity of the harm; he is not however to impose graver penalties, unless the seriousness of the case really demands it. He may not impose penalties which are perpetual. (c. 1349)

The revised canon removed "especially censures" from the previous text of the canon. Therefore, all excommunications for Communist Party membership in Vietnam are doubtful[70] and probably invalid.

Clergy and Religious Sisters' and Brothers' Membership of the Communist Party

Clerics and religious should not be involved in political parties. In the circumstances of a communist country, it is clearly unbecoming and not appropriate for religious and priests to be involved in the party. Canon 285 states,

> §1. Clerics are to refrain completely from all those things which are unbecoming to their state, according to the prescripts of law.
> §2. Clerics are to avoid those things which, although not unbecoming, are nevertheless foreign to the clerical state.
> §3. Clerics are forbidden to assume public offices which entail a participation in the exercise of civil power.

Priests and religious have a religious mission and should be fully devoted to it as representatives of the Church. They are required to foster unity among the faithful, and they cannot be the servants of any particular ideology or political party.[71] Furthermore, according to canon 287,

> §1. Most especially, clerics are always to foster the peace and harmony based on justice which are to be observed among people.
> §2. They are not to have an active part in political parties and in governing labor unions unless, in the judgment of competent ecclesiastical authority, the protection of the rights of the Church or the promotion of the common good requires it.

The canon law is clear. If a priest or religious becomes a member of the Communist Party, they could be given a warning and then a penal precept[72] to leave the party within say a month or they will be suspended. A person must be warned and given a chance to reform before receiving a penalty such as an excommunication or a suspension, as stated in canon 1347 §1: "A censure cannot validly be imposed unless the offender has beforehand received at least one warning to purge the contempt, and has been allowed suitable time to do so."

The warning is for validity, so any penalty imposed without a personal warning is invalid. Furthermore, no parish priest or assistant priest can impose a penalty on any member of the faithful. Any declarations by these priests saying that people are excommunicated are invalid and unlawful.

PAPAL APPROACHES TO CHINA

Since Vatican II, the popes have pursued a very patient, conciliatory approach to dealing with the Chinese authorities. The tone of documents and statements are dramatically different from pre–Vatican II documents such as the 1949 Decree of the Holy Office. The different approach is paralleled by the different approach of the Catholic Church to non-Catholics. Before Vatican II, Protestants were described as heretics and schismatics, but with the "Decree on Ecumenism," they are described as separated brothers and sisters. The Church now emphasizes what we have in common with non-Catholics rather than what separates us. At Vatican II, there was the "Declaration on the Church's Relation to Non-Christian Religions" and a completely different approach to dialogue with these religions. Furthermore, Vatican II's "Declaration on Religious Freedom" enshrined respect for the beliefs and views of other human beings.

Pope John Paul II

Pope John Paul II had a policy of dialogue and seeking constructive progress in the relationship between the Catholic Church and Chinese authorities. John Paul II was also a key figure in the collapse of communism in Eastern Europe. He actively supported the Solidarity movement, but had vicious, personal struggles with the communists in Poland. In 1983, the Polish secret police tried to blackmail Pope John Paul II. They plotted to create a false diary of a deceased woman who used to work for the Archdiocese of Krakow. The contents were to show that she had an affair with the future pope. An operative planted a diary in the home of a priest, but the operative then got drunk and crashed his car. He told the regular Polish police what he had done. Eighteen months later, this operative was involved in beating to death the Solidarity activist Father Jerzy Popieluszko, and then disposing his body in the Vistula River.[73]

George Weigel claims that Soviet bloc intelligence services attempted to manipulate some of the debates at Vatican II.[74] He thought that in Hungary, communists controlled the Church, and they placed moles in places such as Vatican Radio and newspaper offices. At one time, in the Pontifical Hungarian Institute in Rome, all the rectors and half the students were trained Hungarian secret service agents. Pope John Paul II kept Polish papers in the Vatican apartments away from prying eyes at the Secretariat of State. Weigel concludes that Vatican negotiations and compromises with communist powers have not been that beneficial to the Church.[75]

Matteo Ricci (1552–1610) was a preeminent Jesuit missionary in China. He became an official at the imperial court and dialogued with Chinese culture.[76] In a message to the 2001 Matteo Ricci Convention, Pope John Paul II recalled what Ricci wrote from Beijing acknowledging his wisdom:

> So today the Catholic Church seeks no privilege from China and its leaders, but solely the resumption of dialogue, in order to build a relationship based upon mutual respect and deeper understanding.[77]

Pope Benedict XVI

Throughout his pontificate, Pope Benedict XVI was as conciliatory as possible toward the Chinese authorities. On June 30, 2007, he wrote a "Letter to Chinese Catholics":

> It is no secret that the Holy See, in the name of the whole Catholic Church, and, I believe, for the benefit of the whole human family, hopes for the opening of some form of dialogue with the authorities of the People's Republic of China. Once the misunderstandings of the past have been overcome, such a dialogue would make it possible for us to work together for the good of the Chinese people and for peace in the world.[78]

Benedict explained:

> The appointment of bishops...touches the very heart of the life of the Church, in as much as the appointment of bishops by the pope is the guarantee of the unity of the church and of hierarchical communion.[79]

He pointed out,

> Communion and unity...are essential and integral elements of the Catholic Church: Therefore, the proposal for a church that is "independent" of the Holy See in the religious sphere is incompatible with Catholic doctrine.[80]

Nevertheless, Pope Benedict XVI conceded,

> There would not be any particular difficulties with acceptance of the recognition granted by civil authorities on condition that this does not entail the denial of unrenounceable principles of faith and of ecclesiastical communion.[81]

The Holy See obviously wants to bring all bishops into full communion with the Catholic Church. Bishops are selected in various ways in different countries. Some are selected by cathedral chapters. Other bishop selections are covered by procedures in concordats, and there has been the significant involvement of kings during the Middle Ages. If a bishop confers episcopal consecration without a papal mandate, both he and the recipient are excommunicated according to canon 1387 because of the rupture in ecclesial communion and discipline.[82] Pope Benedict wrote,

> The present college of Catholic bishops of China cannot be recognized as an episcopal conference by the Apostolic See: The "clandestine" bishops...are not part of it; it includes bishops who are still illegitimate, and

it is governed by statutes that contain elements incompatible with Catholic doctrine.[83]

However, Benedict allowed concelebration:

> Therefore, it is licit to concelebrate with bishops and with priests who are in communion with the Pope, even if they are recognized by civil authorities and maintain a relationship with entities desired by the state and extraneous to the structure of the church, provided—as was said earlier (cf. section 7 b)—that this recognition and this relationship do not entail the denial of unrenounceable principles of the faith and of ecclesiastical communion.[84]

Pope Francis

Father Jeroom Heyndrickx of Leuven points out that, from the beginning of his papacy, Pope Francis has been committed to dialogue.[85] The pope wants closer relations—an encounter—with China: "Encounter is achieved through dialogue, we must find the way, always through dialogue, there is no other way."[86]

China's population is one-fifth of the world's population, so any dialogue with the Chinese government makes sense. He even indirectly addresses a few words to people worldwide who might be afraid of China's growing influence on the world scene: "Fear is not a good counsellor....I would not be fearful....Let us walk together."[87] And to those in the Church who might be afraid of dialogue with China, he says, "Dialogue does not mean that we end up with a compromise."[88]

He has continued this policy even though there are many struggles and failures concerning papal episcopal appointments in China. On the one hand, in 2016, there were eight illegal bishops in China, of whom three have been excommunicated. On the other hand, Bishops James Su Zhimin and Cosmas Shi Enxiang are in prison.[89] China would not let Pope Francis fly over Chinese territory on his way to a meeting with Asian youth in Korea in August 2014. However, he was allowed to fly over Chinese territory on his return flight. Pope Francis can claim success with the appointments of bishops for Zhouzhi and Anyang dioceses in 2015, after two rounds of negotiations that took place in 2014 in Rome and Beijing, followed by a third round in Rome on January 25–26, 2015.[90]

CONCLUSION

For more than twenty years and at great personal cost, Cardinal József Mindszenty opposed communism in Hungary. Most would say his contribution was irreplaceable. Millions of Christians have suffered in communist persecutions and in many countries have been martyred for the faith. Many Christians are suffering for their faith in China today.

There is a power struggle between the Church and the Chinese authorities and effectively, there is a de facto schism. Nevertheless, the Catholic Church has been in existence almost two thousand years longer than communism and can only be encouraged by the fate of communism in Eastern Europe.

Membership in the Communist Party is different from being a member of the Masons. It has already been noted that the 1949 Declaration concerning communism did not say that those who joined the Communist Party were excommunicated. Joining the party or having one's name on a party list as in Vietnam does not involve a denial of the faith. A person can join without having any interest in or personal commitment to communist doctrines. Also, as Lenin made clear, the philosophy of communism is not atheistic.

It is not possible to make a simple, blanket statement that one can or cannot be a member of the Communist Party in all countries. Implications of membership vary, as do the activities of members. If a person just had their name on a list, without any oath or other involvement, then being a party member could be justified to get, for example, a principal's job. Teaching is very different from a job that involves spying on the Church. Since the Vatican is negotiating to establish diplomatic relations with the Vietnamese government formed by the Party, it is not logical or warranted to excommunicate someone in Vietnam for merely joining the Party.

10

PRESCRIPTION AND ITS IMPACT ON CRIMES OF SEXUAL ABUSE

In most secular jurisdictions there is no prescription or statute of limitations, and a person can be prosecuted for an offense no matter how long ago it took place. For criminal cases, "a statute of limitation is an act of grace, a surrendering of a right to prosecute."[1] If there is no statute of limitations, criminal charges can be laid any time after the alleged crime was committed. For example, in 2011, Father Fernando Karadima was convicted by the Congregation for the Doctrine of the Faith of abusing minors and sentenced to a life of prayer and penance. However, he has not been sentenced by the civil courts because of Chile's statute of limitations.[2]

The institution of prescription is different from the statute of limitations of common law,[3] but because of their similarity, they are often confused with each other. *Prescription* "is a legal method of extinguishing an action….If the libellus is not presented before the terms of prescription expire, the criminal action is extinguished."[4] It is important to distinguish between prescription and statute of limitations. Brian Austin explains:

> In the first place, the canonical institute of prescription must be clearly distinguished from the civil law known in the U.S. as a "statute of limitation." While they bear a certain resemblance to one another, they cannot be simply equated. Specifically, differ as to the effect they have upon criminal action. In US civil law, "A statute of limitation is regarded as barring, or running against, the remedy to which it applies, and not as extinguishing, or even impairing, the right, obligation or cause of action." Therefore, after the time limit of a statute has expired, the "civil action itself exists and continues independently of that statute," the US statute does not extinguish it. But this is precisely what the canonical institute of prescription does—it extinguishes the action, whether contentious (civil) or criminal: "an action is extinguished by prescription" (canon 1492 §1); "a criminal action is extinguished by pre-

scription" (canon 1362 §1). That is to say, "when the time period of prescription has run and reached its terminus, the very cause of action itself is extinguished. It no longer exists."[5]

A criminal action to impose or declare a penalty is extinguished after the prescription time has expired. This means the cause of a criminal action no longer exists. Prescription in canon law allows for the acquiring of rights and the freeing from obligations with the passage of time and under certain conditions.[6] The institute of prescription is not just a procedural law matter but "is in fact a matter of substantive law."[7]

JUSTIFICATION FOR PRESCRIPTION

Prescription of criminal and penal action is usually justified because over time there is often a weakening of the proofs and the loss of witnesses. The reliability of the memory of witnesses can be questioned. Also, some people have argued, perhaps rather optimistically, that over time offenders may well have reformed.[8]

Wernz and Vidal promoted a double reason to justify the institution of criminal prescription. They argued that because of the passage of time, people's memory of the crime faded. For this reason, the harm caused by the crime was reduced, so there was not the same need for criminal and penal action. Also, they argued that, in many cases, claims concerning the Church and the prosecution of a criminal long after the commission of the crime would involve new scandal and astonishment.[9]

There is no doubt that long after a crime has been committed, proof of the offense has reduced, and there are significant, inherent difficulties in defending the accused. Boccafola argues that "the passage of time often makes it difficult to prove or defend against certain charges, because of a person's loss of an exact memory of the events, or because of the death of witnesses."[10] Consequently, there is a grave danger that an innocent person might be condemned, merely because with the passage of time essential proofs of his innocence no longer exist.

Thomas Green elaborates:

> The evidence may become too stale if too long a times lags between the commission of an alleged delict and its formal prosecution. Furthermore, the legal security of the accused is unduly jeopardized if church authorities do not pursue potential criminal actions with reasonable expeditiousness.[11]

The pros and cons of prescription are summarized very well by John Beal, who identifies the complications of delayed prosecutions while acknowledging the seriousness of the crime of sexual abuse:

> It can be argued, of course, that sexual abuse of minors is such a heinous crime that a mere legal technicality should not stand in the way of prosecuting the offence and seeing that justice is done for victims. But the prescription of penal action or a statute of limitations exists because the law, in its wisdom,

recognizes that the passage of time renders prosecution of and defense against complaints increasingly difficult. Over time, potential witnesses disappear, memories dim, relevant documents are lost or inadvertently destroyed, alleged crime scenes are razed or renovated. Given the high burden of proof already placed on priests who are subjects of "credible" accusations of sexual abuse, the elimination of any statute of limitations can raise a nearly insurmountable obstacle to an effective defense.[12]

The Holy See reiterated "moral certainty" as the standard of proof for a conviction when it responded to the Recommendations of the Australian Royal Commission:

> Regarding the standard for conviction in a judicial process, the long tradition of canonical reflection on vital jurisprudential principles, as embodied in the Codes of Canon Law, requires of the judge "moral certainty" in coming to a decision. Such moral certainty is derived from the acts and the proofs of the case (CIC, can. 1608; CCEO can. 1291). The principle of moral certainty gives expression to the need to respect both the presumption of innocence and the ancient legal maxim "in dubio pro reo."[13]

Judges were reminded of this by the change to canon 1342:

> Whenever there are just reasons against the use of a judicial procedure, a penalty can be imposed or declared by means of an extra-judicial decree, observing canon 1720, especially in what concerns the right of defence and the moral certainty in the mind of the one issuing the decree, in accordance with the provision of can. 1608. Penal remedies and penances may in any case whatever be applied by a decree. (c. 1342 §1)

"Moral certainty" is close to the standard of "beyond reasonable doubt." This is a difficult standard of proof to reach after a long passage of time.

THE 1917 CODE

The law on prescription in canon 1703 of the 1917 Code exempted offenses reserved to the Congregation for the Doctrine of the Faith from prescription:

> With due regard for the prescription of canon 1555 §1, concerning delicts reserved to the Sacred Congregation of the Holy Office, the useful time for pursuing a criminal action is three years, unless it concerns:
>
> 1. An action for injuries, which is ended after one year;
> 2. An action from a qualified delict against the sixth or seventh divine precept, which is ended in five years;
> 3. An action for simony or homicide, against which the criminal action lasts for ten years.

As noted, canon 1555 of the 1917 Code exempted delicts reserved to the Congregation for the Doctrine of the Faith from prescription:

§1. The tribunal of the Congregation of the Holy Office proceeds by its own usage and institutes and retains its own proper customs; lower tribunal also, in cases that concern the tribunal of the Holy Office, should follow the norms given out by it.

§2. Other tribunals must observe the prescriptions of the canons that follow.

§3. In a trial about the dismissal of religious the prescriptions of canons 654–658 are observed.

Thomas Green notes that canon 1703 acknowledges the seriousness of each crime by the length of prescription granted for each crime.[14] More serious offenses had longer periods of prescription. Therefore, when the 1917 Code came into effect on May 19, 1918, until 1922—when the instruction *Crimen Sollicitationis* came into effect—prescription for sexual abuse of minors was five years. The Holy Office was then given jurisdiction over pedophilia by the Instruction *Crimen Sollicitationis*,[15] and from 1922 there was no prescription for the crimes of sexual abuse of minors and solicitation until 2001, when *Sacramentorum Sanctitatis Tutela* was promulgated on April 30, 2001, by Pope John Paul II:

> An instruction [of the kind of *Crimen sollicitationis*] had the force of law since the Supreme Pontiff, according to the norm of canon 247 §1 of the *Codex Iuris Canonici* promulgated in 1917, presided over the Congregation of the Holy Office, and the instruction proceeded from his own authority, with the Cardinal at the time only performing the function of a secretary.[16]

Crimen Sollicitationis was promulgated by the pope himself making it law. Then, just a few weeks later, Cardinal Ratzinger stated that the norms of the instruction *Crimen Sollicitationis* had been legally binding until *Sacramentorum Sanctitatis Tutela* came into force.[17]

THE 1983 CODE

When the 1917 Code came into force, previous laws were abrogated. Similarly, with the 1983 Code, except for the juridical norms in the decrees of Vatican II, all universal laws contrary to the Code and all particular and universal penal laws are abrogated. Canon 6 of the 1983 Code stated,

§1. When this Code takes force, the following are abrogated:
1. the Code of Canon Law promulgated in 1917;
2. other universal or particular laws contrary to the prescripts of this Code unless other provision is expressly made for particular laws;
3. any universal or particular penal laws whatsoever issued by the Apostolic See unless they are contained in this Code;
4. other universal disciplinary laws regarding matter which this Code completely reorders.

§2. Insofar as they repeat former law, the canons of this Code must be assessed also in accord with canonical tradition.

Clearly, both universal and particular penal laws were abrogated, changing prescription unless the crimes were reserved to the Congregation for the Doctrine of the Faith as noted in canon 1362:

§1. Prescription extinguishes a criminal action after three years unless it concerns:
1. delicts reserved to the Congregation for the Doctrine of the Faith;
2. an action arising from the delicts mentioned in canons 1394, 1395, 1397, and 1398, which have a prescription of five years;
3. delicts which are not punished in the common law if particular law has established another period for prescription.

§2. Prescription runs from the day on which the delict was committed or, if the delict is continuous or habitual, from the day on which it ceased.

Since canon 1362 only prescribed prescription in universal and particular penal laws, it had no effect on competency to deal with a case. Many crimes have prescription attached so that no prosecution may take place after three or five years.

After the promulgation of the 1983 Code, however, there was confusion about penal law and prescription for sexual abuse cases.[18] It is important that there be certainty about what is the law.

In 1991, John Beal, a distinguished canon lawyer, understood that, from 1983, prescription was for five years for crimes of sexual abuse of minors.[19] His opinion was supported by Juan Arrieta, the secretary of the Pontifical Council for Legislative Texts, who said Cardinal Ratzinger's letter to Cardinal Castillo Lara "presupposes, therefore, that juridical responsibility in [such] matters lies with ordinaries or religious superiors, as is indicated by the letter of the code."[20]

However, under canon 1362 §1 in the 1983 Code, there is no prescription attached to offenses reserved to the Congregation for the Doctrine of the Faith.[21] John Kozlowski explains that prescription for the delicts mentioned in canons 1395, 1397, and 1398 occurs after five years unless the delict is reserved to the Congregation for the Doctrine of the Faith.[22]

Cardinal Ratzinger had written to Cardinal Castillo Lara, president of the Pontifical Commission for the Authentic Interpretation of the Code of Canon Law, on February 19, 1988, asking for a simpler penal process to dismiss clergy.[23] The wording in Cardinal Ratzinger's letter would seem to indicate that he did not seem to think that the Congregation for the Doctrine of the Faith was competent to handle pedophilia cases. Possibly this is because canon 6 of the 1983 Code had abrogated many penal laws.

Three weeks later, on March 10, 1988, Cardinal Castillo Lara of the Pontifical Commission replied in a letter:

> In the current Code, the offences that can lead to loss of the clerical state have been clearly indicated: they are listed in canons 1364 §1, 1367, 1370,

1387, 1394 and 1395. At the same time the procedure has been greatly simplified in comparison with the previous norms of the 1917 Code: it has been speeded up and streamlined, partly to encourage the Ordinaries to exercise their authority through the necessary judgement of the offenders "*ad normam iuris*" and the imposition of the sanctions provided....I can well understand Your Eminence's concern at the fact that the Ordinaries involved did not first exercise their judicial power in order to punish such crimes sufficiently, even to protect the common good of the faithful. Nevertheless, the problem seems to lie not with juridical procedure, but with the responsible exercise of the task of governance.[24]

At other difficult times in the life of the Church, when there has been confusion of consciences and relaxation of ecclesiastical discipline, the sacred Pastors have not failed to exercise their judicial power in order to protect the supreme good of the "*salus animarumi.*"[25]

Soon afterward, in 1988, Pope John Paul II restructured the Roman curia with the promulgation of the Apostolic Constitution *Pastor Bonus*,[26] which replaced *Regimini Ecclesiae Universae*.[27] Article 52 of *Pastor Bonus* gave exclusive penal jurisdiction to the Congregation for the Doctrine of the Faith headed by Cardinal Ratzinger. This ensured that the Congregation for the Doctrine of the Faith was not only competent regarding offenses against the faith or in the celebration of the sacraments, but also regarding "more serious offences against morals." However, there was no public statement or advice to bishops explaining how to deal with pedophilia, and there was no action from the Congregation.

The existence of the instruction *Crimen Sollicitationis* in 1962 was not a complete secret, as is shown when the officers of the Canon Law Society of America visited the Congregation for the Doctrine of the Faith in 1996. In its June 1996 Newsletter, the president reported,

> The norms on solicitation cases issued in 1962 are currently under review by a commission within the CDF. New norms are required in light of the revision of canon law. In the interim, the 1962 norms should be followed with obvious adaptations.[28]

On January 28, 1998, Archbishop Philip Wilson, the then bishop of Wollongong, wrote to the Congregation for the Doctrine of the Faith asking if *Crimen Sollicitationis* was restricted to confession. On February 28, 1998, Archbishop Bertone, the secretary of the Congregation for the Doctrine of the Faith replied to Bishop Wilson:

> Your Excellency,
> With your letter of January 28, 1998, regarding the case of a priest accused of sexually abusing a minor, you asked whether the procedure of the *Instructio de modo Procendi in causis sollicitationis* should be followed, or whether these procedures only concern actions which are alleged to have occurred in

the context of the Sacrament of Confession.

This Congregation responds that in the above-mentioned case, the procedure of the *Instructio* should be followed as indicated in the fifth chapter of the document (*De crimine pessimo*).

Archbishop Bertone stated clearly that *Crimen Sollicitationis* was not confined just to solicitation and was still in force when dealing with child sexual abuse crimes. However, there seems to be little evidence of action by bishops in Australia on this information.

Many bishops around the world thought that the penal process was too difficult to implement, one reason being the lack of qualified, competent, and experienced priests. The procedural law of *Crimen Sollicitationis* remained unknown because it had not been publicly promulgated. Most bishops and religious superiors were ignorant of the law, and many did not deal with sexual abuse crimes appropriately.

Few people were certain of the law and procedures for prosecuting cases involving pedophilia. In the 1980s and 1990s, most of the publicity about sexual abuse crimes was concentrated in North America. After negotiations with officials at the Holy See by representatives of the US Catholic Bishops' Conference, particular law was legislated for the United States. On April 25, 1994, as a trial for five years, prescription for sexual abuse crimes in the United States was set at ten years from when the minor had completed eighteen years of age.[29]

PRESCRIPTION AFTER *SACRAMENTORUM SANCTITATIS*

As noted above, on April 30, 2001, Pope John Paul II promulgated the *motu proprio Sacramentorum Sanctitatis Tutela*. As universal law, this document listed the sexual abuse of a minor under eighteen years of age committed by a cleric as a more grave crime (*delicta graviora*) reserved to the Congregation for the Doctrine of the Faith. Prescription for this crime delict was fixed at ten years beginning at the completion when the victim turned eighteen years of age, meaning that the victim had until age twenty-eighth to lay a complaint.[30] The Promotor of Justice at the Congregation for the Doctrine of the Faith, Msgr. Charles Scicluna, explains:

> The question of prescription regarding *graviora delicta* is once again much discussed after the *motu proprio* because, for the first time in history, a time limit has been imposed, after which the *actio criminalis* is extinguished for these delicts. Art. 5 §1 indicates that a delict is bound by prescription after ten years, while Art. 5 §2 establishes that this period of ten years runs according to the norm of can. 1362 §2 CIC or of can. 1152 §3 CCEO: Prescription runs from the day on which the delict was committed or, if the delict is continuous or habitual, from the day on which it ceased....
>
> In cases of sexual abuse, the period of ten years begins to run the day on which the minor completes his eighteenth year. Experience has shown that

a term of ten years is inadequate for these types of cases and that it would be desirable to return to the former system in which these delicts were not subject to prescription at all.[31]

On November 2, 2002, Pope John Paul II granted the Congregation for the Doctrine of the Faith the faculty to derogate from prescription on a case-by-case basis. Charles Scicluna acknowledges, "There is a tendency supporting a return to the previous norm, which simply stated that *graviora delicta* were not subject to prescription."[32]

On May 21, 2010, Pope Benedict XVI revised the *Sacramentorum Sanctitatis Tutela* norms so that prescription in the case of abuse of minors was now set as twenty years calculated from the completion of when the victim turned eighteen years of age, so that the victim had until age thirty-eight to complain. The Congregation for the Doctrine of the Faith continued to be able to derogate from prescription in individual cases. The canonical delict of acquisition, possession, or distribution of pedopornography was also included in this revised *motu proprio*.[33]

The Congregation for the Doctrine of the Faith Norms of 2001, and as revised in 2010, reserved to the exclusive competence of the Congregation for the Doctrine of the Faith all clerical offenses against the sixth commandment with a minor aged under eighteen years.[34] When a member of a clerical religious institute commits an offense reserved to the Congregation for the Doctrine of the Faith, the religious institute remains involved in the process. The supreme moderator and council of the religious institute decide whether the offense was committed. The supreme moderator forwards the acts of the case with his *Vota* to the Congregation for the Doctrine of the Faith. Then the Congregation for the Doctrine of the Faith determines how the case should be handled and the process to be used.

Charles Scicluna stated that with the promulgation of *Sacramentorum Sanctitatis Tutela*, "for the first time in history, a time limit has been imposed, after which the *action criminalis* is extinguished for those delicts [i.e. those reserved to the Congregation for the Doctrine of the Faith]."[35] Kozlowski is also of the opinion that prescription of canon 1362 did not apply to clerical offenses against the sixth commandment with a minor when the 1983 Code went into effect.[36]

ISSUES WITH DISPENSATIONS FROM PRESCRIPTION

"Prescription" cannot be dispensed, but it can be derogated. A dispensation relaxes the law, while derogation means that the law does not apply in this particular case.[37]

Charles Renati points out that the faculty granted to the Congregation for the Doctrine of the Faith to derogate from prescription "did not give the Congregation for the Doctrine of the Faith the power to dispense from the law of prescription itself, but only to set aside the [terms] of prescription"[38] on a case-by-case basis.

Thomas Green and Ladislas Orsy strongly oppose dispensations or derogations from prescription.[39] They remind everyone that retroactive penal laws are prohibited in many countries and legal systems according to the legal maxim *nulla poena sine lege*.[40] The 1948 *Universal Declaration of Human Rights* stated,

> No one shall be held guilty of any penal offence on account of any act or omission which did not constitute a penal offence, under national or international law, at the time when it was committed.[41]

Furthermore, changing a law concerning prescription is completely contrary to canon 1313:

> §1. If a law is changed after an offence has been committed, the law more favourable to the offender is to be applied. §2. If a later law removes a law, or at least a penalty, the penalty immediately lapses. (c. 1313)

Ex post facto laws are also contrary to the natural law.[42] Changes in canon law are not retroactive.

Renati is much more nuanced in his interpretation of the Congregation for the Doctrine of the Faith power to derogate. He explains that the power of the Congregation for the Doctrine of the Faith applies only in those cases "for which prescription is still running."[43] He thinks that a derogation could apply to a case in which the preliminary investigation has been started, but the time limit applies before the investigation or penal action is completed. This is reflected in the changes to canon 1362:

> §3. When the offender has been summoned in accordance with canon 1723, or informed in the manner provided in canon 1507 §3 of the presentation of the petition of accusation according to canon 1721 §1, prescription of the criminal action is suspended for three years; once this period has expired or the suspension has been interrupted through the cessation of the penal process, time runs once again and is added to the period of prescription which has already elapsed. The same suspension equally applies if, observing canon 1720 no. 1, the procedure is followed for imposing or declaring a penalty by way of an extra-judicial decree. (c. 1362)

In 2002, norm 8a of *Sacramentorum sanctitatis tutela* stated,

> If the case would otherwise be barred by prescription, because sexual abuse of a minor is a grave offence, the bishop/eparch [*sic*] shall apply to the Congregation for the Doctrine of the Faith for a dispensation from the prescription, while indicating appropriate pastoral reasons.[44]

Three changes were made to this paragraph in the 2006 version:

> If the case would otherwise be barred by prescription, because sexual abuse of a minor is a grave offence, the bishop/eparch [*sic*] may apply to the Congregation for the Doctrine of the Faith for a

derogation from the prescription while indicating relevant grave reasons.⁴⁵

The bishop/eparch does not have to ask for a derogation and the Congregation for the Doctrine of the Faith can derogate from the terms of prescription in individual cases but cannot dispense from the law of prescription itself.⁴⁶ The motivating "relevant grave reasons" would have to be founded on both law and fact.

Derogations are not automatically granted. On June 6, 2017, the Congregation for the Doctrine of the Faith (Prot. No. 274/2017-60703) refused to grant derogation in a long-standing case where there had never been sufficient proof, and where the accused brother had not offended again.⁴⁷ The Congregation said his ministry could be restricted using a precept:

> However, the public exercise of sacred orders of the brother can be limited by disciplinary means. If it is opportune and necessary you could impose on the brother a precept according to canons 49–51, 1319 and 1339 *CIC* citing canon 1371 no. 2 warning that the violation of the same would carry the imposition of a punishment.⁴⁸
>
> Should a precept emanate, I ask you to ensure a copy of the aforementioned precept comes to this Dicastery signed by the brother at the moment of his notification.⁴⁹

Francis Morrisey quotes another decision from the Congregation of the Clergy:

A response from the Congregation of the Clergy, April 12, 2017 Prot. No. 20171421 indicates that if a judicial process is underway, the Apostolic Signatura is to be approached for an eventual authorisation to derogate from prescription. However, a response from the Signatura, September 2, 2017 (Prot. No. 53109/17 VT) indicates that it considers prescription to be a constitutive part of penal law, and, therefore, cannot be subject to dispensation; furthermore, it indicates that a dispensation is to be applied for more favourable circumstances, not to be able to impose penalties on a person.⁵⁰

LAY RELIGIOUS

The prescription for twenty years in canon 1362 and how it is calculated is the law for dismissal of lay religious for crimes of sexual abuse of minors under canon 695 §1, no. 2.⁵¹ *Crimen Sollicitationis* only applied to clerical sexual abuse of minors. So, the period of prescription for clerical offenses against a minor was not applicable when the 1983 Code went into effect, and it was only *Sacramentorum Sanctitatis Tutela* of 2001 that established a period of prescription. Only the Dicastery for the Doctrine of the Faith can derogate from prescription. The Dicastery for Religious and Societies of Apostolic Life, for Clergy and the Dicastery for Divine Worship and the Discipline of the Sacraments do not have the same faculty or right to derogate from prescription in cases before them.

CONCLUSION

Knowledge of prescription is essential to know what law applies when an accusation is made. The accused is to be punished in accordance with the canon law that applies at the time (see c. 221 §3). The law on prescription that applies at the time of the offense will determine if a prosecution can take place. Only the Dicastery for the Doctrine of the Faith can derogate from prescription in individual cases when appropriate.[52] This derogation can also apply to the canonical delict of acquisition, possession, or distribution of pedopornography.[53]

The Australian Royal Commission into Institutional Responses to Sexual Abuse in the Final Report concerning Religious Institutions stated,

> In private sessions held up to 31 May 2017, of the 4,029 survivors who told us about child sexual abuse in religious institutions, the majority (3,588 survivors or 89.1 per cent) told us when they first disclosed the abuse. Of these, 2,181 survivors (60.8 per cent) disclosed for the first time when they were an adult and 1,407 survivors (39.2 per cent) disclosed as a child. These figures are broadly consistent with those for survivors who experienced child sexual abuse in institutions under other management. They are also consistent with research which suggests that many people who were sexually abused as children do not disclose their experience of abuse until adulthood. Some survivors who told us they had been sexually abused as children said they had not previously disclosed the abuse. Of the 4,029 survivors who told us in private sessions about child sexual abuse in religious institutions, 3,342 survivors (82.9 per cent) provided information on who they had disclosed to. Of those, 284 survivors (8.5 per cent) said they had not disclosed their experience of sexual abuse to anyone prior to telling the Royal Commission.[54]

The data of the complaints to the Catholic Church showed the average length of time between the first incident of abuse and a victim reporting it was, on average, thirty-three years:

> The Catholic Church claims data showed that the time between the first alleged incident of child sexual abuse and the date when the claim was received by the relevant Catholic Church authority was more than 30 years in 59 per cent of claims, and more than 20 years in 81 per cent of claims. The average time between the first alleged incident date and the date the claim was received was 33 years.[55]

The Australian Royal Commission has demonstrated that minors take on average thirty years to complain about being sexually abused. Sexual abuse is a heinous crime that does enormous damage to the victims. Therefore, the Catholic Church needs to revert to previous law so that there is no prescription for cases of sexual abuse involving clerics, religious brothers and sisters. It needs to be explicitly stated in canon 1362 that there is no prescription for crimes of sexual abuse of minors.

11

THE SEAL OF CONFESSION FOR VICTIMS AND PERPETRATORS

The Australian Royal Commission into Institutional Responses to Child Abuse recommended "no excuse, protection, nor privilege" should apply for priests who failed to report information about child abuse to the police after it was reported during confession. The Commission had heard evidence of pedophile priests receiving absolution and continuing to abuse minors.

The Commission also heard of child victims telling confessors that they were sexually abused, and yet nothing was done to stop the abuser. How does the seal of confession apply both to a penitent who is a pedophile confessing his crime of abuse and a child victim reporting abuse or seeking help? A famous case involving the seal of confession was that of Father Francis Douglas, a New Zealand Columban priest. In 1938, Father Douglas was appointed to Pililla, a town near Manila in the Philippines. It was a difficult assignment, made worse by the Japanese occupation of the country in January 1942. In July 1943, he was asked to visit some guerrillas who said that they needed his priestly services. Afterward, the Japanese thought he was a spy. He was tortured for three days and killed because, among other things, he would not break the seal of confession.[1] Many people regard him as a martyr for being faithful to his priestly obligations.

"The 'seal of confession' is the obligation on the part of the confessor to maintain confidentiality with respect to information disclosed to him by a penitent within the context of the sacrament of penance as it is known in the Catholic Church."[2] The Apostolic Penitentiary quotes De Paolis explaining that the seal includes

all the sins of both the penitent and others known from the penitent's confession, both mortal and venial, both occult and public, as manifested in order to obtain absolution and therefore known to the confessor by virtue of sacramental science.³

For Father Francis Douglas, this would have meant that, if a guerrilla told him the name of a girlfriend with whom he had had sex, her name would be protected under the seal of confession.

The Congregation for the Doctrine of the Faith defines the "seal of confession" as "the obligation of strict confidentiality imposed by divine law on a confessor in the sacrament of penance not to reveal to any person, under pain of excommunication, the sins confessed."⁴

There are many issues concerning the seal of confession that are misunderstood. In 1215, the Fourth Lateran Council became the first Church Council to address the issue. It explicitly taught the doctrine of the seal of confession in canon 21:

> Let him take the utmost care, however, not to betray the sinner at all by word or sign or in any other way. If the priest needs wise advice, let him seek it cautiously without any mention of the person concerned. For if anyone presumes to reveal a sin disclosed to him in confession, we decree that he is not only to be deposed from his priestly office but also to be confined to a strict monastery to do perpetual penance.⁵

This Council attached the penal sanctions of removal from office and confinement for violating the seal of confession. The priest would be barred from having any offices in future, and the penances would have included fasting. Saint Thomas Aquinas (1224–74) taught that the sacrament of penance signified the action of Christ within the person forgiving them their sins.

Saint Thomas taught that since God does not reveal the sins of the penitent, neither should the priest.⁶ The priest acquires his knowledge as God's representative⁷ because he acts in the person of Christ himself.⁸ Because of this role, the priest must keep what is confessed secret. For Saint Thomas, the seal covered the sins confessed as well as any information that would reveal the identity of the penitent and what sins they confessed.⁹

Pope Innocent III (1160–1216) argued that the obligation of the secrecy of confession was derived from the fact that the priest had no human knowledge of events from what he had seen, but only knew about events from acting as God's representative.¹⁰

Following this teaching, canon 983 of the 1983 Code specified,

> §1. The sacramental seal is inviolable; therefore, it is a crime for a confessor in any way to betray a penitent by word or in any other manner or for any reason. §2. The interpreter, if there is one present, is also obliged to preserve the secret, and also all others to whom knowledge of sins from confession shall come in any way. (c. 983)

This canon makes a distinction between "the sacramental seal" and "the penitential secret."¹¹ Only the minister of the sacrament of penance has the obligation of upholding the seal of confession. In paragraph 2, the obligation of someone who overhears the confession, or an interpreter, is to uphold the penitential secret. Interpreters are rarely used in the sacrament of penance. If an interpreter is involved in the confession, canon 1386 §2 states, "An interpreter and other persons mentioned in canon 983 §2, who violate this secrecy are to be punished with a just penalty, not excluding excommunication."[12] Their knowledge is more of a professional secret and the seal of confession strictly applies to the priest alone.

A priest confessor cannot violate the seal of confession to save his own life, someone else's life, or for other reasons to protect someone's good reputation.[13] The confessor who directly violates the seal of confession incurs the penalty of an automatic excommunication. The confessor who indirectly violates the seal of confession is to be punished according to the seriousness of the violation.[14]

Pope John Paul II's apostolic letter *Sacramentorum Sanctitatis Tutela* reserved competence in the external forum for dealing with direct violations of the seal of confession to the Congregation for the Doctrine of the Faith.[15] Then on February 7, 2003, Pope John Paul II reserved the delict of indirect violation of the seal of confession to the Congregation for the Doctrine of the Faith.

There is also a penalty of excommunication for recording a confession. There was the 1998 case of Conan Hale's confession being recorded in the United States.[16] Furthermore, there have been cases of confessions being recorded for publishing the reactions of priests to what is confessed. Consequently, Charles Scicluna stated,

The recording, or divulging by means of social communication, of that which has been said, whether by the priest or by the penitent, in confession (Art. 3, n. 4 Decretum CDF, 23 September 1988, *AAS*, 80(1988), 1367). This *delictum gravius* was added by the Holy Father in a decision dated 7 February 2003. The decree of the CDF, establishing an excommunication *latae sententiae*, was published in 1988.[17]

In 2010, Pope John Paul II, in Article 4 of the substantive norms that were included in the revised *Sacramentorum Sanctitatis Tutela*, also reserved to the Congregation for the Doctrine of the Faith the crime of recording and publishing in the media statements by penitents or priests during the celebration of the sacrament of penance:

§2. With due regard for §1, no. 5, also reserved to the Congregation for the Doctrine of the Faith is the more grave delict which consists in the recording, by whatever technical means, or in the malicious diffusion through communications media, of what is said in sacramental confession, whether true or false, by the confessor or the penitent. Anyone who commits such a delict is to punished according to the gravity of the crime, not excluding, if he be a cleric, dismissal or deposition.[18]

The grave crime involves both the recording of what is said or its distribution with malicious intent in the media. When Pope Francis revised Book VI of the Code of Canon Law in 2021, a new paragraph was added to canon 1386 that replaced canon 1388, effectively incorporating the 1988 legislation into the Code:

> §3. Without prejudice to the provisions of §§ 1 and 2, any person who by means of any technical device makes a recording of what is said by the priest or by the penitent in a sacramental confession, either real or simulated, or who divulges it through the means of social communication, is to be punished according to the gravity of the offence, not excluding, in the case of a cleric, by dismissal from the clerical state. (c. 1386)

DIRECT AND INDIRECT VIOLATION

The Congregation for the Doctrine of the Faith defined the *Seal of Confession* as "the obligation of strict confidentiality imposed by divine law on a confessor in the sacrament of penance not to reveal to any person, under pain of excommunication, the sins confessed."[19] Direct violation of the seal requires the confessor to violate the seal of confession deliberately. Gregory Zubacz explains: "Direct violation occurs when a confessor reveals: a) to a third party, b) the identity of the penitent, c) the confessed sin."[20] An example of an indirect violation of the seal would be a priest commenting, based on knowledge gained in a confession, that the person was not to be trusted. Criteria for interpreting and judging the indirect violation were published by the Apostolic Penitentiary in 1983.[21]

Indirect violation of the seal of confession "occurs when the sin and the sinner can be deduced from the words, gestures, deeds, or omission of the confessor."[22] Juan Arias notes that an indirect violation could occur when the confessor speaks of a sin confessed when only a small number of people have been to confession—for example, a priest in a homily in a small country town referring to a sin confessed. The confessor could also indirectly violate the seal by telling a friend not to invest in the company shares of a penitent who confessed dishonesty.

Priests must be very careful about how they use knowledge of sins obtained during confessions. In 1915, the Holy Office issued an instruction:

> In future, not only in theological classes but also in conferences on moral "cases" as they are called, and in public and private talks and exhortations to the clergy, they carefully see to it that the priests subject to them be taught never to dare to mention anything which pertains to the matter of sacramental confession in any form or under any pretext, especially on the occasion of sacred missions or spiritual exercises, nor even incidentally, directly or indirectly in public or private speech (except the case of necessary consultation to be made according to the rules laid down by approved authors).[23]

Confessors must be clear about their obligations of confidentiality. In 1682, Pope Blessed Innocent XI presided over the Holy Office when it replied to a question concerning confidentiality. He prohibited the use of information obtained in confession that could be to the detriment of the penitent even though the seal of confession was maintained.[24] Information gained in confession can never be used to the harm or detriment of the penitent, but implicitly without breaking the seal, information can be used for the good of the penitent. Thus, canon 984 of the 1983 Code legislates,

> §1. Even if every danger of revelation is excluded, a confessor is absolutely forbidden to use knowledge acquired from confession when it might harm the penitent. (c. 984)

Specifically, paragraph 2 of canon 984 of the Code rules out the use of confessional knowledge by religious superiors or those who are later in a position to use it:

> §2. One who is placed in authority can in no way use for external governance knowledge about sins which he has received in confession at any time. (c. 984)

Both superiors at the time and confessors who later become superiors and who have knowledge concerning sins from confession, cannot use this knowledge in any way for external governance.

According to canon 240, seminary staff are specifically required to protect knowledge acquired in the sacrament of penance or the internal forum:

> §2. In making decisions about the admission of students to orders or their dismissal from the seminary, the opinion of the spiritual director and confessors can never be sought. (c. 240)

THE PENITENT WHO IS A VICTIM

Priest confessors must uphold the seal of confession. They must know and be committed to implementing policies and procedures concerning disclosure of sexual abuse. Priests must affirm the person for doing the right thing and seeking help. In a confession involving disclosure of abuse, the penitent/victim might think the seal of confession applies to them personally. The penitent/victim may also think that the seal applies to everything said when going to confession. The priest must clarify these matters for the penitent. Furthermore, the penitent/victim might think mistakenly that he or she has in some way sinned, caused the abuse, or have acted wrongly. The priest must clarify for the victim that that they have not done anything wrong, and that the abuser is responsible for the crime. The priest/confessor must do his best to get help for the penitent/victim.

For example, a thirteen-year-old boy rides to the church to go to confession. On the way, he is knocked off his bike by a car whose driver does not stop. When he arrives at the confessional, the boy tells the priest about the incident. The priest would not be breaking the seal of confession if he phones the police or the boy's parents and tells them that the boy has been a victim of a hit-and-run accident. The boy has done nothing wrong. What happened to him was not a sin on his part. He is an innocent victim and needs help. Similarly, if a boy, for example, has been sexually abused, he has not committed any sin. He is an innocent victim and needs help. The priest's role is not to engage in counseling in the context of the sacrament of penance. The priest confessor must encourage and help the penitent/victim to obtain help from an appropriate person.

When a person comes to confession to confess his/her sins, the priest is only acting in the person of Jesus Christ. The confession of sins made to the priest are understood as being made to God. The confession of sins is not for the priest to reveal. The seal of confession outlined in canons 983 and 1386 applies only to the priest/confessor, not to the penitent. Nor does the seal of confession apply to matters that are not sinful. For example, if a penitent during the confession tells the priest that his horse is going to win and suggests backing it, the priest is not breaking the seal when he suggests to a third party that they back this horse as well.

Many people think that the seal of confession applies to everything that is said on the occasion of going to confession. For example, when going to confession, a penitent changes the day for the priest to bring her mother communion. This is not covered by the seal of confession. Priests must make it clear to penitents when sexual abuse is not covered by the seal of confession. The priest must advise the penitent/victim to seek help and to inform civil authorities. The Apostolic Penitentiary advises confessors with older victims in the confessional:

> If a penitent is present who has been a victim of the evil of others, it will be the concern of the confessor to instruct them regarding their rights, as well as about the concrete juridical instruments to use to denounce the fact in civil and/or ecclesiastical forum and invoke his justice.[25]

On July 16, 2020, the Congregation for the Doctrine of the Faith published the *Vademecum: On Certain Points of Procedure in Treating Cases of Sexual Abuse of Minors Committed by Clerics*.[26] The seal of confession is briefly addressed by the *Vademecum*:

> It must be pointed out that a report of a *delictum gravius* received in confession is placed under the strictest bond of the sacramental seal (cf. canon 983 §1 CIC; canon 733 §1 CCEO; art. 4 §1, 5° SST). A confessor who learns of a *delictum gravius* [more grave delict] during the celebration of the sacrament should seek to convince the penitent to make that information known by other means, in order to enable the appropriate authorities to take action. (no. 14)

It would have been better if the Congregation addressed in more detail the situations of an abuser, an adult abused as a child, or a recent child victim disclosing sexual abuse in the sacrament of penance. The situation of an innocent child seeking help when going to confession is very different to an abuser confessing his abuse.[27] In 2020, the Holy See replied to the recommendation of the Australian Royal Commission concerning the seal of confession:

However, even if the priest is bound to scrupulously uphold the seal of the confessional, he certainly may, and indeed in certain cases should, encourage a victim to seek help outside the confessional or, when appropriate, to report an instance of abuse to the authorities.[28]

The priest must be careful to uphold the seal of confession. After confession, if the child victim states what had been earlier stated in confession, obviously now the knowledge is in the external forum and not only in the internal sacramental forum. Care must be taken not to confuse what is under the seal and what is not under the seal. The priest could then accompany the child to speak to his or her parents or help the child to inform civil authorities.

THE PENITENT WHO IS AN ABUSER

Many people go to confession anonymously and confess behind a screen or grill. The priest has no idea who is confessing, and he is not allowed to ask the identity of the person with whom the penitent sinned.[29]

The essential element of a sacramental confession, at least as far as the seal is concerned, is the penitent's intention of receiving absolution. If the penitent is a pedophile confessing his personal sin of sexual abuse of a minor, the seal of confession applies to the priest/confessor.

Priests can delay or even deny absolution to a pedophile confessing his sin of sexual abuse of minors. Pope Blessed Innocent XI condemned the proposition that a priest could grant absolution to a penitent when there appeared no hope of amendment.[30] Experience demonstrates that pedophiles often repeat sexual abuse.

The Royal Commission in Australia heard evidence of priest abusers receiving absolution many times for sexual abuse of children.[31] In France, there have been similar cases.[32] Penitents, such as pedophiles, who are judged by the confessor to have no real intention of reforming and avoiding the occasions of sin, can have absolution deferred or refused until the confessor judges their intention of amendment to be sincere.[33] A confessor can never require a penitent to hand himself into civil authorities, as the Apostolic Penitentiary points out:

> In the presence of sins that involve criminal offenses, it is never permissible, as a condition for absolution, to place on the penitent the obligation to turn himself in to civil justice, by virtue of the natural principle, incorporated in every system, according to which "*nemo tenetur se detegere.*"[34]

In delaying absolution, the confessor could ask the pedophile to seek help from a psychologist or psychiatrist before granting absolution.

As noted above, in 2020, the Holy See replied to the recommendation of the Australian Royal Commission concerning the seal of confession:

> Concerning absolution, the confessor must determine that the faithful who confess their sins are truly sorry for

them and that they have a purpose of amendment (cfr. CIC, can. 959). Since repentance is, in fact, at the heart of this sacrament, absolution can be withheld only if the confessor concludes that the penitent lacks the necessary contrition (cfr. CIC, can. 980). Absolution then, cannot be made conditional on future actions in the external forum.[35]

A penitent can be encouraged to hand himself in to civil authorities. However, a confessor cannot require a penitent to hand himself into civil authorities. The granting of absolution cannot be conditional on handing himself in. A parallel example is a confessor should not require an unfaithful husband to tell his wife of the affair. The "Note" issued on July 1, 2019, by the Apostolic Penitentiary explains this.[36]

If an abuser/penitent later discloses abuse outside the sacrament of penance, obviously the knowledge is now in the external forum (not in the internal sacramental forum), but care must be taken not to confuse what is under the seal of confession and what is not. The matter is in the external forum and must be dealt with accordingly.[37] The priest must prevent further sexual abuse of minors.

If a priest learns of the abuse from a source outside the confessional, the seal of confession does not apply to the information he has learned in the external forum. Because of the complexity of such situations, bishops, major superiors of clerical religious institutes, and members of sexual abuse protocol committees should not hear the confessions of priests to avoid any potential conflict of interest.

CONCLUSION

Upholding the seal of confession is a serious obligation for priests. The seal is not just to protect the privacy of the penitent. It is founded on the necessity to protect the dignity of the sacrament. Montini explains:

> The sacramental seal is to protect (even) the sacrament itself, and, therefore, the removal of the confessor from the seal is not at the discretion of the penitent. If at all the seal is at the discretionary power of the penitent, then the latter may be indirectly subject to such pressures (moral, social, etc.) so that the confessor is freed from the bond of the secrecy, which in reality would be equivalent to shift the actual guardian of the sacramental seal.[38]

The seal of confession applies to mortal and venial sins. The sacrament of penance is the only way the faithful receive forgiveness of their sins in normal circumstances. Therefore, priests must be very careful not to discourage the faithful from going to receive the sacrament of penance or reconciliation by giving the impression that the seal of confession is not absolute.

A young child seeking help has not sinned, so when he or she comes to the confessional/reconciliation room seeking help, the priest must encourage the child to seek help from a person such as a parent, or if necessary, talk to the priest himself again outside after the confession. Because upholding the seal of confession is such a grave obligation for priests, when there is doubt about whether information is under the seal or not, the priest must keep the information confidential under the seal of confession. On the other hand, if the person who came to confession divulges the information again outside the context of the confession, it is clear the information divulged in the external forum is not under the seal of confession. Priests having a clear understanding of these principles should always be able to help victims who divulge in confession that they have been abused.

12

DISMISSAL FROM THE CLERICAL STATE

The term *defrocked* is often used by the media to refer to a priest dismissed from the clerical state, but the term is no longer used in canon law. In 2010, the *New York Times* reported, "Top Vatican officials—including the future Pope Benedict XVI—did not defrock a priest who molested as many as 200 deaf boys."[1] On March 11, 2018, the *Sunday Star Times* in New Zealand ran a story advising, "Catholic priest defrocked after affair in the US now in charge of Auckland parish."[2] In the 1917 Code of Canon Law, a penalty that could be imposed upon a cleric was the prohibition to wear ecclesiastical dress. The penalty could be imposed either as a temporary or a perpetual privation. Perpetual privation was a very serious penalty, but it did not include the cleric being dismissed from the clerical state. The penalty of degradation alone had that effect.[3] The 1917 Code was replaced by the 1983 Code. Hence *defrocked* is not a term applicable to the Catholic Church for the dismissal from the clerical state.

Once a priest has been dismissed from the clerical state, he remains an ordained priest while losing all rights and privileges of being a cleric,[4] but can function if someone is in danger of death.[5]

HISTORICAL PRECEDENTS

The Church has always been aware of the sexual abuse of children and, until the twentieth century, has severely punished perpetrators of the sexual abuse of minors. Priests who had abused children were dismissed from the clerical state immediately.

Sexual abuse of girls or boys was always seen by Christians as being contrary to the sixth commandment. Polycarp (ca. 69–155), the second bishop of Smyrna, wrote to the Philippians:

The younger men must be blameless in all things, caring of purity before everything and curbing themselves from every evil...whether whoremongers nor effeminate persons nor defilers of themselves with men and boys shall inherit the Kingdom of God.[6]

Sexual abuse by a priest was considered especially evil. Canon 71 of the Council of Elvira (305–6) in Spain, condemned those who rape little boys:[7] "People who sexually abuse boys shall not be given communion even at the end."[8] Refusing communion to a dying perpetrator of sexual abuse demonstrates how evil the Council judged sexual abuse.

The Council of Nicaea (325) was the first ecumenical council and began placing Church norms into canons. Canon 9 ordered that an unchaste priest before or after ordination could not exercise ministry.[9]

The Books of Penitentials that were common between the sixth and eleventh centuries give us an important insight into how the Church of that time viewed sins, especially sins of homosexuality and pedophilia. In England, the Penitential of Bede defined effeminacy and sodomy as capital sins with resulting penalties of seven years for deacons, ten years for priests, and twelve years for bishops.[10]

Bishop Burchard of Worms compiled a twenty-volume collection of canon law[11] that he completed in 1012. He wrote,

A cleric or monk who is a perverter of young boys or adolescents, who has been caught kissing or in another occasion of base behaviour with young boys or adolescents, shall be whipped in public, shall lose his crown (tonsure), and so basely shorn, shall have his face spit on, shall be bound in iron chains, shall waste in prison for six months, and for three days of each week, shall be fed only on barley bread at evening time. After this, for another six months, he is to be kept apart in an enclosure, under the watch of a spiritual elder, intent on manual labour and prayer, subject to vigils and prayers, and he is always to walk under the guard of two spiritual brothers, not being allowed to engage in private speech or counsel with any young men.[12]

In *The Book of Gomorrah*, Peter Damian condemns sexual misconduct by clerics stating "that those who are addicted to impure practices should be neither promoted to orders nor, if already ordained, should be allowed to continue."[13]

The Third Lateran Council of 1179 taught,

All those who are caught to be laboring under that incontinence which is against nature and because of which the wrath of God visited the sons of infidelity and burnt down five cities: if they are clerics, they will be dismissed from the clerical state or else be confined to monasteries to do penance; if they are lay people they will be excommunicated and they will be considered as totally estranged from the assembly of the faithful.[14]

The Fourth Lateran Council of 1215 stated,

In order that the behavior and actions of the clergy may be reformed the better, let all, especially those who are constituted in Holy Orders, strive to live in continence and chastity avoiding every lustful vice especially that vice for which the wrath of God descends from heaven upon the sons of infidelity. May they be able to minister before the almighty God with a pure heart and unblemished body.[15]

The Fifth Lateran Council in 1514 taught,

> If anyone indeed, whether a lay person or cleric were to be convicted of the crime for which the wrath of God descends upon the sons of infidelity, let him be punished by the penalties respectively imposed by the sacred canons or the civil law.[16]

On October 11, 1551, the Council of Trent forbade priests to be sexually active and required bishops to deprive offenders of office and to punish them.[17] In session 13, the Council decreed in canon 3,

> There are occasions when crimes of such gravity have been committed by ecclesiastical persons that, on account of their heinous nature, these persons have to be removed from sacred orders and handed over to the secular tribunal.[18]

Clerics who sexually abused minors were dismissed from the clerical state and lost the privilege of the forum and the right to be tried in a church court. Offending clerics were then tried and punished in a secular court. In the sixteenth century, five bishops were usually required by canon law to dismiss a priest. If there was difficulty getting the required number of bishops to dismiss them, canon 4 of canon law allowed a bishop to enlist his vicar general and other senior clerics to do it:

> It shall be lawful for a bishop in person, or through his vicar general in spirituals, to proceed against a cleric in recognized orders, including those of the priesthood, even to his condemnation and verbal deposition, and when acting in person even to the actual and solemn reduction from the orders themselves and from ecclesiastical status...if he has other persons of recognized ecclesiastical rank who are available, are of mature years and are commendable by their knowledge of the law.[19]

There was no delay in punishing grave crimes. The first recorded case after the Council of Trent was in 1570. A church court in Florence judged the case of Luigi Fontino, a canon of the Church of Our Lady of Loreto. He had sodomized a fifteen- or sixteen-year-old choir boy. After Luigi Fontino was threatened with torture, he pleaded guilty. The church court dismissed him and handed him over to secular authorities, who had him beheaded. The choir boy was whipped and exiled from the Papal States.[20]

In 1726, the Sacred Congregation for the Council was more specific about crimes and penalties as it sentenced any priest to the galleys[21] and forbade him from celebrating Mass again for sodomizing boys.[22]

THE 1917 CODE

Minor and Major Clerics

According to the 1917 Code, not all clerics were clerics by ordination.[23] A distinction was made between those who were installed as minor clerics by receiving the tonsure, and major clerics such as bishops, priests, or deacons who had received the sacrament of holy orders.[24]

A person became a cleric by receiving the tonsure. A tonsured cleric in minor orders was usually in a seminary where his suitability for ordination was examined.[25] If he was not later ordained, a minor cleric would be returned to the lay state because of a canonical reason such as being unsuitable for ordination,[26] attempting marriage,[27] failing to wear clerical dress after receiving a precept,[28] enlisting in the army,[29] or by asking to leave the seminary and cease training to be a priest.

Clerics through ordination who were reduced to the lay state lost all offices, benefices, clerical rights and privileges, and were prohibited from wearing clerical dress or tonsure.[30] Privileges included the privilege of the forum so that a cleric was tried in an ecclesiastical court rather than a secular court.[31] The faithful no longer had to show him reverence.[32] In many countries, being a cleric freed him from compulsory military service, so a cleric reduced to the lay state could be conscripted.[33]

However, after a major cleric was reduced to the lay state, he was still bound by the obligations of celibacy unless it was judged he had been ordained under the pressure of grave fear and had not ratified the ordination through the exercise of Holy Orders. In such a case the Sacred Congregation for the Sacraments could investigate in a judicial or administrative manner and release him from the obligations of celibacy.[34]

Loss of the Clerical State

Canon 211 of the 1917 Code listed three possible ways to lose the clerical state:

§1. Although sacred ordination, once validly received, can never be invalidated, nevertheless, a major cleric can be returned to the lay state by a rescript of the Holy See, by a decree or sentence according to the norm of canon 214, or finally as a penalty of degradation.

§2. A minor cleric can be returned to the lay state not only automatically as a result of the causes described in law but also upon his own will, having informed the local ordinary, or by a decree of the same ordinary given for a just cause, if namely the ordinary, all things considered, prudently judges that the cleric is not [sufficiently] consistent with the decorum of the clerical state to be promoted to sacred orders.

Therefore, a cleric could lose the clerical state by his ordination being declared null; receiving a reduction to the lay state, or dismissal from the clerical state.

1. *An ordination could be declared null.* This means that the person was not validly ordained because the sacrament was not administered properly, or not received by the ordinand (perhaps not wanting to be ordained). If an ordination was declared null, the ordinand lost all rights and was released from all obligations of the clerical state.
2. *A rescript could be obtained from the Holy See.*[35] These rescripts from the Apostolic See used to say the cleric was "reduced to the lay state." The ordinand may not have been free to decide to be ordained. This situation is addressed by canon 214:
   §1. A cleric who, coerced by grave fear, receives sacred ordination, and does not later, once the fear has passed, ratify that ordination at least tacitly by the exercise of orders, [and] wanting by such an act to subject himself to clerical obligations is returned to the lay state by sentence of a judge, upon legitimate proof of coercion and lack of ratification, [by which sentence] all obligations of celibacy and canonical hours cease.

   Therefore, a cleric could be reduced to the lay state by a church court and dispensed from the obligations of celibacy and praying the office if it was decided
   a) he received ordination under external pressure
   b) but with sufficient freedom to receive the sacrament of holy orders validly.
3. A person could be dismissed from the clerical state under the 1917 Code for the offenses stated in canon 2359 §2:
   If they engage in a delict against the sixth precept of the Decalogue with a minor below the age of sixteen, or engage in adultery, debauchery, bestiality, sodomy, pandering, incest with blood-relatives or affines in the first degree, they are suspended, declared infamous, and are deprived of any office, benefice, dignity, responsibility, if they have such, whatsoever, and in more serious cases they are to be deposed.

Canon law has traditionally distinguished between the loss of the clerical state and release from the obligations of the clerical state.[36] "Dismissal from the clerical state as a penalty in the Pio-Benedictine Code (1917) was called degradation."[37] When a cleric was dismissed, he no longer had the rights and privileges of the clerical state. However, unless he was dispensed from the obligations of celibacy and praying the divine office, the dismissed cleric was still bound by these obligations. Abbo and Hannan explain that "in the juridical sense, the reduction of clerics to the lay state means the perpetual deprivation of the rights, the privileges, and the juridical status of clerics, especially of the right of lawfully exercising the power of orders possessed."[38]

One of the privileges of clerics in the 1917 Code was the privilege of the forum. Canon 120 §1 stated,

> Clerics shall in all cases, whether contentious or criminal, be brought before an ecclesiastical judge, unless it has been legitimately provided otherwise in certain places.

Canon 120 §2 did provide that a priest could also be brought before the secular courts if the bishop granted permission.[39] The law said that such permission could only be refused with a just and serious reason.

The privilege of the forum never applied in Germany,[40] Australia, New Zealand, Canada[41] and the United States of America because of contrary custom. In Australia any charge of sexual abuse of a minor committed by a priest, such as Michael Glennon in 1978, was dealt with in secular courts. The privilege of the forum was abolished everywhere when the revised Code of Canon Law came into effect on November 27, 1983.[42]

Penalty of Degradation

A major cleric could be reduced to the lay state for committing a crime, defined in ecclesiastical law as "an external and morally imputable violation of a law to which a canonical sanction, at least an indeterminate one, is attached."[43] A deposed cleric lost his office and benefice, all titles, and his pension. However, the deposed or degraded cleric could continue to receive financial support as a charitable grant from the bishop.

If the cleric still failed to reform, then a second penalty of deprivation of ecclesiastical dress was imposed.[44] At this stage the deposed cleric had the status of a layman.

Finally, the third level of penalty of actual degradation outlined in canon 2305 could then be imposed.[45]

> §1. Degradation contains within itself deposition, the perpetual deprivation of ecclesiastical habit, and the reduction of the cleric to the lay state.
> §2. This penalty can only be carried out for a delict expressed in law, or if it is a cleric who is already deposed and deprived of ecclesiastical habit, and if he continues to give out grave scandal for a year.
> §3. One form is *verbal*, that is, by *edict*, which can only be imposed by sentence so that all its juridic effects take place immediately without execution; the other form is *real*, if the solemn prescripts in the Roman Pontifical are observed.

The penalty of actual degradation occurred because the offender continued to offend or because he gave grave scandal.[46] This third level of degradation took place in a public ceremony using the *Roman Pontifical* where the superior gradually divested him of his sacred vestments, before he was handed over to a secular judge.[47] The sentence of degradation was given by five judges in a judicial process[48] for the crimes of apostasy, heresy, schism (c. 2314 §1, no. 3); violence to the pope (c. 2343 §1, no. 3); marriage and continuing in the married state (c. 2388 §1); solicitation (c. 2368 §1); or culpable homicide (c. 2354 §2).

CRIMEN SOLLICITATIONIS

On March 16, 1962, Pope John XXIII issued the Instruction *Crimen Sollicitationis*, which was a slightly amended version of the 1922 Instruction issued by Pope Pius XI. As the title indicated, *Crimen Sollicitationis* dealt almost entirely with the crime of solicitation—that is, the solicitation of sex by a priest hearing confession. The final section[49] of both the 1922 and the 1962 versions of *Crimen Sollicitationis* reads, "What is established herein on the crime of solicitation is also valid, *mutatis mutandis*, for the worst crime *crimen pessimum* [of paedophilia]."[50] The instruction stated that the punishment for more serious cases was reduction to the lay state.[51]

The instruction guided the judge in his evaluation of the seriousness of the crime by "the connection of the solicitation with other crimes; the duration of the immoral conduct; the repetition of the crime; recidivism following an admonition, and the obdurate malice of the solicitor."[52] Therefore, dismissal from the clerical state usually resulted from the commission of a grave crime as well as the perpetrator giving no indication of reforming his life.

VATICAN II AND POST–VATICAN II DOCUMENTS

In 1964, the Sacred Congregation for the Holy Office announced that a commission had been formed to deal with reductions to the lay state and dispensations from celibacy.[53]

After Vatican II, it was theologically incorrect and inappropriate to speak of clergy being reduced to the lay state. Vatican II taught the fundamental equality of all the people of God in the Dogmatic Constitution on the Church:

> Therefore, the chosen People of God is one....There is the common dignity of the members from their regeneration in Christ; they share in common the grace of being heirs, the call to perfection, one salvation, one hope, and one undivided charity. There is, therefore, no inequality in Christ and in the Church....And if some members are appointed, by the will of Christ, as teachers, dispensers of the mysteries, and pastors for others, yet there is a true equality of all with regard to the dignity and action common to all the faithful concerning the building up of the body of Christ....[54] Everyone is called to holiness.[55]

The fundamental equality of all the baptized was emphasized by this teaching. This led to new terminology of "dispensations from celibacy" or clerics being "dismissed from the clerical state."

DISPENSATIONS FROM CELIBACY

In 1971, the Congregation for the Doctrine of the Faith issued New Norms for dispensation from celibacy as well as providing norms for dismissal from the clerical state:

> By observing due proportions, in those cases in which, after the necessary investigation, it was seen that a certain priest, through his improper life or due to doctrinal errors or for some other grave cause, ought to be reduced to the lay state and given a dispensation at the same time, prompted by feelings of compassion, so that he would not be exposed to the danger of eternal damnation.[56]

The cleric's return to the lay state was simplified:

> In place of the "juridical process" instructed in a tribunal, there now is a simple investigation whose purpose it is to discover whether the reasons alleged in the petition for a dispensation from the obligations of celibacy are valid and whether the assertions made by the petitioner are based on the truth. This kind of investigation, therefore, has less of juridical rigor and is governed more by pastoral considerations and proceeds in a simpler way.[57]

In this administrative procedure, the reasons for granting a dispensation were to be very serious and not just a desire to get married or because the petitioner had contempt for the law of celibacy.

MINISTRIES DOCUMENT

In 1972, Pope Paul VI completely revised the minor orders. Previously, a person became a cleric with tonsure, but from 1972 onwards, when a person received the ministries of lector or acolyte, the person remained a layperson until the reception of diaconate.[58] Tomas Rincon explained that Vatican II restricted the notion of who is a cleric:

> The reform carried out by Paul VI has been included in the new Code: nowadays, a person is a cleric or a sacred minister—both terms are equivalent (canon 207) from the diaconate onwards (canon 266).[59]

REVISION OF THE PENAL LAW OF THE 1917 CODE

The 1967 Synod of Bishops discussed the revision of the Code of Canon Law. The Synod gave a guiding principle in no. 9 concerning penalties:

> It is generally agreed that penal laws should be imposed (*ferendae sententiae*), only in the external forum, and remitted likewise only in the external forum. As for penal law automatic penalties (*latae sententiae*), while abolition

of all of these has been proposed by not a few canonists, we suggest that they be reduced to the smallest possible number and concern only the gravest crimes.[60]

During the revision of the 1917 Code, the schema on penalties[61] was completed in 1973 after seven years of work. The *praenotanda* outlined the significant changes from the previous law.[62] Thomas Green explained that when clerics are dismissed from the clerical state, it will have been for committing serious offenses:

> As "delinquents" such individuals may be justifiably liable to sanction of one type or another because of their destructive violations of profound community values, e.g. betrayal of trust and psychological trauma occasioned by paedophilic activity. However, as "Christifideles" such individuals still maintain a fundamental dignity and relationship to Christ and his Church which is to be respected and which grounds continuing efforts to call such individuals to conversion and reintegration within the life of the community.[63]

While the 1917 Code used the terms "reduction to the lay state" and "degradation," the drafts of the 1983 Code favoured the term "loss of the clerical state," or "dismissal from the clerical state."

THE 1983 CODE

Pope John Paul II promulgated the 1983 Code on January 25, 1983. Clerics were required to observe perfect and perpetual continence and be celibate.[64]

Canons 290 to 292 of the 1983 Code deal with loss of the clerical state. Canon 290 now states the three ways that a cleric can lose the clerical state:

> Once validly received, sacred ordination never becomes invalid. A cleric, nevertheless, loses the clerical state:
> No. 1. by a judicial sentence or administrative decree, which declares the invalidity of sacred ordination;[65]
> No. 2. by the legitimate infliction of the penalty of dismissal;
> No. 3. by rescript of the Apostolic See which grants it to deacons only for grave causes and to presbyters only for most grave causes.

A cleric who has been validly ordained always remains a priest but could be prohibited from exercising the power of orders by being excommunicated or suspended.[66]

Dismissal from the Clerical State

The 1983 Code uses the term "dismissal from the clerical state" rather than "degradation." Dismissal from the clerical state cannot be established as a penalty by a diocesan bishop,[67] but can only be imposed[68] administratively by the Holy See or judicially by a college of three judges for the offenses mentioned in the Code.[69] Dismissal from the clerical state is an imposed *ferendae sententiae* penalty rather than an automatic *latae sententiae* penalty.

Dismissal from the clerical state can be a penalty for the following crimes:

1. Ongoing scandal given in apostasy, heresy, or schism (c. 1364 §2)
2. Violation of the sacred species (c. 1382)
3. Physical force against the Roman Pontiff (c. 1370 §1)
4. Solicitation in the sacrament of penance (c. 1385)
5. Attempted marriage and continuing after a warning (c. 1394 §1)
6. Offenses against the sixth commandment with a minor below sixteen years (c. 1398)[70]

John Alesandro notes that a sexual offense violating canon 1398 "need not be a complete act of intercourse, nor should the term be equated with the definitions of sexual abuse or other sexual crimes in civil law...[but] an external act which qualifies as an objectively grave violation of the Sixth Commandment."[71] If the pope dismisses a priest from the clerical state for a canonical crime reserved to the Dicastery for the Doctrine of the Faith, the Dicastery issues the decree of dismissal.[72]

American Norms

A joint commission of the United States Bishops' Conference and the Apostolic See was established by the Apostolic See in 1993. The commission agreed to derogations in canon law concerning raising the age to eighteen years in canon 1395 and changing the time for prescription in sexual abuse cases in canon 1362.

Pope John Paul II made these derogations or changes to the law for an experimental period of five years for the United States of America on April 25, 1994.[73] This was renewed. Canon 1395 §2, 2° was modified so that the age limit for crimes of sexual abuse was raised from age sixteen to age eighteen years. The statute of limitations in canon 1362 was changed so that instead of only five years from the commission of an offense, a victim had until age twenty-three years to lay a complaint about being sexually abused while still a child or a minor.[74]

SACRAMENTORUM SANCTITATIS TUTELA

As noted, on April 30, 2001, Pope John Paul II promulgated as universal law *Sacramentorum Sanctitatis Tutela* (*SST*). The 2001 document was revised in 2010.[75]

The document included the possible crimes in the 1983 Code that might result in dismissal from the clerical state:

1. heresy, apostasy, and schism;[76]
2. a priest or religious: sexually abusing a person under 18 years of age; raping a person of any age; engaging in public sexual activity; continuing to live in concubinage or persisting in a sexual relationship (c. 1395);
3. acquiring, possessing, or distributing child pornography of minors under age 14 (*SST*, 6);[77]
4. violation of the seal of confession;[78]
5. recording what is said in confession;[79]

6. engaging in solicitation in the sacrament of penance (c. 1387);[80]
7. absolving an accomplice in a sin against the sixth commandment (cc. 977, 1384);[81]
8. the consecration of the Eucharist for a sacrilegious purpose;[82]
9. the taking or retaining for a sacrilegious purpose or the throwing away of the consecrated species;[83]
10. attempting the liturgical action of the Eucharistic Sacrifice when not a priest;[84]
11. the simulation of the Eucharistic celebration;[85]
12. concelebration of the Eucharist with those not validly ordained;[86]
13. attempting to absolve when one is not a priest but pretending to be one;[87]
14. attempting to ordain a woman.[88]

The norms were then revised in 2010 and included the faculty for the Congregation of the Doctrine of the Faith to dispense from a trial in the most serious of cases, so that the offending cleric could be dismissed from the clerical state without a penal trial:

> The faculty to dispense from a judicial trial and therefore to proceed *per decretum extra iudicium*. In these cases, the Congregation for the Doctrine of the Faith, after a careful examination of the facts, decides on a case-by-case basis when to authorize an extrajudicial (administrative) process at the request of the ordinary or local hierarch or ex officio (in any of these cases the imposition of a perpetual, expiatory penalty requires the mandate of the Congregation for the Doctrine of the Faith) (Art. 21 §2 n. 1).

For the faculty to present cases directly to the Holy Father *for dimissio e statu clericali or depositio, una cum dispensatione a lege caelibatus*; to proceed in this manner, in addition to the extreme gravity of the particular case, the commission of the delict in question must be manifest, and the right to a proper defense of the accused must be guaranteed (Art. 21 §2 n. 2).[89] To qualify for an extrajudicial or administrative process, the case must be an extremely grave one, and the accused priest must still be heard to provide for his right of defense.

SPECIAL FACULTIES FOR THE CONGREGATION FOR THE EVANGELIZATION OF THE PEOPLES

Many mission territories do not have functioning tribunals. In those territories, Pope John Paul II granted the Congregation for the Evangelization of the Peoples[90] a special faculty to deal with priests living in concubinage and causing scandal.[91] The special faculties allowed dismissal from the clerical state through an abbreviated process that also granted a dispensation from celibacy.

First, the bishop had to have suspended the priest. Then the bishop had to require the priest to reside in another place from where he had ministered. If the priest showed no signs of reforming his life, the bishop could then request the pope to dismiss the priest from the clerical state. The petition for the dismissal was addressed to the pope and had to be signed by the diocesan bishop and two of his consultors.[92] In the bishop's *votum* at the conclusion of the case, there needed to be a statement advising he had no functioning tribunal. The dismissal was granted by the pope *in forma specifica*, so it was not possible to appeal the decision.

When a priest was dismissed from the clerical state, he was not automatically allowed to marry by receiving the favor of a dispensation from celibacy. A dispensation was not granted because the Church intended to facilitate the dismissed priest's eternal salvation. The dismissed priest was not rewarded for causing scandal and committing a serious ecclesiastical crime. However, a priest who was dismissed from the clerical state could still absolve someone in danger of death.[93]

More Special Faculties

On December 19, 2008, Pope Benedict XVI granted the Congregation for the Evangelization of the Peoples special faculties concerning clergy violating canons 1394 and 1395.[94] The special faculties encompassed the cases of priests:

1. who had attempted a civil marriage,[95]
2. who were living in concubinage or had committed sexual crimes,[96] and
3. who had abandoned ministry for more than five consecutive years.[97]

The faculties enabled the Congregation to proceed administratively and bring the cases to the Holy Father to decide.[98]

The special faculties also enabled cases of deacons to be dealt with:

> The same penalty could also be applied to a deacon who has caused scandal in the moral field and is therefore judged by the competent superior not fit to be promoted to the order of priesthood, but does not intend to ask for the pontifical dispensation from the obligations arising from the diaconate ordination.[99]

These faculties apply in mission countries such as New Zealand.

SPECIAL FACULTIES FOR THE CONGREGATION FOR THE CLERGY

Because clerical misconduct was a worldwide problem, Pope Benedict XVI granted almost identical faculties to the Congregation for the Clergy on January 30, 2009, as had been granted to the Congregation for the Evangelization of the Peoples. These faculties enabled the Congregation to treat and present to the Holy Father cases for dismissal from the clerical state:

> 1. The special faculty to treat and present to the Holy Father, for his approval *in forma specifica* and his decision, cases of dismissal from the clerical state *in poenam* with dispensation from the obligations consequent to ordination, including that of celibacy,

of clerics who have attempted marriage, even if only civilly, and who, having been admonished, have not withdrawn from this state, therefore persisting in an irregular and scandalous life (cf. canon 1394 § 1) [also Book VI, 2021 c. 1395]; and of clerics guilty of grave sins against the Sixth Commandment (cf. canon 1393 §§1–2) [Book VI, 2021 c. 1395].

The special faculty to intervene in accord with canon 1399, either by taking direct action in a case or by confirming the decisions of ordinaries, were the competent authority so to request, due to the especial gravity of the violation of law and the need or urgency to avoid an objective scandal.

2. This is granted along with the derogation from the prescriptions of canons 1317, 1319, 1342 §2 and 1349, with respect to the application of perpetual penalties, to be applied to deacons only for grave reasons and to priests for the gravest reasons, always requiring that such cases are presented to the Holy Father for his approval *in forma specifica*.
3. The special faculty to handle cases of clerics, who having freely abandoned the ministry for a period of more than five consecutive years and who, after careful verification of the facts insofar as this is possible, persist in such freely chosen and illicit absence from the ministry; taking this situation into account, to declare then their dismissal from the clerical date, with dispensation from the obligations consequent to ordination, including that of celibacy.[100]

These faculties apply in countries such as Australia. Faculty 1 has clear terms of reference regarding marriage or long-term concubinage. Faculty 2 would apply to a variety of cases including disobeying laws and precepts concerning safeguarding or not returning to an appointment in the diocese of incardination (c. 1371), conduct unbecoming to the clerical state giving scandal (c. 285 §1), or repeated sexual misconduct (c. 1399). The 1983 Code did not provide for dismissal of clerics from the clerical state for clerics abandoning ministry. This faculty was now granted to the Congregation. A dismissed cleric could take recourse against a decision of the Congregation.[101] Faculty 3 gives the initiative to ordinaries to regularize the state of clergy who have left active ministry without seeking a dispensation from celibacy.

Furthermore, the changes in penal law in 2021 include the crime of voluntarily and unlawfully abandoning ministry for six months continuously:

A cleric who voluntarily and unlawfully abandons the sacred ministry, for six months continuously, with the intention of withdrawing himself from the competent Church authority, is to be punished, according to the gravity of the offence, with suspension or additionally with the penalties established in can. 1336 §§2–4, and in the more serious cases may be dismissed from the clerical state. (Pope Francis, Book VI, 2021, c. 1392)

This canon reinforces and strengthens the ability of the ordinary to deal with these offenders.

PROCESS FOR HANDLING CASES THAT MAY LEAD TO DISMISSAL

When a complaint is received alleging a cleric[102] committed a grave crime in canon law, the ordinary must decree the opening of the preliminary investigation and appoint a delegate to investigate the complaint. Alesandro notes that the delegate has the same powers as an auditor and "the investigation should include a search of the archives (including the secret archives) of the dioceses (and religious institutes, if applicable) where the accused cleric has served in order to determine if previous accusations were made against the cleric."[103]

The ordinary may withdraw the faculties of the accused immediately using canon 1722 and consulting the promotor of justice.

The delegate, according to canon 1718, is to provide a report concerning the complaint and a recommendation to the ordinary.

If the complaint has a "semblance of truth about it," the ordinary must send the acts of the case to the Congregation of the Doctrine of the Faith. The ordinary will attach his *votum* to the acts. The *votum* shall request the Congregation to authorize one of the following:

1. An administrative process for dismissal from the clerical state.[104] Both in law and in practice the Congregation for the Doctrine of the Faith has moved in this direction.
2. A penal trial of the accused.[105]
3. An ex officio dismissal from the clerical state because of the gravity of the case and the scandal surrounding it.
4. The imposition of a nonpenal remedy.
5. The dismissal of the case because it is not proven.

DECISIONS IN A PENAL PROCESS

There are three types of penal processes: a judicial penal process; an extrajudicial penal process; or the Congregation for the Doctrine of the Faith presenting the most grave cases to the decision of the Roman Pontiff (see Article 21 §2, 2° *SST*).

The Congregation for the Doctrine of the Faith has identified that a judicial or extrajudicial process concludes with one of the following decisions:

- conviction ("constat"), if with moral certainty the guilt of the accused is established regarding the delict ascribed to him. In this case, the decision must indicate specifically the type of canonical sanction imposed or declared.

- acquittal ("constat de non"), if with moral certainty the innocence of the accused is established, since no offence was committed, the accused did not commit the offence, or the offence is not deemed a delict by the law or was committed by a person who is not imputable.
- dismissal ("non constat"), whenever it has not been possible to attain moral certainty regarding the guilt of the accused, due to lack of evidence or to insufficient or conflicting evidence that the offence was in fact committed, that the accused committed the offence, or that the delict was committed by a person who is not imputable.[106]

The judicial decision or administrative decree must use one of these three terms, so that it is definite whether the decision is *constat, constat de non,* or *non constat*.[107]

CONCLUSION

Dismissal from the clerical state is the most serious penalty that may be inflicted upon a cleric. It is a penalty to punish the most serious crimes, or as a penalty of last resort for an offending cleric who refuses to reform. If a cleric commits several crimes of which one is reserved to the competency of the Dicastery for the Doctrine of the Faith, this Dicastery deals with all crimes of the cleric. After the Dicastery for the Doctrine of the Faith has studied the acts of the case and the *votum* of the ordinary, these are the ways that guilty clerics may be dismissed from the clerical state:

1. The Dicastery of the Doctrine of the Faith refers the case to a local tribunal to hold a judicial trial.
2. The Dicastery of the Doctrine of the Faith tries the case in its own tribunal.[108]
3. The Dicastery of the Doctrine of the Faith instructs the bishop to proceed with an extrajudicial process that may involve dismissal from the clerical state, and then the case will be returned to the Dicastery of the Doctrine of the Faith for confirmation of the penalty.
4. The Dicastery of the Doctrine of the Faith may recommend an ex officio dismissal to the Holy Father.[109]
5. The Dicastery of the Doctrine of the Faith may "pre-authorize" the diocesan bishop "to impose a perpetual expiatory penalty, not excluding dismissal from the clerical state" if the accused cleric has multiple civil convictions for child sexual abuse.
6. The Dicastery for Clergy and the Dicastery for the Evangelization of the Peoples have special faculties to dismiss clerics who have abandoned ministry for more than five consecutive years, or who persist in concubinage or attempted marriage after a warning, or who are causing grave scandal.

The Special Faculties have granted several derogations from the 1983 Code. The 1983 Code did not allow for dismissal from the clerical state through an administrative process[110] before 2021.[111] When it is morally certain that the cleric is guilty of a more grave crime and the penalty of dismissal from the clerical state is appropriate, dismissal from the clerical state protects the rights of victims and the Church itself.[112] Bishops and superiors have a duty to apply the penal law of the Church to such situations.[113]

NOTES

CHAPTER 1

1. Francis, address, "To Participants in the Plenary Assembly of the Pontifical Council for Legislative Texts," Friday, February 21, 2020, http://www.vatican.va.

2. Francis, apostolic constitution *Pascite Gregem Dei*, May 23, 2021, http://www.vatican.va.

3. See Pope Benedict XVI, audience, January 26, 2011, http://www.vatican.va.

4. Lesley O'Brien, *Mary MacKillop Unveiled* (Melbourne: Collins Dove, 1994), 94.

5. R. Bentley Anderson, *Black, White, and Catholic: New Orleans Interracialism, 1947–1956* (Nashville: Vanderbilt University Press, 2005), 146.

6. See Code of Canon Law, c. 1350, in *The Code of Canon Law: Latin-English Edition* (Washington, DC: Canon Law Society of America, 1983), http://www.vatican.va.

7. Pope Benedict XVI, "Pastoral Letter to the Catholics of Ireland," March 19, 2010, http://www.vatican.va.

8. Code of Canon Law, c. 1344, no. 1.

9. Code of Canon Law, c. 1311 §2.

10. *Catechism of the Catholic Church*, 2nd ed. (Washington DC: United States Catholic Conference, 2011), sec. 2284. Note: sec. 2285: Scandal takes on a particular gravity by reason of the authority of those who cause it or the weakness of those who are scandalized. It prompted our Lord to utter this curse: "Whoever causes one of these little ones who believe in me to sin, it would be better for him to have a great millstone fastened round his neck and to be drowned in the depth of the sea." Scandal is grave when given by those who by nature or office are obliged to teach and educate others. Jesus reproaches the scribes and Pharisees on this account: he likens them to wolves in sheep's clothing.

11. John Paul II, apostolic letter, issued *motu proprio*, *Sacramentorum Sanctitatis Tutela*, April 30, 2001, http://www.vatican.va.

12. "Substantive Norms," http://www.vatican.va/resources/resources_norme_en.html.

13. See Chris Gillon and Damian Grace, *Reckoning: The Catholic Church and Child Sexual Abuse* (Adelaide, AU: ATF Press, 2014), 115. Bishop Jarratt never reported any cases to the CDF.

14. Congregation for the Doctrine of the Faith (July 22, 2010), "Revised Norms on Dealing with Clerical Sex Abuse of Minors and Other Grave Offenses," *Origins* 40, no. 10 (2010): 145–52.

15. Congregation for the Doctrine of the Faith, *Revised Norms on Dealing with Clerical*

Sex Abuse of Minors and Other Grave Offenses, 148.

16. Code of Canon Law, c. 1329 §2. In the case of a *latae sententiae* penalty attached to an offense, accomplices, even though not mentioned in the law or precept, incur the same penalty if, without their assistance, the crime would not have been committed, and if the penalty is of such a nature as to be able to affect them; otherwise, they can be punished with *ferendae sententiae* penalties.

17. Francis, apostolic letter issued *motu proprio*, *Vos Estis Lux Mundi*, May 7, 2019; http://www.vatican.va.

18. Dicastery for the Doctrine of Faith, *Vademecum* on Certain Points of Procedure in Treating Cases of Sexual Abuse of Minors Committed by Clerics, June 5, 2022, nos. 11–12, http://www.vatican.va.

19. *Vademecum*, no. 19. Even in these cases, however, it is advisable that the ordinary or hierarch communicate to the DDF the *notitia de delicto* and the decision made to forego the preliminary investigation due to the manifest lack of the semblance of truth.

20. Francis, *Vos Estis Lux Mundi*, Art. 3 §1. The local ordinary means the diocesan bishop, apostolic or diocesan administrator; see c. 134.

21. The term *metropolitan* goes back to the early days of the church when a Roman organizational model was borrowed by the Church. The word comes from the Greek words for "mother city." The original metropolitan diocese normally had other smaller dioceses divided off from it, so it was in a sense the mother diocese.

22. Frank G. Morrisey, OMI, "Papal and Curial Pronouncements: Their Canonical Significance in Light of the 1983 Code of Canon Law," *The Jurist*, 50 (1990), 118, notes, "The general legislation of the Church does not provide for circular letters as an authentic source of law. Nevertheless, we find this form used more often in recent years to outline procedures and to indicate new obligations....At times, though, a circular letter will accompany a set of norms on a given subject. An example of this can be found in the letter and norms regarding the procedures to be observed in petitioning the Holy See for a dispensation from priestly obligations. In these and in other similar instances it is quite clear that the norms constitute the legislative portion of the communication; the circular letter explains the intention, spirit, and purpose of the rules."

23. Congregation for the Doctrine of the Faith, "Circular Letter to Help Episcopal Conferences Prepare Guidelines for the Treatment of Cases of Sexual Abuse against Minors by Clerics," May 3, 2011, I, e: "Cooperation with Civil Authority."

24. Jason Horowitz, "Pope Issues First Rules for Catholic Church Worldwide to Report Sex Abuse," *New York Times*, May 8, 2019, https://www.nytimes.com.

25. Chris McGreal, "Somalian Rape Victim, 13, Stoned to Death," *The Guardian*, November 2, 2008, https://www.theguardian.com.

26. Francis, *Vos Estis Lux Mundi*, Art. 1 §1b.

27. Carol Glatz, "Days of Covering Up Abuse Allegations Are Over, Says Vatican Adviser," Catholic News Service, May 9, 2019, https://www.catholicnews.com.

28. Carol Glatz, "Days of Covering Up Abuse Allegations Are Over."

29. Jason Horowitz, "Pope Issues First Rules for Catholic Church."

30. Carol Glatz, "Days of Covering Up Abuse Allegations Are Over."

31. Carol Glatz, "Days of Covering Up Abuse Allegations Are Over."

32. Editorial Opinion, "Two Steps Forward and One Step Back Won't Cleanse the Catholic Church," *Washington Post*, May 11, 2019, https://www.washingtonpost.com.

33. "How Italian Data Protection Law Differs from the GDPR," https://www.activemind.legal/law/it-data-protection/.

34. Francis, *Vos Estis Lux Mundi*, Art. 6.

35. *Vademecum*, no. 50: "Whenever civil judicial authorities issue a legitimate executive order requiring the surrender of documents regarding cases, or order the judicial seizure of such documents, the Ordinary or Hierarch must cooperate with the civil authorities."

36. Code of Canon Law, c. 22: "Civil laws to which the law of the Church yields are to be observed in canon law with the same effects, insofar as they are not contrary to divine law and unless canon law provides otherwise."

37. Code of Canon Law, c. 1378 §§1–2. The 1917 Code, c. 2404 states, "Abuse of ecclesiastical power, in the prudent judgment of the Legitimate Superior, shall be punished according to the gravity of the fault, with due regard for the prescriptions of those canons that establish certain penalties for various abuses."

38. Francis, *Vos Estis Lux Mundi*, Art. 1 §§1–4.

39. See Juan Arrieta, secretary of the Pontifical Council for Legislative Texts, quoted in Cindy Wooden, "Official Looks at Meaning, Role of 'Metropolitan Archbishop,'" *Crux*, June 1, 2019, www.cruxnow.com.

40. Francis, *Vos Estis Lux Mundi*, Art. 12 §6.

41. Scicluna quoted in Carol Glatz, "Days of Covering Up Abuse Allegations Are Over."

42. Canon 2195 §1, 1917 *Codex Iuris Canonicis*, trans. Edward Peters, *The 1917 Pio-Benedictine Code of Canon Law* (San Francisco, Ignatius Press, 2001). Hereinafter, all translations of the 1917 Code from this source.

43. *Catechism of the Catholic Church*, sec. 1857: "For a sin to be mortal, three conditions must together be met: 'Mortal sin is sin whose object is grave matter and which is also committed with full knowledge and deliberate consent.'"

44. *Catechism of the Catholic Church*, sec. 1858: "Grave matter is specified by the Ten Commandments, corresponding to the answer of Jesus to the rich young man: 'Do not kill, Do not commit adultery, Do not steal, Do not bear false witness, Do not defraud, Honor your father and your mother.' The gravity of sins is more or less great: murder is graver than theft. One must also take into account who is wronged: violence against parents is in itself graver than violence against a stranger."

45. In the 1983 Code the word *delict* occurs 72 times and the word *crime* 7 times.

46. Linus Neli, *Delicta Graviora: "More Grave Delicts" in the Catholic Church* (Bengaluru: ATC Publishers, 2018), 11.

47. *Catechism of the Catholic Church*, sec. 1859: "Mortal sin requires full knowledge and complete consent. It presupposes knowledge of the sinful character of the act, of its opposition to God's law. It also implies a consent sufficiently deliberate to be a personal choice. Feigned ignorance and hardness of heart do not diminish, but rather increase, the voluntary character of a sin."

48. Code of Canon Law, c. 1321 §1. "Any person is considered innocent until the contrary is proved. §2. No one can be punished unless the commission by him or her of an external violation of a law or precept is gravely imputable by reason of malice or of culpability."

49. Juan I. Arias, ed., in *Code of Canon Law Annotated*, 4th ed. (Montreal: Wilson & LaFleur, 2022), 1029.

50. Code of Canon Law, c. 1321 §3.

51. Velasio de Paolis, "*De Sanctionibus*," in *Exegetical Commentary on the Code of Canon Law*, ed. A Marzoa, J. Miras, and R. Rodrigues-Ocana, vol. IV/l, (Montreal: Wilson & LaFleur, 2004), 271.

52. Juan I. Arias, *Exegetical Commentary*, vol. IV/l, 272. Cf. *Communicationes* 8 (1976): 176.

53. Code of Canon Law, c. 1341. "The Ordinary must start a judicial or an administrative procedure for the imposition or the declaration of penalties when he perceives that neither by the methods of pastoral care, especially fraternal correction, nor by a warning or correction, can justice be sufficiently restored, the offender reformed, and the scandal repaired."

54. Code of Canon Law, c. 1347 §1. "A censure cannot validly be imposed unless the offender has beforehand received at least one warning to purge the contempt and has been allowed suitable time to do so." §2. "The offender is said to have purged the contempt if he or she has truly repented of the offence and has made suitable reparation for the scandal and harm, or at least seriously promised to make it."

55. See Code of Canon Law, c. 1752.

56. See Code of Canon Law, c. 1336. "§1. Expiatory penalties can affect the offender either for ever or for a determined or an indeterminate period. Apart from others which the law may perhaps establish, they are those enumerated in §§2–5. §2. An order: 1° to reside in a certain place or territory; 2° to pay a fine or a sum of money for the Church's purposes, in accordance with the guidelines established by the Episcopal Conference. §3. A prohibition: 1° against residing in a certain place or territory; 2° against exercising, everywhere or inside or outside a specified place or territory, all or some offices, duties, ministries or functions, or only certain tasks attaching to offices or duties; 3° against performing all or some acts of the power of order; 4° against performing all or some acts of the power of governance; 5° against exercising any right or privilege or using insignia or titles; 6° against enjoying an active or passive voice in canonical elections or taking part with a right to vote in ecclesial councils or colleges; [new] 7° against wearing ecclesiastical or religious dress. §4. A deprivation: 1° of all or some offices, duties, ministries or functions, or only of certain functions attaching to offices or duties; 2° of the faculty of hearing confessions or of preaching; 3° of a delegated power of governance; 4° of some right or privilege or insignia or title; 5° of all ecclesiastical remuneration or part of it, in accordance with the guidelines established by the Episcopal Conference, without prejudice to the provision of can. 1350 §1. §5. Dismissal from the clerical state. [cf. canon 1336 §1 5°]."

57. Code of Canon Law, cc. 291–93 specify the consequences including loss of all rights as a cleric.

58. Code of Canon Law, c. 1317. "Penalties are to be established only insofar as they are truly necessary to provide more suitably for ecclesiastical discipline. Particular law, however, cannot establish a penalty of dismissal from the clerical state."

59. Code of Canon Law, c. 1347 §1. "A censure cannot validly be imposed unless the offender has beforehand received at least one warning to purge the contempt and has been allowed suitable time to do so."

60. See Code of Canon Law, cc. 1350; 1365; 1371; 1376; 1377; 1378; 1396; 1398.

61. Code of Canon Law, c. 1361 §4. "Remission must not be granted until, in the prudent judgement of the Ordinary, the offender has repaired any harm caused. The offender may be urged to make such repara-

tion or restitution by one of the penalties mentioned in canon 1336 §§2–4; the same applies also when the offender is granted remission of a censure under canon 1358 §1."

62. Code of Canon Law, cc. 1357; 1361; 1368; 1376; 1377; 1378; 1393.

63. Josemaria Sanchis, in *Exegetical Commentary*, vol. IV/l, 238.

64. Josemaria Sanchis, in *Exegetical Commentary*, vol. IV/l, 238.

65. Note: the Code of Canon Law for the Oriental churches does *not have any automatic penalties*. A list of *Latae sententiae penalties* is in Woestman, *Ecclesiastical Sanctions*, 275.

66. Code of Canon Law, c. 1318. "*Latae sententiae* penalties are not to be established, except perhaps for some outstanding and malicious offences which may be either more grave by reason of scandal or such that they cannot be effectively punished by *ferendae sententiae* penalties; censures, however, especially excommunication, are not to be established, except with the greatest moderation, and only for offences of special gravity. *Latae sententiae* penalties are incurred ipso facto by the very fact of the offense having been committed."

67. Code of Canon Law, c. 1335 §2. "If a censure prohibits the celebration of sacraments or sacramentals or the placing of an act of governance, the prohibition is suspended whenever it is necessary to care for the faithful in danger of death. If a *latae sententiae* censure has not been declared, the prohibition is also suspended whenever a member of the faithful requests a sacrament or sacramental or an act of governance; a person is permitted to request this for any just cause."

68. Congregation for the Doctrine of the Faith, "General Decree," December 19, 2007, no. 1, in *L'Osservatore Romano*, May 30, 2008, "With due regard for what has been established by canon 1378 of the Code of Canon Law, both he who has attempted to confer holy orders on a woman, and the woman who has attempted to receive the said sacrament, incurs a *latae sententiae* excommunication, reserved to the Apostolic See."

69. Archbishop Lefebvre was formally warned by the Congregation of the Bishops before consecrating bishops, and formally excommunicated even though the penalty is *latae sententiae*. See William Woestman, OMI, *Ecclesiastical Sanctions and the Penal Process* (Ottawa, Saint Paul University, 2000), 191–97.

70. Congregation for the Doctrine of the Faith, Prot. No. 57/73, in *AAS* 80 (1988): 1367.

71. Judith Hahn, "What Does It Mean to Be 'Morally Certain'? How Secular Standards of Proof Help to Understand Canonical Decision Making," *The Canonist* 11, no. 2 (2020): 242, and Judith Hahn, "Moral Certitude: Merits and Demerits of the Standard of Proof Applied in Roman Catholic Jurisprudence," *Oxford Journal of Law and Religion* 8 (2019): 324.

72. See Code of Canon Law, c. 1321. "§1. Any person is considered innocent until the contrary is proved. §2. No one can be punished unless the commission by him or her of an external violation of a law or precept is gravely imputable by reason of malice or of culpability. §3. A person who deliberately violated a law or precept is bound by the penalty prescribed in that law or precept. If, however, the violation was due to the omission of due diligence, the person is not punished unless the law or precept provides otherwise. [This was §2 in original canon.] §4. Where there has been an external violation, imputability is presumed, unless it appears otherwise."

73. See Margaret Poll, *The Reparation of Harm: A Canonical Analysis of Canon 128*

with Reference to its Common Law Parallels (Ottawa. St. Paul University, 2002), 386.

74. Pope Benedict XVI, "Address to the US Bishops," April 16, 2008, http://www.vatican.va.

75. Francis, apostolic letter issued *motu proprio*, "As a Loving Mother," June 4, 2016, http://www.vatican.va.

76. Jason Horowitz, "Pope Issues First Rules for Catholic Church," https://www.nytimes.com.

77. Francis, "Instruction On the Confidentiality of Legal Proceedings," attached to the present *Rescriptum ex audientia SS.mi*, December 6, 2019, http://www.vatican.va/roman_curia/secretariat_state/2019/documents/rc-seg-st-20191206_rescriptum_en.html.

78. Francis, "Instruction *On the Confidentiality of Legal Proceedings*."

79. Francis, apostolic constitution, *Pascite Gregem Dei*—Reforming Book VI of the Code of Canon Law, June 4, 2021, http://www.vatican.va.

CHAPTER 2

1. John Paul II, apostolic letter *Sacramentorum Sanctitatis Tutela*, April 30, 2001, https://www.vatican.va.

2. Code of Canon Law, c. 1379 §1. "The following incur a *latae sententiae* interdict or, if a cleric, also a *latae sententiae* suspension: §3. Both a person who attempts to confer a sacred order on a woman, and the woman who attempts to receive the sacred order, incur a *latae sententiae* excommunication reserved to the Apostolic See; a cleric, moreover, may be punished by dismissal from the clerical state."

3. The Royal Commission into Institutional Responses to Child Sexual Abuse, *Final Report*, December 15, 2017, https://www.childabuseroyalcommission.gov.au/final-report.

4. Francis, "New Book VI of the Code of Canon Law," June 1, 2021, https://press.vatican.va/content/salastampa/en/bollettino/pubblico/2021/06/01/210601b.html. (Hereafter, all translations of the revised Book VI are taken from this source.)

5. See "Offences against Chastity," in *Catechism of the Catholic Church*, Section 3, Part 2, secs. 2351–56, https://www.usccb.org/sites/default/files/flipbooks/catechism/562/.

6. Dicastery for the Doctrine of the Faith, "*Vademecum*: On Certain Points of Procedure in Treating Cases of Sexual Abuse of Minors Committed by Clerics," June 5, 2022, https://www.vatican.va.

7. CDF, "*Vademecum*," Art. 1.

8. Francis, New Book VI, 2021, c. 1398 §2.

9. Francis, *Vos Estis Lux Mundi*, Art. 1, §1.

10. "Bishop Arrieta: How Book VI of Canon Law Has Changed," Vatican News, June 1, 2021, https://www.vaticannews.va/en/vatican-city/news/2021-06/book-vi-vatican-penal-code-apostolic-constitution.html.

11. "Bishop Arrieta: How Book VI of Canon Law Has Changed."

12. Francis, New Book VI, 2021, c. 1398 §1.

13. Nirmala Carvalho, "Cardinal Says Church Law on Abuse Will Need 'Continuous Updating,'" interview with Cardinal Gracias, Crux, June 15, 2021, https://cruxnow.com/vatican/2021/06/cardinal-says-church-law-on-abuse-will-need-continuous-updating/.

14. Francis, *Vos Estis Lux Mundi*, Art. 1, §2 b).

15. DDF, "*Vademecum*," no. 5.

16. Code of Canon Law, c. 1378 §§1–2.

17. Code of Canon Law, c. 128. "Whoever unlawfully causes harm to another by a juridical act, or indeed by any other act which is malicious or culpable, is obliged to repair the damage done." In "Title VII: Juridical Acts" (cc. 124–28).

18. Francis, New Book VI, 2021, c. 1392.

19. Francis, apostolic letter issued *motu proprio*, *Communis Vita*, March 19, 2019, www.vatican.va. See also John Renken, *The Penal Law of the Roman Catholic Church: Commentary on Canons 1311–1399 and 1717–1731 and Other Sources of Penal Law* (Ottawa: Saint Paul University, 2015), 485–99.

20. See Congregation for the Doctrine of the Faith, "Revised Norms on Dealing with Clerical Sex Abuse of Minors and Other Grave Offenses," *Origins* 40 (2010): 146–51.

21. Congregation for the Doctrine of the Faith, "Revised Norms on Dealing with Clerical Sex Abuse of Minors and Other Grave Offenses," 148. See 4. "Crimes against Catholic Morals," Art. 6, §1, No. 2. The text of the Norms on *delicta graviora* currently in force is the text approved by Benedict XVI on May 21, 2010, that was published by the Vatican press office on July 15, 2010.

22. Code of Canon Law, c. 1329.

23. Francis, *Vos Estis Lux Mundi*, Art. 1, §2 c).

24. Francis, Rescriptum ex audientia SS.mi: Rescript of the Holy Father Francis with which the "Instruction *On the Confidentiality of the Causes*" is promulgated, December 6, 2019, https://www.vatican.va/roman_curia/secretariat_state/2019/documents/rc-seg-st-20191203_rescriptum_en.html.

25. Francis, New Book VI, 2021, c. 1398 §1.

26. Code of Canon Law, c. 1397 §2. "A person who actually procures an abortion incurs a *latae sententiae* excommunication" [formerly canon 1398], and §3. "If offences dealt with in this canon are involved, in more serious cases the guilty cleric is to be dismissed from the clerical state."

27. Francis, apostolic letter, *Misericordia et misera*, November 20, 2016, https://www.vatican.va.

28. Code of Canon Law, c. 915. "Those upon whom the penalty of excommunication or interdict has been imposed or declared, and others who obstinately persist in manifest grave sin, are not to be admitted to holy communion."

29. Code of Canon Law, c. 1368. "A person is to be punished with a just penalty who, at a public event or assembly, or in a published writing, or by otherwise using the means of social communication, utters blasphemy, or gravely harms public morals, or rails at or excites hatred of or contempt for religion or the Church."

30. Joseph Ratzinger, "Worthiness to Receive Holy Communion. General Principles," no. 6, https://chiesa.espresso.repubblica.it/articolo/7055%26eng%3Dy.html.

31. Thomas Petri, "Priests, prudence, Politics: Why Joe Biden was refused Holy Communion at a Catholic Mass," *USA Today*, November 3, 2019, https://www.usatoday.com/story/opinion/2019/11/03/joe-biden-catholic-mass-holy-communion-refused-column/4123123002/.

32. Cardinal Luis Ladaria, Letter to Archbishop Gomez, May 7, 2021, Prot. No. 3277/70-82755, https://www.scribd.com/document/507399449/Pillar-Media-CDF-Letter-5-7-21.

33. Cardinal Luis Ladaria, Letter to Archbishop Gomez.

34. Cardinal Luis Ladaria, Letter to Archbishop Gomez.

35. Cardinal Luis Ladaria, Letter to Archbishop Gomez.

36. The Australian Royal Commission into Institutional Responses to Child Sexual Abuse, *Final Report*, 2017, https://www.childabuseroyalcommission.gov.au/final-report.

37. Code of Canon Law, c. 1323. "No one is liable to a penalty who, when violating a law or precept: 1° has not completed the sixteenth year of age; 2° was, without fault, ignorant of violating the law or precept; inadvertence and error are equivalent to ignorance; 3° acted under physical force, or under the impetus of a chance occurrence which the person could not foresee or if foreseen could not avoid; 4° acted under the compulsion of grave fear, even if only relative, or by reason of necessity or grave inconvenience, unless, however, the act is intrinsically evil or tends to be harmful to souls; 5° acted, within the limits of due moderation, in lawful self-defence or defence of another against an unjust aggressor; 6° lacked the use of reason, without prejudice to the provisions of canons 1324 §1 n. 2 and 1326 §1 n. 4; 7° thought, through no personal fault, that some one of the circumstances existed which are mentioned in nn. 4 or 5."

38. Code of Canon Law, c. 1324 §1–3. "§1. The perpetrator of a violation is not exempted from penalty, but the penalty prescribed in the law or precept must be diminished, or a penance substituted in its place, if the offence was committed by: 1° one who had only an imperfect use of reason; 2° one who was lacking the use of reason because of culpable drunkenness or other mental disturbance of a similar kind, without prejudice to the provision of can. 1326 §1 no. 4; 3° one who acted in the heat of passion which, while serious, nevertheless did not precede or hinder all mental deliberation and consent of the will, provided that the passion itself had not been deliberately stimulated or nourished; 4° a minor who has completed the sixteenth year of age; 5° one who was compelled by grave fear, even if only relative, or who acted by reason of necessity or grave inconvenience, if the offence is intrinsically evil or tends to be harmful to souls; 6° one who acted in lawful self-defence or defence of another against an unjust aggressor, but did not observe due moderation; 7° one who acted against another person who was gravely and unjustly provocative; 8° one who erroneously, but culpably, thought that some one of the circumstances existed which are mentioned in can. 1323 nn. 4 or 5; 9° one who through no personal fault was unaware that a penalty was attached to the law or precept; 10° one who acted without full imputability, provided it remained grave. §2. A judge can do the same if there is any other circumstance present which would reduce the gravity of the offence. §3. In the circumstances mentioned in § 1, the offender is not bound by a *latae sententiae* penalty, but may have lesser penalties or penances imposed for the purposes of repentance or repair of scandal."

39. See excellent advice in D. Miller and Eileen Jaramillo, *Procedural Handbook for Institutes of Consecrated Life and Societies of Apostolic Life* (Washington, Canon Law Society of America, 2021).

CHAPTER 3

1. Antonio Viana, in *Exegetical Commentary*, vol. 1, 835.

2. Code of Canon Law, c. 883 3°. "'As regards those who are in danger of death, the pastor or indeed any presbyter' may administer the sacrament of confirmation"; c. 976. "Even though a priest lacks the faculty to hear confessions, he absolves validly and

licitly any penitents whatsoever in danger of death from any censures and sins, even if an approved priest is present"; c. 1003 §2. "All priests to whom the care of souls has been entrusted have the duty and right of administering the anointing of the sick for the faithful entrusted to their pastoral office. For a reasonable cause, any other priest can administer this sacrament with at least the presumed consent of the priest mentioned above"; c. 1352 §1. "If a penalty prohibits the reception of the sacraments or sacramentals, the prohibition is suspended as long as the offender is in danger of death."

3. Code of Canon Law, c. 132. "§1. Habitual faculties are governed by the prescripts for delegated power. §2. Nevertheless, unless the grant expressly provides otherwise or the ordinary was chosen for personal qualifications, a habitual faculty granted to an ordinary is not withdrawn when the authority of the ordinary to whom it was granted expires, even if he has begun to execute it, but the faculty transfers to any ordinary who succeeds him in governance."

4. Viana, *Exegetical Commentary*, vol. 1, 836.

5. Code of Canon Law, c. 970. "The faculty to hear confessions is not to be granted except to presbyters who are found to be suitable through an examination or whose suitability is otherwise evident."

6. Rodger Austin, "Submission on Canon Law to the Royal Commission into Institutional Responses to Child Sexual Abuse in Australia," October 2016. See Canon 966.

7. Code of Canon Law, cc. 156, 474.

8. Code of Canon Law, c. 1025. "§1. To confer the presbyteral or diaconal orders licitly, it is required that the candidate, having completed the period of probation according to the norm of law, is endowed in the judgment of his own bishop or of the competent major superior with the necessary qualities, is prevented by no irregularity and no impediment, and has fulfilled the prerequisites according to the norm of canons 1033-1039. Moreover, the documents mentioned in canon 1050 are to be obtained and the investigation mentioned in canon 1051 is to be completed. §2. Furthermore, it is required that he is considered in the judgment of the same legitimate superior as useful for the ministry of the Church. §3. The bishop ordaining his own subject who is destined to the service of another diocese must be sure that the one to be ordained is going to be attached to this other diocese."

9. Code of Canon Law, c. 1052. "§1. For a bishop conferring ordination by his own right to proceed to the ordination, he must be sure that the documents mentioned in canon 1050 are at hand and that, after the investigation has been conducted according to the norm of law, positive arguments have proven the suitability of the candidate. §2. For a bishop to proceed to the ordination of someone who is not his subject, it is sufficient that the dimissorial letters mention that the same documents are at hand, that the investigation has been performed according to the norm of the law, and that the suitability of the candidate has been established. Moreover, if the candidate is a member of a religious institute or a society of apostolic life, the same letters must also attest that he has been received definitively into the institute or society and is a subject of the superior who gives the letters. §3. If, all these notwithstanding, the bishop doubts for specific reasons whether a candidate is suitable to receive orders, he is not to promote him."

10. Francis G. Morrisey OMI, "Suitability for Ministry," *The Canonist* 3, no. 2 (2012): 224; see cc. 281, 274, 1025; CCEO 371.

11. Code of Canon Law, c. 51. "A decree is to be issued in writing, with the reasons at least summarily expressed if it is a decision."

12. Code of Canon Law, c. 974 §1. "The local ordinary and the competent superior are not to revoke the faculty to hear confessions habitually except for a grave cause."

13. Congregation for the Clergy, Prot. No. 37937/05 CA, June 23, 2007, quoted in Francis G. Morrisey OMI, "Violations of Canon 277 (with an Adult) Appropriate and Just Responses," *The Canonist* 1, no. 2 (2010): 62.

14. David Price, "Open Forum," *Newsletter of the Canon Law Society Australia and New Zealand*, (2000/1): 27–28; John Beal, "To Be or Not to Be That Is the Question: The Rights of the Accused in the Canonical Penal Process," *Canon Law Society of America Proceedings* 53 (1991): 77–97.

15. DDF, "*Vademecum*," no. 62.

16. Norm 6 of the "Essential Norms for Diocesan/Eparchial Policies Dealing with Allegations of Sexual Abuse of Minors by Priests or Deacons" *Origins* 32, no. 25 (2002): 415ff.

17. See Sentence Apostolic Signatura, Petrus Card. Erdo, March 18, 2006, in Wollongong case, Prot. No. 32108/01 CA: "The decision…is in no way the inflicting of a penalty, for which is required moral certainty concerning a gravely imputable crime committed, but a non-penal disciplinary decision, which may be imposed because of a positive and probable doubt concerning the suitability of the cleric in the matter concerned."

18. See footnotes 33–36 and text concerning expiatory penalties.

19. Peter O. Akpoghiran, *The Catholic Formulary in Accordance with the Code of Canon Law*, vol. 5, *Penal Acts*, (New Orleans, Guadalupe Book Publishers, 2014), 63.

20. Akpoghiran, *The Catholic Formulary*, 47.

21. Code of Canon Law, c. 221. "§1. The Christian faithful can legitimately vindicate and defend the rights which they possess in the Church in the competent ecclesiastical forum according to the norm of law. §2. If they are summoned to a trial by a competent authority, the Christian faithful also have the right to be judged according to the prescripts of the law applied with equity. §3. The Christian faithful have the right not to be punished with canonical penalties except according to the norm of law."

22. Giuseppe Di Mattia, OFM, in *Exegetical Commentary*, vol. IV/I, Commentary on canon 1336, 345.

23. Code of Canon Law, c. 1717. "§1. Whenever an ordinary has knowledge, which at least seems true, of a delict, he is carefully to inquire personally or through another suitable person about the facts, circumstances, and imputability, unless such an inquiry seems entirely superfluous. §2. Care must be taken so that the good name of anyone is not endangered from this investigation. §3. The person who conducts the investigation has the same powers and obligations as an auditor in the process; the same person cannot act as a judge in the matter if a judicial process is initiated later."

24. Code of Canon Law, c. 1717.

25. See Congregation for the Clergy, Prot. No. 37937/05 CA, June 23, 2007, quoted in Morrisey, *Violations of Canon 277*, 62.

26. Pat Lagges, "The Penal Process: The Preliminary Investigation in Light of the Essential Norms of the United States," in *Sacerdotes iuris*, ed. P. Cogan (Ottawa: Saint Paul University, 2005), 255–96.

27. Code of Canon Law, c. 1341. "An ordinary is to take care to initiate a judicial or administrative process to impose or declare penalties only after he has ascertained that fraternal correction or rebuke or other means of pastoral solicitude cannot sufficiently repair the scandal, restore justice, reform the offender."

28. Code of Canon Law, c. 1720. "If the ordinary thinks that the matter must proceed by way of extrajudicial decree: 1° he is to inform the accused of the accusation and the proofs, giving an opportunity for self-defence, unless the accused neglected to appear after being properly summoned; 2° he is to weigh carefully all the proofs and arguments with two assessors; 3° if the delict is certainly established and a criminal action is not extinguished, he is to issue a decree according to the norm of canons 1342–1350, setting forth the reasons in law and in fact at least briefly."

29. Code of Canon Law, c. 1721 §1. "If the ordinary has decreed that a judicial penal process must be initiated, he is to hand over the acts of the investigation to the promoter of justice who is to present a libellus of accusation to the judge according to the norm of canons 1502 and 1504." Innocent III in the Decretals of Gregory IX (X 5.39.35) said *Rei Publicae interest, ne crimina remaneant impunita*—"It is in the public interest that crimes do not remain unpunished."

30. Code of Canon Law, c. 1722. "To prevent scandals, to protect the freedom of witnesses, and to guard the course of justice, the ordinary, after having heard the promoter of justice and cited the accused, at any stage of the process can exclude the accused from the sacred ministry or from some office and ecclesiastical function, can impose or forbid residence in some place or territory, or even can prohibit public participation in the Most Holy Eucharist. Once the cause ceases, all these measures must be revoked; they also end by the law itself when the penal process ceases."

31. Code of Canon Law, c. 221.

32. Some people wanted to eliminate this preference during the Code revision process, cf. *Communicationes* IX (1977): 161. See V. de Paolis, "Il Processo penale del nuovo codice," in *Dilexit iustitiam*, ed. Z. Grocholewski and V. Carcel Orti (Vatican City: Libreria Editrice Vaticana, 1984), 473–94.

33. Code of Canon Law, c. 1342 §2.

34. Code of Canon Law, c. 1338 §2. "There can be no deprivation of the power of order, but only a prohibition against the exercise of it or of some of its acts; neither can there be a deprivation of academic degrees."

35. Code of Canon Law, c. 904. "Remembering always that in the mystery of the Eucharistic sacrifice the work of redemption is exercised continually, priests are to celebrate frequently; indeed, daily celebration is recommended earnestly since, even if the faithful cannot be present, it is the act of Christ and the Church in which priests fulfil their principal function."

Code of Canon Law, c. 906. "Except for a just and reasonable cause, a priest is not to celebrate the Eucharistic sacrifice without the participation of at least some member of the faithful."

36. Code of Canon Law, c. 764. "Without prejudice to the prescript of canon 765, presbyters and deacons possess the faculty of preaching everywhere; this faculty is to be exercised with at least the presumed consent of the rector of the church, unless the competent ordinary has restricted or taken away the faculty or particular law requires express permission."

37. Code of Canon Law, c. 976. "Even though a priest lacks the faculty to hear confessions, he absolves validly and licitly any penitents whatsoever in danger of death from any censures and sins, even if an approved priest is present."

38. Code of Canon Law, c. 966 §1. "The valid absolution of sins requires that the minister have, in addition to the power of orders, the faculty of exercising it for the faithful to whom he imparts absolution."

39. Code of Canon Law, cc. 47–58.

40. USCCB, "Essential Norms for Diocesan/Eparchial Policies Dealing with Allegations of Sexual Abuse of Minors by Priest or Deacons," May 5, 2006, http://www.usccb.org/issues-and-action/child-and-youth-protection/upload/Charter-for-the-Protection-of-Children-and-Young-People-revised-2011.pdf.

41. Code of Canon Law, c. 701. "By legitimate dismissal, vows as well as the rights and obligations deriving from profession cease ipso facto. Nevertheless, if the member is a cleric, he cannot exercise sacred orders until he finds a bishop who receives him into the diocese after an appropriate probation according to the norm of canon 693 or at least permits him to exercise sacred orders."

42. "The Revocation of Ministerial Faculties" in *Ministerium Iustitiae: Jurisprudence of the Supreme Tribunal of the Apostolic Signatura*, trans. William Daniel, (Montreal: Wilson & Lafleur, 2011), 417.

43. "The Revocation of Ministerial Faculties," 417.

44. Code of Canon Law, c. 1362. "§1. Prescription extinguishes a criminal action after three years unless it concerns: 1° delicts reserved to the Congregation for the Doctrine of the Faith; 2° an action arising from the delicts mentioned in canons 1394, 1395, 1397, and 1398, which have a prescription of five years."

45. "The Revocation of Ministerial Faculties," 214.

46. Code of Canon Law, c. 764.

47. Code of Canon Law, c. 974 §1.

48. Code of Canon Law, c. 1003.

49. "The Revocation of Ministerial Faculties," 217.

50. Daniel, *Ministerium Iustitiae*, 219.

51. Code of Canon Law, c. 1722.

52. Daniel, *Ministerium Iustitiae*, 221.

53. Daniel, *Ministerium Iustitiae*, 222: Case from Pamplona, Pro. No. 22785/91 CA, no. 8 p. 6.

54. Congregatio pro Clericis, 23 August 2001, Prot. No. 2001/1099, quoted in Augustine Mendonça, "The Bishop as the Mirror of Justice and Equity in the Particular Church: Some Practical Reflections on Episcopal Ministry," *Canonical Studies* (2002): 28.

55. Mendonça, "The Bishop as the Mirror of Justice and Equity in the Particular Church," 28.

56. Congregatio pro Clericis, August 23, 2001, Prot. No. 2001/0081. See Mendonça, "The Bishop as the Mirror of Justice and Equity in the Particular Church," 30.

57. Congregatio pro Clericis, December 21, 2000, Prot. No. 2000/1201. See Mendonça, "The Bishop as the Mirror of Justice and Equity in the Particular Church," 31.

58. Code of Canon Law, c. 1608 §1. "For the pronouncement of any sentence, the judge must have moral certitude about the matter to be decided by the sentence."

59. Judith Hahn, "What Does It Mean to Be 'Morally Certain'? How Secular Standards of Proof Help to Understand Canonical Decision Making," *Canonist* 11, no. 2 (2020): 242 and Judith Hahn, "Moral Certitude: Merits and Demerits of the Standard of Proof Applied in Roman Catholic Jurisprudence," *Oxford Journal of Law and Religion* 8 (2019): 324; See also James Q. Whitman, *The Origins of Reasonable Doubt: Theological Roots of the Criminal Trial* (New Haven, CT: Yale University Press, 2008).

60. DDF, "*Vademecum*," 29.

61. Morrisey, *Suitability for Ministry*, 232.

CHAPTER 4

1. Functioning privately would include celebrating Mass alone, or celebrating with family or friends, while celebrating publicly would mean celebrating in a parish church.

2. Jose Bernal, in *Exegetical Commentary*, vol. IV/l, 335.

3. Code of Canon Law, c. 1398 §2. Canon 1331 had the phrase "which can only affect clerics" removed in 2021.

4. Francisco X. Wernz, *Ius Decretalium*, 3rd ed., vol. IV (Prati: Ex Officina Libraria Giachetti, 1912), no. 144.

5. Eligius Rainer, *Suspension of Clerics: An Historical Synopsis and Commentary*, Canon Law Studies 111 (Washington, DC: The Catholic University of America, 1937), 11.

6. Rainer, *Suspension of Clerics*, 4.

7. Karl Hefele, *A History of the Councils from the Original Documents*, vol. 1 (Edinburgh: T & T Clark, 1883), 201 states, "Canon 1. Priests who sacrificed [during the persecution], but afterwards repenting, resumed the combat not only in appearance, but in reality, shall continue to enjoy the honours of their office, but they may neither sacrifice or preach, nor fulfil any priestly office."

8. Rainer, *Suspension of Clerics*, 7.

9. Karl Hefele, *A History of the Councils from the Original Documents*, vol. 3 (Edinburgh, T & T Clark, 1883), 158 states, "Canon 3 said he could receive the support of the Church 'but must never offer the sacrifice in towns or in the absence of the bishop, or ordain nay cleric, or, generally discharge any episcopal function in the church which is granted him. Only in his own church he may confirm the newly baptised.'"

10. Migne, *Patrologia Latina*, vol. IV (Alexandria. VA: Chadwyck-Healey Inc, 1995), 347; Rainer, *Suspension of Clerics*, 6.

11. Third Synod of Carthage, c. 49: "Clericus qui absque corpusculi sui inaequalitate vigiliis deest stipendiis privetur," in Rainer, *Suspension of Clerics*, 10.

12. Medicinal penalties, including excommunication and suspension, aim to bring about the reform of the offender.

13. Wernz, *Ius Decretalium*, 3rd ed., vol. VI (Prati: Ex Officina Libraria Giachetti, 1912), no. 203.

14. Expiatory penalties specifically aim to reestablish Church order, repair scandal, remedy the damage done to the Church by the offender, as well as to deter other offenders.

15. Rainer, *Suspension of Clerics*, 10: Novellae. (123.1) "2: …Per unum annum separi a sacro ministerio;" Novellae, (1232.10) "L: …jubemus eum per tres annos ab omni reigioso ministerio prohiberi et in monasterium immitti."

16. Council of Epaon, c. IV: "Si Episcopus est, tribus mensibus se a Commune suspendat duobus presbyter abstineat." Rainer, *Suspension of Clerics*, 6.

17. "Si quis re Ecclesiae debitas vel proprias sacerdotis horrendae cuspiditatis occupaverit…tam diu a commune ecclesiastica suspendatur," in Hefele, *A History of the Councils from the Original Documents*, vol. 2, 277.

18. Council of Narbonne, c. 10. "Non solum a stipendio sed uno anno a commune privetur"; Cabassutius, *Notitia Ecclesiastica*, 302, quoted by Rainer, *Suspension of Clerics*, 12.

19. Council of Lerida, c. 15: "...post primam et secundam commotionem si emendare neglexerit, donec in vitio perseverat officii sui dignitate privetur; (quod in vitio perseverat officii sui dignitate privetur) quod si se De juvante correxerit, sancto ministerio restauretur," Mansi, VIII, 614.

20. Rainer, *Suspension of Clerics*, 12.

21. Gratian, *Decretum*, C. 13, C. 11, q. 5.

22. *Liber* 9, *Epist*. l; Migne, *P.L.* LXXVII; quoted in Rainer, *Suspension of Clerics*, 13.

23. Council of Toledo, c. XI: "Transgressor institutonis paternae tanto tempore excommunicatum et remotum se a suis officiis noverit esse, quanto eium qui fugiit sub sua potestate contingerit remorasse," Mansi, IX, 17.

24. Council of Chalcedon, c. VI: "No one, whether presbyter or deacon or anyone at all who belongs to the ecclesiastical order, is to be ordained without title, unless the one ordained is specially assigned to a city or village church or to martyr's shrine or a monastery. This sacred synod has decreed that the ordination of those ordained without title is null, and that they cannot operate anywhere, because of the presumption of the one who ordained them." English translation from Norman Tanner, *Decrees of the Ecumenical Councils*, vol. 1 (London: Sheed and Ward, 1990), 90.

25. English Translation in Tanner, *Decrees of the Ecumenical Councils*, vol. 1, 214: "If a bishop ordains someone as deacon or priest without a definite title from which he may draw the necessities of life, let the bishop provide him with what he needs until he shall assign him the suitable wages of clerical service in some church, unless it happens that the person ordained is in such a position that he can find the support of life from his own or family inheritance."

26. Innocent III, C. 20, X, *de verborum significatione*, V, 40; see Rainer, *Suspension of Clerics*, 14; Kevin Knight, "Ecclesiastical Censures," in *Catholic Encyclopedia*: "Innocent III, who in 1200 (cap. 13, X De judicious, II, 1) had used the term for punishment in general, at a later date (1214), answering a query as to the meaning of ecclesiastical censure in pontifical documents, expressly distinguished (cap. 20, X De verb, signif. V, 40) censure from any other ecclesiastical penalty (respondemus quod per eam non solum interdicti, sed suspensionis et excommunicationis sententia valet inteligi), thereby authentically declaring that by ecclesiastical censure were meant the penalties of interdict, suspension, and excommunication." http://www.newadvent.org/cath en/03527a.htm.

27. Council of Trent, session 25, chapter 14: "If after being warned by superiors they still have such relationships...they are automatically to be deprived of a third of the revenues....If they persevere in the same sin with the same or another woman...they are to be suspended from the administration of their benefices....If even when suspended they do not cast them out, or even return to them, they are to be deprived permanently of all ecclesiastical benefices...." Translation in Tanner, *Decrees of the Ecumenical Councils*, vol. 2, 793.

28. Session 23, de. ref. c. 10, Mansi XXXIII, 144.

29. Council of Trent, session 14, de reform., canon 1; John Carr, *The Suspension of a Cleric by the Administrative Procedure According to the 1983 Code of Canon Law* (Ottawa: Saint Paul University, 1989), 45.

30. Pope Pus IX, apostolic constitution, *Apostolicae Sedis*, October 12, 1869; in Rainer, *Suspension of Clerics*, 35; *Fontes*, no. 552.

31. Jose Bernal, *Exegetical Commentary on the Code of Canon Law*, vol. IV/1, 335.

32. Sacred Congregation for the Propagation of the Faith, Instruction, October 20, 1884, *Coll.* S.C.P.F. no 1628; *Fontes*, 4907.

33. Rainer, *Suspension of Clerics*, 35 notes that a suspension was a "penalty, either medicinal or vindictive [expiatory] in its nature, by which a cleric guilty of a crime is temporarily forbidden (*prohibetur*), in whole or in part, the use or exercise of rights which he possesses, either by reason of his orders, or by reason of his office or benefice considered separately, or by reason of his office and benefice taken conjointly."

34. 1917 Code of Canon Law, cc. 2341, 2366, 2371, 2384, 2386, 2387, 2400, 2402.

35. General Synod of Bishops, October 4, 1967, "Principia quae codicis iuris canonici recognitionem dirigant" in *Communicationes* (Pontificia commissio codici iuris canonici recognoscendo), vol 1, (Vatican City: Libreria Editrice Vaticana, 1969), 77–85; English translation in R. Schoenbechler, "Principles Which Govern the Revision of the Code of Canon Law," in *Readings, Cases, Materials in Canon Law*, ed. J. Hite et al. (Collegeville, MN: Liturgical Press, 1986), 70–78.

36. English translation in R. Schoenbechler, "Principles Which Govern the Revision of the Code of Canon Law," 86.

37. *Communicationes* 1 (1969), 84–85; English Translation in R. Schoenbechler, "Principles Which Govern the Revision of the Code of Canon Law," 92.

38. *Communicationes* 7 (1975), 171.

39. Armstrong, *A Critical Appraisal of Latae Sententiae Penalties in the 1983 Code of Canon Law*, 351; including such things as hearing confessions without faculties and absolving from reserved sins canon 2366.

40. 1973 Schema, c. 28 §1. "Whenever there are grave reasons why a judicial process cannot take place, and there are evident proofs of a crime and the time for a criminal action has not run out, then the penalty may be inflicted or declared by an extrajudicial decree. On the other hand, penances and penal remedies may be imposed in any kind of case." English translation from Carr, *The Suspension of a Cleric by the Administrative Procedure According to the 1983 Code of Canon Law*, 107.

41. *Communicationes* 9 (1977), 161.

42. See 1983 Code of Canon Law, c. 145. "§1. An ecclesiastical office is any post which by divine or ecclesiastical disposition is established in a stable manner to further a spiritual purpose. §2. The duties and rights proper to each ecclesiastical office are defined either by the law whereby the office is established, or by a decree of the competent authority whereby it is at one and at the same time established and conferred."

43. Bernal, *Exegetical Commentary on the Code of Canon Law*, vol. IV/1, 336.

44. 1983 Code of Canon Law, c. 1388. A bishop who, contrary to the provision of canon 1015, ordained someone else's subject without the lawful dimissorial letters, is prohibited from conferring orders for one year. The person who received the order is ipso facto suspended from the order received.

45. Josemaria Sanchis, in *Exegetical Commentary*, vol. IV/1, 238: "*Latae sententiae* penalties…are incurred ipso facto by the very fact of the offense having been committed." Once it is verified that the crime has in fact been committed, the legislator imposes the penalty on the offender by the law itself. This canon also allows for the fact that some crimes cannot be effectively punished by *ferendae sententiae* penalties.

46. V. de Paolis, "De recognoscendo iure poenali canonico," *Periodica* 63 (1974): 54–

58; Tom Green, "The Future of Penal Law in the Church," *The Jurist* 35 (1975): 224–27.

47. Josemaria Sanchis, in *Exegetical Commentary*, vol. IV/l, 238: "*Ferendae sententiae* penalties...are applied by a sentence from a judge or a decree from a superior, following a penal procedure (judicial or administrative, depending on the case) to obtain juridical certainty that there was an offense and to ascertain the author's guilt."

48. 1983 Code of Canon Law, c. 1314. "A penalty is ordinarily *ferendae sententiae*, that is, not binding upon the offender until it has been imposed. It is, however, *latae sententiae* if the law or precept expressly lays this down, so that it is incurred automatically upon the commission of an offence."

49. 1983 Code of Canon Law, c. 1370. "§1. A person who uses physical force against the Roman Pontiff incurs a *latae sententiae* excommunication reserved to the Apostolic See; if the offender is a cleric, another penalty, not excluding dismissal from the clerical state, may be added according to the gravity of the crime. §2. One who does this against a Bishop incurs a *latae sententiae* interdict and, if a cleric, he incurs also a *latae sententiae* suspension."

50. 1983 Code of Canon Law, c. 1379 §1. "The following incur a *latae sententiae* interdict or, if a cleric, also a *latae sententiae* suspension: [cf. former canon 1378]. 1° a person who, not being an ordained priest, attempts the liturgical celebration of the Eucharistic Sacrifice,"

51. 1983 Code of Canon Law, c. 1379 §1. "2° a person who, apart from the case mentioned in can. 1384, though unable to give valid sacramental absolution, attempts to do so, or hears a sacramental confession. The following incur a *latae sententiae* interdict or, if a cleric, a *latae sententiae* suspension. N.B. There are exceptions with canon 976 and danger of death, or canon 144 and common error."

52. 1983 Code of Canon Law, c. 1380. A person who through simony celebrates or receives a sacrament is to be punished with an interdict or suspension or the penalties mentioned in canon 1336 §§2–4.

53. 1983 Code of Canon Law, c. 1385. A priest who in confession, or on the occasion or under the pretext of confession, solicits a penitent to commit a sin against the sixth commandment of the Decalogue, is to be punished, according to the gravity of the offense, with suspension, prohibitions, and deprivations; in the more serious cases he is to be dismissed from the clerical state. Igino Tarocchi, "Solicitation," in *Dictionary of Moral Theology*, compiled under the direction of Francesco Cardinal Roberti, ed. Pietro Palazzini, trans. Henry Yannone (Westminster: The Newman Press, 1962), defines the crime of *solicitation* as "any act by which a confessor in the sacrament of penance either induces a penitent to sin seriously against chastity or accepts the inducements of a penitent against chastity (1917 canon 904)." Solicitation can be either active or passive. Therefore, solicitation leads another to commit sinful acts by means of explicit words, advice, promises, signs, actions or any other method that reveals the intention of the solicitor to solicit.

54. 1983 Code of Canon Law, c. 1395. "§1. A cleric living in concubinage, other than in the case mentioned in can. 1394, and a cleric who continues in some other external sin against the sixth commandment of the Decalogue which causes scandal, is to be punished with suspension. To this, other penalties can progressively be added if after a warning he persists in the offence, until eventually he can be dismissed from the clerical state. §2. A cleric who has offended in other ways against the sixth commandment of the Decalogue, if

the offence was committed in public, is to be punished with just penalties, not excluding dismissal from the clerical state if the case so warrants. [part omitted now in new canon 1398]. §3. A cleric who by force, threats or abuse of his authority commits an offence against the sixth commandment of the Decalogue or forces someone to perform or submit to sexual acts is to be punished with the same penalty as in §2."

55. "Nullum crimen nulla poena sine lege poenali praevia."

56. Thomas Green, *New American Commentary*, 1604.

57. 1983 Code of Canon Law, c. 1341. "The Ordinary must start a judicial or an administrative procedure for the imposition or the declaration of penalties when he perceives that neither by the methods of pastoral care, especially fraternal correction, nor by a warning or correction, can justice be sufficiently restored, the offender reformed, and the scandal repaired."

58. That is, a "rebellious inclination against authority and discipline." V. De Paolis, "De recognoscendo iure poenali canonico," 69.

59. 1983 Code of Canon Law, c. 1339 §3.

60. 1983 Code of Canon Law, c. 1339. "§4. If on one or more occasions warnings or corrections have been made to someone to no effect, or if it is not possible to expect them to have any effect, the Ordinary is to issue a penal precept in which he sets out exactly what is to be done or avoided. §5. If the gravity of the case so requires, and especially in a case where someone is in danger of relapsing into an offence, the Ordinary is also to subject the offender, over and above the penalties imposed according to the provision of the law or declared by sentence or decree, to a measure of vigilance determined by means of a singular decree."

61. 1983 Code of Canon Law, c. 1323, no. 2 "…was, without fault, ignorant of violating the law or precept; inadvertence and error are equivalent to ignorance."

62. "If the ordinary thinks that the matter must proceed by way of extrajudicial decree: 1° he is to inform the accused of the accusation and the proofs, giving an opportunity for self-defense, unless the accused neglected to appear after being properly summoned."

63. 1983 Code of Canon Law, c. 1717. "§1. Whenever the Ordinary receives information, which has at least the semblance of truth, about an offence, he is to enquire carefully, either personally or through some suitable person, about the facts and circumstances, and about the imputability of the offence, unless this enquiry would appear to be entirely superfluous. §2. Care is to be taken that this investigation does not call into question anyone's good name. §3. The one who performs this investigation has the same powers and obligations as an auditor in a process. If, later, a judicial process is initiated, this person cannot take part in it as a judge." "Can. 1718 §1. When the facts have been assembled, the Ordinary is to decree: 1° whether a process to impose or declare a penalty can be initiated; 2° whether this would be expedient, bearing in mind Canon 1341; 3° whether a judicial process is to be used or, unless the law forbids it, whether the matter is to proceed by means of an extra-judicial decree. §2. The Ordinary is to revoke or change the decree mentioned in §1 whenever new facts indicate to him that a different decision should be made. §3. In making the decrees referred to in §§1 and 2, the Ordinary, if he considers it prudent, is to consult two judges or other legal experts. §4. Before making a decree in accordance with §1, the Ordinary is to consider whether, to avoid useless trials, it would be expedient, with the parties' consent, for himself or

the investigator to make a decision, according to what is good and equitable, about the question of damages. Can. 1719. The acts of the investigation, the decrees of the Ordinary by which the investigation was opened and closed, and all those matters which preceded the investigation, are to be kept in the secret curial archives, if they are not necessary for the penal process."

64. 1983 Code of Canon Law, c. 221. "§1. Christ's faithful may lawfully vindicate and defend the rights they enjoy in the Church before the competent ecclesiastical forum in accordance with the law. §2. If any members of Christ's faithful are summoned to trial by the competent authority, they have the right to be judged according to the provisions of law, to be applied with equity. §3. Christ's faithful have the right that no canonical penalties be inflicted upon them except in accordance with the law."

65. 1983 Code of Canon Law, c. 1311. "§2. The one who is at the head of a Church must safeguard and promote the good of the community itself and of each of Christ's faithful, through pastoral charity, example of life, advice and exhortation and, if necessary, also through the imposition or declaration of penalties, in accordance with the provisions of the law, which are always to be applied with canonical equity and having in mind the restoration of justice, the reform of the offender, and the repair of scandal."

66. Congregation for the Clergy, Decree, Prot. No. 2001/1099, August 23, 2001, quoted in Augustine Mendonça, "The Bishop as the Mirror of Justice and Equity in the Particular Church: Some Practical Reflections on Episcopal Ministry," *Canonical Studies* (2002), 28.

67. Congregation for the Clergy, Decree, Prot. No. 37937/05 CA. June 23, 2007, quoted in Francis Morrisey OMI, "Violations of Canon 277 (with an Adult) Appropriate and Just Responses," *The Canonist* 1 (2010), no. 2.

68. Pat Lagges, "The Penal Process: The Preliminary Investigation in Light of the Essential Norms of the United States," in *Sacerdotes iuris*, ed. P. Cogan (Ottawa: Saint Paul University, 2005), 255–96. It must be ascertained if canons 1323 and 1324 apply.

69. James Provost, *Roman Replies and CLSA Advisory Opinions 1995* (Washington DC: Canon Law Society of America. 1995), 99–100.

70. Bernal, in *Exegetical Commentary*, vol. IV/1, 337; 1983 Code of Canon Law, c. 1109. "Within the limits of their territory, the local Ordinary and the parish priest by virtue of their office validly assist at the marriages not only of their subjects, but also of non-subjects, provided one or other of the parties is of the Latin rite. They cannot assist if by sentence or decree they have been excommunicated, placed under interdict or suspended from office, or been declared to be such."

71. 1983 Code of Canon Law, c. 1335 §2. "If a censure prohibits the celebration of the sacraments or sacramentals or the performance of an act of governance, the prohibition is suspended whenever this is necessary to provide for the faithful who are in danger of death. If a *latae sententiae* censure has not been declared, the prohibition is also suspended whenever one of the faithful requests a sacrament or sacramental or an act of the power of governance; for any just reason it is lawful to make such a request."

72. Juan Arias, in *Code of Canon Law Annotated*, ed. E. Caparros, M. Theriault, and J. Thorn (Montreal: Wilson & Lafleur Ltd, 1993), 835.

73. 1983 Code of Canon Law, c. 1352. "§1. If a penalty prohibits the reception of the sacraments or sacramentals, the prohibition is suspended for as long as the offender is in

danger of death. §2. The obligation of observing a *latae sententiae* penalty which has not been declared, and is not notorious in the place where the offender actually is, is suspended either in whole or in part to the extent that the offender cannot observe it without the danger of grave scandal or loss of good name."

74. 1983 Code of Canon Law, c. 976. "Any priest, even though he lacks the faculty to hear confessions, can validly absolve any penitents who are in danger of death, from any censures and sins, even if an approved priest is present."

75. V. de Paolis, "De recognoscendo iure poenali canonico," 69.

76. 1983 Code of Canon Law, c. 1358. "§1. The remission of a censure cannot be granted except to an offender whose contempt has been purged in accordance with can. 1347. §2. However, once the contempt has been purged, the remission cannot be refused, without prejudice to the provision of can. 1361 §4."

77. 1983 Code of Canon Law, c. 1347. "§1. A censure cannot validly be imposed unless the offender has beforehand received at least one warning to purge the contempt, and has been allowed suitable time to do so. §2. The offender is said to have purged the contempt if he or she has truly repented of the offence and has made, or at least seriously promised to make, appropriate reparation for the damage and scandal."

78. 1983 Code of Canon Law, c. 1354. "§3. If the Apostolic See has reserved the remission of a penalty to itself or to others, the reservation is to be strictly interpreted."

79. 1983 Code of Canon Law, c. 1355. "§1. Provided it is not reserved to the Apostolic See, a penalty established by law which is *ferendae sententiae* and has been imposed, or which is *latae sententiae* and has been declared, can be remitted by the following: 1° the Ordinary who initiated the judicial proceedings to impose or declare the penalty, or who by a decree, either personally or through another, imposed or declared it; 2° the Ordinary of the place where the offender actually is, after consulting the Ordinary mentioned in n. 1, unless because of extraordinary circumstances this is impossible. §2. Provided it is not reserved to the Apostolic See, a penalty established by law which is *latae sententiae* and has not yet been declared can be remitted by the following: 1° the Ordinary in respect of his subjects; 2° the Ordinary of the place also in respect of those actually in his territory or of those who committed the offence in his territory; 3° any Bishop, but only in the course of sacramental confession."

80. 1983 Code of Canon Law, c. 134 includes the Roman Pontiff, diocesan bishops, diocesan administrators, vicars general, some episcopal vicars, major superiors of clerical religious institutes of pontifical right and major superiors of clerical societies of apostolic life of pontifical right.

81. 1983 Code of Canon Law, c. 1361. "§1. A remission can be granted even to a person who is not present, or conditionally. §2. A remission in the external forum is to be granted in writing, unless a grave reason suggests otherwise. §3. The petition for remission or the remission itself is not to be made public, except in so far as this would either be useful for the protection of the good name of the offender, or be necessary to repair scandal. §4. Remission must not be granted until, in the prudent judgement of the Ordinary, the offender has repaired any harm caused. The offender may be urged to make such reparation or restitution by one of the penalties mentioned in canon 1336 §§2–4; the same applies also when the offender is granted remission of a censure under canon 1358 §1."

82. Green, *New American Commentary*, 802; Canon 1356 "§1. A *ferendae* or a *latae sententiae* penalty established in a precept not issued by the Apostolic See, can be remitted by the following: 1° the author of the precept; 2° the Ordinary who initiated the judicial proceedings to impose or declare the penalty, or who by a decree, either personally or through another, imposed or declared it; 3° the Ordinary of the place where the offender actually is. §2. Before the remission is granted, the author of the precept, or the one who imposed or declared the penalty, is to be consulted, unless because of extraordinary circumstances this is impossible." Canon 1357 "§1. Without prejudice to the provisions of Canons 508 and 976, a confessor can in the internal sacramental forum remit a *latae sententiae* censure of excommunication or interdict which has not been declared, if it is difficult for the penitent to remain in a state of grave sin for the time necessary for the competent Superior to provide. §2. In granting the remission, the confessor is to impose upon the penitent, under pain of again incurring the censure, the obligation to have recourse within one month to the competent Superior or to a priest having the requisite faculty, and to abide by his instructions. In the meantime, the confessor is to impose an appropriate penance and, to the extent demanded, to require reparation of scandal and damage. The recourse, however, may be made even through the confessor, without mention of a name. §3. The same duty of recourse, when they have recovered, binds those who in accordance with Canon 976 have had remitted an imposed or declared censure or one reserved to the Apostolic See."

83. 1983 Code of Canon Law, c. 1354. "§1. Besides those who are enumerated in Canons 1355-1356, all who can dispense from a law which is supported by a penalty or exempt from a precept which threatens a penalty, can also remit the penalty itself. §2. Moreover, a law or precept which establishes a penalty can also grant to others the power of remitting the penalty. §3. If the Apostolic See has reserved the remission of a penalty to itself or to others, the reservation is to be strictly interpreted."

CHAPTER 5

1. Pope Francis, Homily, Calabria, June 21, 2014, http://w2.vatican.va.

2. Documents in *CLD.*, vol. 8, 793–809.

3. *Light of the World: The Pope, the Church, and the Signs of the Times; Pope Benedict XVI: A Conversation with Peter Seewald*, trans. M. Miller and A. Walker (San Francisco: Ignatius Press, 2010), 121.

4. Congregation for Bishops, "Decree Remitting the Excommunication *Latae Sententiae* of the Bishops of the Society of St. Pius X," January 21, 2009, https://www.vatican.va; Pope Benedict XVI explained his actions in "A Word of Clarification for Peace within the Church," *L' Osservatore Romano* 42, no. 11, March 18, 2009, 3–4. The pope said that if he had known about Bishop Richard Williamson's views on the Holocaust, he would not have lifted the excommunications.

5. 1983 Code of Canon Law, c. 1398. "A person who procures a completed abortion incurs a *latae sententiae* excommunication."

6. 1983 Code of Canon Law, c. 1329. "§2. In the case of a *latae sententiae* penalty attached to an offence, accomplices, even though not mentioned in the law or precept, incur the same penalty if, without their assistance, the crime would not have been committed, and if the penalty is of such a nature as to

be able to affect them; otherwise, they can be punished with *ferendae sententiae* penalties."

7. Michael Clancy, "Nun Excommunicated for Allowing Abortion," *NCR*, May 18, 2010, https://www.ncronline.org/news/justice/nun-excommunicated-allowing-abortion (accessed September 21, 2022).

8. "Pope Francis Excommunicates Pro-Gay Marriage Priest. He's Not the Liberal the Media Wants," *The Telegraph*, September 23, 2013, www.telegraph.co.uk (accessed August 1, 2015).

9. Craig Keener, *1–2 Corinthians*, The New Cambridge Bible Commentary (New York: Cambridge University Press, 2005), 48.

10. Cyprian, *de lapsis*, 15, 16, *PL*, 4, 479; de oratione dominica, c. 8, *PL*, 4, 531: "hunc autem panem dari nobis quotidie postulamus, ne qui in Christo sumus et eucharisticam quotidie ad cibum salutis accipimus, intercedente aliquot graviori delicto, dum ansenti et non communicantes a caelesti pane prohibemur, a Christi corpore separemur."

11. Alphonse Borras, *L'Excommunication dans le nouveau code de droit canonique*, 230, in 56 and 57.

12. Alphonse Borras, *L'Excommunication dans le nouveau code de droit canonique*, 230, in 17:7–10.

13. Irenaeus of Lyon, *Adversus Haereses* 1, 13, 7, quoted in Borras, *L'Excommunication dans le nouveau code de droit canonique*, 235.

14. Canon 53 in Charles Joseph Hefele, *A History of the Councils from the Original Documents*, vol. 1 (Edinburgh: T&T Clark, 1883), 159: "One excommunicated by a bishop can only be restored by the bishop who condemned him. Another bishop receiving him into communion, unless the first bishop acts at the same time, or approves of the reconciliation, must answer for it before his brethren, that is to say, before the provincial synod, and must run the danger of being deprived of his office."

15. Charles Joseph Hefele, *A History of the Councils*, 445–46.

16. See the Council of Nicaea, c. 11, in Norman Tanner, *Decrees of the Ecumenical Councils*, vol. 1 (London: Sheed and Ward, 1990), 11.

17. Borras, *L'Excommunication dans le nouveau code de droit canonique*, 24.

18. Eligius Rainer, *Suspension of Clerics*, Canon Law Studies, no. 111 (Washington DC: Catholic University of America, 1937), 7.

19. F. Kober, *Die Suspension der Kirchendiener* (Tubingen: Nabu Press, 1862), 15.

20. Charles Joseph Hefele, *A History of the Councils from the Original Documents*, vol. 3 (Edinburgh: T&T Clark, 1883), 158: canon 3 stated that he could receive the support of the Church "but must never offer the sacrifice in towns or in the absence of the bishop, or ordain any cleric, or, generally discharge any episcopal function in the church which is granted him. Only in his own church he may confirm the newly baptised."

21. "Decree of Gratian," in Francis Hyland, *Excommunication: Its Nature, Historical Development and Effects* (Washington, DC: Catholic University of America, 1928), Canon Law Studies 49, 24; Gratian, C. 13, C. III, q. 4, (translated in the Catholic Encyclopedia, 1, 456).

22. Borras, *L'Excommunication dans le nouveau code de droit canonique*, 52.

23. Third Lateran Council, canon 6, in Tanner, *Decrees of the Ecumenical Councils*, vol. 1, 214.

24. J. Bernal, in *Exegetical Commentary*, vol. 4/1, 325.

25. Hyland, *Excommunication*, 42.

26. "Council of Trent, 'Decree on General Reform,'" in Norman Tanner, *Decrees of the*

Ecumenical Councils, vol. 2 (London: Sheed and Ward, 1990), 785–86.

27. Christopher Armstrong, *A Critical Appraisal of Latae Sententiae Penalties in the 1983 Code of Canon Law*, Canon Law Studies, no. 548 (Washington, DC: Catholic University of America, 1996), 30.

28. *Fontes*, vol. 3, 24–31.

29. 1917 Code, c. 2258. "§1. Some excommunicates are banned, others tolerated. §2. No one is banned unless so named as an excommunicate by the Apostolic See, the excommunication is publicly announced, and it is expressly stated in the decree or sentence that he must be avoided with due regard for the prescription of canon 2343, §1 no 1."

30. 1917 Code, c. 2343. "§1. Whoever lays violent hands on the person of the Roman Pontiff: 1° Contracts automatic excommunication most specially reserved to the Apostolic See; and is by that fact banned; 2° Is infamous by the law; 3° [If] a cleric, he shall be degraded."

31. 1917 Code, c. 2262. "§1. One excommunicated is not able to participate in the indulgences, suffrage, and other public prayers of the Church. §2. Nevertheless, it is not prohibited: 1° For the faithful to pray privately for him; 2° For priests privately and avoiding scandal to apply Mass for him; but, if he is banned, only for his conversion."

32. 1917 Code, c. 2259. "§1. Anyone excommunicated lacks the right of assisting at divine offices, but not of [attending the] preaching of the word of God. §2. If a tolerated [excommunicate] passively assists [at these], it is not necessary that he be expelled; if [he is] banned, he should be expelled or if he does not wish to be expelled, there should be a cessation of the [divine] offices, provided this can be done without grave inconvenience; but from active assistance that includes any participation in the celebration of divine offices, not only should one banned be repelled, but [so should] any [one excommunicated] after a declared or condemnatory sentence or who is otherwise notoriously excommunicated."

33. 1917 Code, c. 2260. "§1. Nor can one excommunicated receive the Sacraments; or, indeed, after a declaratory or condemnatory sentence, the Sacramentals. §2. In what applies to ecclesiastical burial, the prescription of canon 1240§1 no 2 is observed." Can. 1240 "§1. Unless they gave before death a sign of repentance, the following are deprived of ecclesiastical burial: 2.° Excommunicates or those under interdict after a condemnatory or declaratory sentence."

34. 1917 Code, c. 2261. "§1. One excommunicated is prohibited from confecting and administering licitly the Sacraments and Sacramentals, except for the exceptions that follow. §2. The faithful, with due regard for the prescription of §3, can for any just cause seek the Sacraments and Sacramentals from one excommunicated, especially if other ministers are lacking, and then the one who is excommunicated and approached can administer these and is under no obligation of inquiring the reasons from the one requesting. §3. But from a banned excommunicate and from others excommunicated after a condemnatory or declaratory sentence has come, only the faithful in danger of death can ask for sacramental absolution according to the norm of canons 882 and 2252 and even, if other ministers are lacking, other Sacraments and Sacramentals."

35. 1917 Code, c. 882. "In danger of death all priests and bishops, even those not approved for confessions, validly and licitly absolve all penitents whatsoever of all sins and censures whatsoever, no matter how reserved or notorious, even if there is present an approved priest, with due regards for the prescription of canons 884 and 2252."

36. 1917 Code, c. 2263. "One excommunicated is removed from legitimate ecclesias-

tical acts within his limits and in the places defined by law; nor can he act in ecclesiastical cases, except according to the norm of canon 1654; he is prohibited from conducting ecclesiastical offices or responsibilities, and from enjoying earlier concessions and privileges from the Church."

37. 1917 Code, c. 2264. "Acts of jurisdiction, whether for the external forum or the internal forum, placed by one excommunicated are illicit; and if a condemnatory or declaratory sentence has been laid down, they are also invalid with due regard for the prescription of canon 2261 §3; otherwise, they are valid, and, indeed, are even licit if they are sought by a member of the faithful according to the norm of the mentioned canon 2261 §2."

38. 1917 Code, c. 2266. "After a condemnatory or declaratory sentence, one excommunicated remains deprived of the fruits of the dignity, office, benefice, pension, and duty if had one in the Church; and a banned [excommunicate is deprived] of the dignity, office, benefice pension and duty itself." Can. 2267. "The faithful must avoid association in profane things with a banned excommunicate, unless it concerns a spouse, parents, children, householders, subjects, and so on, unless reasonable cause excuses."

39. 1917 Code, c. 2265. "§1. Anyone excommunicated: 1° Is prohibited from the right of electing, presenting or appointing; 2° Cannot obtain dignities, offices benefices, ecclesiastical pensions, or other duties in the Church; 3° Cannot be promoted to orders. §2. An act posited contrary to the prescription of §1 numbers 1 and 2, however, is not null, unless it was posited by a banned excommunicate or by another excommunicate after a condemnatory or declaratory sentence; but if this sentence has been given, the one excommunicated cannot validly pursue any pontifical favor, unless in the pontifical rescript mention is made of the excommunication."

40. Christopher Armstrong, *A Critical Appraisal of Latae Sententiae Penalties in the 1983 Code of Canon Law,* Canon Law Studies, no. 548, 348–50. These *latae sententiae* excommunications included heresy, apostasy, and schism (c. 2314); violating the sacred species (c. 2320); marriage before a non-Catholic minister or having children baptized or educated non-Catholics (c. 2319); crime in a papal election (c. 2330); and abortion (c. 2350).

41. Armstrong, *A Critical Appraisal of Latae Sententiae Penalties,* 351; including such things as hearing confessions without faculties and absolving from reserved sins (c. 2366).

42. Armstrong, *A Critical Appraisal of Latae Sententiae,* 352; including giving an ecclesiastical burial to an excommunicated person (c. 2339).

43. R. Schoenbechler, "Principles Which Govern the Revision of the Code of Canon Law," in *Readings, Cases, Materials in Canon Law,* ed. J. Hite et al. (Collegeville, MN: Liturgical Press, 1986), 70–78.

44. Schoenbechler, "Principles," 86.

45. Schoenbechler, "Principles," 92.

46. Schoenbechler, "Principles," 86.

47. Schoenbechler, "Principles," 92.

48. *Communicationes* 7 (1975): 171.

49. 1983 Code of Canon Law, c. 19. "If on a particular matter there is not an express provision of either universal or particular law, nor a custom, then, provided it is not a penal matter, the question is to be decided by taking into account laws enacted in similar matters, the general principles of law observed with canonical equity, the jurisprudence and practice of the Roman Curia, and the common and constant opinion of learned authors."

50. Cf. *Communicationes* 2 (1970): 101; *Communicationes* 9 (1977): 147–48; *Schema Documenti quo disciplina sanctionum seu poenarum in Ecclesia Latina denuo ordinatur* (Rome: Typis Polyglottis Vaticanis, 1973), 5–6.

51. Albert Gauthier OP, *Roman Law and its Contribution to the Development of Canon Law* (Ottawa: St. Paul University, 1996), 108.

52. Javier Otaduy, in *Exegetical Commentary*, vol. 1, 339.

53. See 1983 Code of Canon Law, c. 16. "§1. Laws are authentically interpreted by the legislator and by that person to whom the legislator entrusts the power of authentic interpretation. §2. An authentic interpretation which is presented by way of a law has the same force as the law itself, and must be promulgated. If it simply declares the sense of words which are certain in themselves, it has retroactive force. If it restricts or extends a law or explains a doubtful one, it is not retroactive. §3. On the other hand, an interpretation by way of a court judgement or of an administrative act in a particular case, does not have the force of law. It binds only those persons and affects only those matters for which it was given."

54. Council for the Interpretation of Legislative Texts, authentic interpretation, January 19, 1988, in *AAS* 80 (1988): 1818; Javier Otaduy, in *Exegetical Commentary*, vol. 1, 341. See canon 1397.

55. Council for the Interpretation of Legislative Texts, authentic interpretation, January 19, 1988, in *AAS* 80 (1988): 1818.

56. Canon 1341. The ordinary must start a judicial or an administrative procedure for the imposition or the declaration of penalties when he perceives that neither by the methods of pastoral care, especially fraternal correction, nor by a warning or correction, can justice be sufficiently restored, the offender reformed, and the scandal repaired.

57. Cf. Edward Peters, "Canon 1324: Exemption from a Penalty," in *Roman Replies*, 2010, 169–74.

58. Juan Arias, *Code of Canon Law Annotated* (Montreal: Wilson & LaFleur, 2004), 1033.

59. Austin Fagothey, *Right and Reason: Ethics in Theory and Practice* (Saint Louis: C.V. Mosby Company, 1967), 97–98.

60. See 1983 Code of Canon Law, c. 1347.

61. See 1983 Code of Canon Law, c. 1321. "§1. Any person is considered innocent until the contrary is proved. §2. No one can be punished unless the commission by him or her of an external violation of a law or precept is gravely imputable by reason of malice or of culpability."

62. See 1983 Code of Canon Law, c. 1318. "*Latae sententiae* penalties are not to be established, except perhaps for some outstanding and malicious offences which may be either more grave by reason of scandal or such that they cannot be effectively punished by *ferendae sententiae* penalties; censures, however, especially excommunication, are not to be established, except with the greatest moderation, and only for offences of special gravity."

63. Borras, *L'Excommunication dans le nouveau code de droit canonique*, 34.

64. See 1983 Code of Canon Law, cc. 1341 and 1342; see Armstrong, *A Critical Appraisal of Latae Sententiae Penalties*, 275.

65. De Paolis, *Exegetical Commentary* IV/1, 383: The proposed requirement for an independent warning of the possibility that an automatic censure was going to be declared formally was dropped during the revision of penal canon law. See also Edward Peters, *Incrementa in Progressu 1983 Codicis Iuris*

Canonici (Montreal: Wilson & Lafleur, 2005), 1168.

66. See 1983 Code of Canon Law, c. 1387.

67. See 1983 Code of Canon Law, c. 1350. "§1. In imposing penalties on a cleric, except in the case of dismissal from the clerical state, care must always be taken that he does not lack what is necessary for his worthy support. §2. If a person is truly in need because he has been dismissed from the clerical state, the Ordinary is to provide in the best way possible, but not by the conferral of an office, ministry or function."

68. See 1983 Code of Canon Law, c. 209. "§1. Christ's faithful are bound to preserve their communion with the Church at all times, even in their external actions. §2. They are to carry out with great diligence their responsibilities towards both the universal Church and the particular Church to which they belong."

69. Juan Arias, *Code of Canon Law Annotated* (Montreal: Wilson & LaFleur, 2004), 1033.

70. Armstrong, *A Critical Appraisal of Latae Sententiae Penalties in the 1983 Code of Canon Law*, 280.

71. 1983 Code of Canon Law, cc. 908 and 1352.

72. 1983 Code of Canon Law, cc. 1335 and 1352.

73. 1983 Code of Canon Law, c. 1352 §2.

74. 1983 Code of Canon Law, c. 145. "§1. An ecclesiastical office is any post which by divine or ecclesiastical disposition is established in a stable manner to further a spiritual purpose."

75. J. Bernal, in *Exegetical Commentary*, vol. 4/1, 328.

76. Borras, *L'Excommunication dans le nouveau code de droit canonique*, 102.

77. 1983 Code of Canon Law, c. 1109. "Within the limits of their territory, the local Ordinary and the parish priest by virtue of their office validly assist at the marriages not only of their subjects, but also of non-subjects, provided one or other of the parties is of the Latin rite. They cannot assist if by sentence or decree they have been excommunicated, placed under interdict or suspended from office, or been declared to be such."

78. 1983 Code of Canon Law, c. 1364. "§1. An apostate from the faith, a heretic or a schismatic incurs a *latae sententiae* excommunication, without prejudice to the provision of can. 194 § 1 n. 2; he or she may also be punished with the penalties mentioned in can. 1336 §§ 2–4. §2. If a long-standing contempt or the gravity of scandal calls for it, other penalties may be added, not excluding dismissal from the clerical state."

79. 1983 Code of Canon Law, c. 1382. "§1. One who throws away the consecrated species or, for a sacrilegious purpose, takes them away or keeps them, incurs a *latae sententiae* excommunication reserved to the Apostolic See; a cleric, moreover, may be punished with some other penalty, not excluding dismissal from the clerical state."

80. 1983 Code of Canon Law, c. 1385. "A priest who in confession, or on the occasion or under the pretext of confession, solicits a penitent to commit a sin against the sixth commandment of the Decalogue, is to be punished, according to the gravity of the offence, with suspension, prohibitions and deprivations; in the more serious cases he is to be dismissed from the clerical state."

81. 1983 Code of Canon Law, c. 1387. "Both the Bishop who, without a pontifical mandate, consecrates a person a Bishop, and the one who receives the consecration from him, incur a *latae sententiae* excommunication reserved to the Apostolic See."

82. 1983 Code of Canon Law, c. 1386. "§1. A confessor who directly violates the sacramental seal incurs a *latae sententiae*

excommunication reserved to the Apostolic See; he who does so only indirectly is to be punished according to the gravity of the offence. prohibitions and deprivations; in the more serious cases he is to be dismissed from the clerical state. §2. Interpreters, and the others mentioned in canon 983 §2, who violate the secret are to be punished with a just penalty, not excluding excommunication."

83. 1983 Code of Canon Law, c. 1370. "§1. A person who uses physical force against the Roman Pontiff incurs a *latae sententiae* excommunication reserved to the Apostolic See; if the offender is a cleric, another penalty, not excluding dismissal from the clerical state, may be added according to the gravity of the crime."

84. 1983 Code of Canon Law, c. 1397 §2.

85. 1983 Code of Canon Law, c. 1347. "§2. The offender is said to have purged the contempt if he or she has truly repented of the offence and has made suitable reparation for the scandal and harm, or at least seriously promised to make it."

86. 1983 Code of Canon Law, c. 1358. "§1. The remission of a censure cannot be granted except to an offender whose contempt has been purged in accordance with can. 1347. §2. However, once the contempt has been purged, the remission cannot be refused, without prejudice to the provision of canon 1361 §4. §2 The one who remits a censure can make provision in accordance with can. 1348, and can also impose a penance."

87. Borras, *L'Excommunication dans le nouveau code de droit canonique*, 131.

88. 1983 Code of Canon Law, c. 134. "§1. In law the term Ordinary means, apart from the Roman Pontiff, diocesan Bishops and all who, even for a time only, are set over a particular Church or a community equivalent to it in accordance with Can. 368, and those who in these have general ordinary executive power, that is, Vicars general and episcopal Vicars; likewise, for their own members, it means the major Superiors of clerical religious institutes of pontifical right and of clerical societies of apostolic life of pontifical right, who have at least ordinary executive power. §2. The term local Ordinary means all those enumerated in §1, except Superiors of religious institutes and of societies of apostolic life. §3. Whatever in the canons, in the context of executive power, is attributed to the diocesan Bishop, is understood to belong only to the diocesan Bishop and to those others in Can. 381 §2 who are equivalent to him, to the exclusion of the Vicar general and the episcopal Vicar except by special mandate."

89. 1983 Code of Canon Law, cc. 1354 §1; 1355; 1356.

90. Borras, *L'Excommunication dans le nouveau code de droit canonique*, 135.

91. 1983 Code of Canon Law, c. 1355.

92. 1983 Code of Canon Law, c. 1356.

93. Armstrong, *A Critical Appraisal of Latae Sententiae Penalties in the 1983 Code of Canon Law*, 309.

94. Borras, *L'Excommunication dans le nouveau code de droit canonique*, 135–36; Velasio de Paolis, *De Sanctionibus in Ecclesia: Ad notationes in Codicem*, vol. VI (Rome: Editrice Pontificia Universita Gregoriana, 1986), 99–100.

95. 1983 Code of Canon Law, c. 980.

96. Tom Green, "Sanctions in the Church," in *The Code of Canon Law: A Text and Commentary*, ed. J. Coriden et al. (New York, Paulist Press, 1985), 916.

97. 1983 Code of Canon Law, c. 508 §1.

98. Coriden et al., *The Code of Canon Law: A Text and Commentary*, 409.

99. 1983 Code of Canon Law, c. 976.

100. 1983 Code of Canon Law, c. 1357 §3.

101. 1983 Code of Canon Law, c. 566 §2.

102. 1983 Code of Canon Law, c. 1357 §1.

103. 1983 Code of Canon Law, c. 1357 §3.

104. 1983 Code of Canon Law, c. 1361 "§4. Remission must not be granted until, in the prudent judgement of the Ordinary, the offender has repaired any harm caused. The offender may be urged to make such reparation or restitution by one of the penalties mentioned in canon 1336 §§2–4; the same applies also when the offender is granted remission of a censure under canon 1358 §1."

105. Borras, *L'Excommunication dans le nouveau code de droit canonique*, 143; Armstrong, *A Critical Appraisal of Latae Sententiae Penalties in the 1983 Code of Canon Law*, 303.

106. 1983 Code of Canon Law, c. 1357 §3.

107. 1983 Code of Canon Law, c. 1357. "§1. Without prejudice to the provisions of Canons 508 and 976, a confessor can in the internal sacramental forum remit a *latae sententiae* censure of excommunication or interdict which has not been declared, if it is difficult for the penitent to remain in a state of grave sin for the time necessary for the competent Superior to provide. §2. In granting the remission, the confessor is to impose upon the penitent, under pain of again incurring the censure, the obligation to have recourse within one month to the competent Superior or to a priest having the requisite faculty, and to abide by his instructions. In the meantime, the confessor is to impose an appropriate penance and, to the extent demanded, to require reparation of scandal and damage. The recourse, however, may be made even through the confessor, without mention of a name. §3. The same duty of recourse, when they have recovered, binds those who in accordance with Canon 976 have had remitted an imposed or declared censure or one reserved to the Apostolic See."

108. Borras, *L'Excommunication dans le nouveau code de droit canonique*, 144–45; Armstrong, *A Critical Appraisal of Latae Sententiae Penalties in the 1983 Code of Canon Law*, 321.

109. 1983 Code of Canon Law, c. 1331. "§1. An excommunicated person is prohibited: 1° from celebrating the Sacrifice of the Eucharist and the other sacraments; 2° from receiving the sacraments; 3° from administering sacramentals and from celebrating the other ceremonies of liturgical worship; 4° from taking an active part in the celebrations listed above; 5° from exercising any ecclesiastical offices, duties, ministries or functions; 6° from performing acts of governance."

110. Velasio de Paolis, "Penal Sanctions, Penal Remedies and penances in Canon Law," in Dugan, *The Penal Process*, 168.

111. 1983 Code of Canon Law, c. 1331. "§2. If a *ferendae sententiae* excommunication has been imposed or a *latae sententiae* excommunication declared, the offender: 1° proposing to act in defiance of the provision of §1 nn. 1–4 is to be removed, or else the liturgical action is to be suspended, unless there is a grave reason to the contrary; 2° invalidly exercises any acts of governance which, in accordance with §1 n. 6, are unlawful; 3° is prohibited from benefiting from privileges already granted; 4° does not acquire any remuneration held in virtue of a merely ecclesiastical title; 5° is legally incapable of acquiring offices, duties, ministries, functions, rights, privileges or honorific titles." The declared *ferendae sententiae* penalty could be imposed by a bishop or tribunal after a penal process concerning a crime. A *latae sententiae* penalty could be declared by a bishop in the case of a catholic doctor performing abortions. Then priests in their parishes would have to implement the decisions and refuse communion.

112. 1983 Code of Canon Law, c. 1350.

113. 1983 Code of Canon Law, c. 1109. "Unless the local ordinary and pastor have

been excommunicated, interdicted, or suspended from office or declared such through a sentence or decree, by virtue of their office and within the confines of their territory they assist validly at the marriages not only of their subjects but also of those who are not their subjects provided that one of them is of the Latin rite."

CHAPTER 6

1. Judith Hahn, *Church Law in Modernity* (Cambridge: Cambridge University Press. 2019), 105ff.

2. William D'Antonio, James Davidson, Dean Hoge, and Mary Gauthier, "American Catholics and Church Authority," in *The Crisis of Authority in Catholic Modernity*, ed. Michael Lacey and Francis Oakley (Oxford: Oxford University Press, 2011), 273–90; Hahn, *Church Law in Modernity*, 108–9.

3. Hahn, *Church Law in Modernity*, 97.

4. Pope John Paul II, "Letter to Priests Holy Thursday 1979," April 8, 1979, http://www.vatican.va.

5. J. Bernal, in *Exegetical Commentary*, vol. IV/l, 252.

6. Pope Leo I, *Ep. Ad Angst*, Letter 14 to Anastasius, *P.L.* 54, 669; chap. 6 D. XLV, Fr 1, 162; quoted in Council of Trent, Session 13, "Decree of Reform," in Tanner, *Decrees of the Ecumenical Councils*, vol. 2, 699.

7. *Decretals,* II, 28 (Fr 2, 410).

8. S.C. Episcoporum et Regularium, instruction, June 11, 1880, no. 7, in Emi Petri Card. Gasparri, ed., *Codicis Iuris Canonici Fontes*, vol. IV (Rome: Typis Polyglottis Vaticanis, 1926), 1022.

9. S.C. Congregation de Propaganda Fide, instruction ad Vicar Apostolic Sin., October 18, 1883, in Gasparri, *Codicis Iuris Canonici Fontes*, vol. VII, 500.

10. S.C. Congregation de Propaganda Fide, instruction, *Cum Magnopere*, in S. B. Smith, *The New Procedure in Criminal and Disciplinary Causes of Ecclesiastics in the United States*, 2nd ed. (New York: Fr. Pustet & Co., 1888), no. VII, 257: "Quod si monitiones in irritum cedant, Ordinarius jubet, per Curiam delinquent analogum praeceptum intimari ita, ut in hoc explicetur, quid ipse vel facere vel vitare debeat, addita respectivae poenae ecclesiasticae comminatione, quam si praeceptum transgrediatur, incurret."

11. S. B. Smith, *The New Procedure in Criminal and Disciplinary Causes*, 32–33.

12. *Cum Magnopere*, in Smith, *The New Procedure in Criminal and Disciplinary Causes* 257: "VIII 1°. Actus injunctionis praecepti signatura partibus praesentibus, et a delinquent etiam, si velit."

13. *Codex Iuris Canonici,* Pii X Pontificis Maximi iussu digestus, Benedict Papae XV auctoritate promulgatus, praefatione Petri Card. Gasparri et indice analytico-alphabetico auctus (Rome: Typis Polyglottis Vaticanis, 1917).

14. 1983 Code of Canon Law, c. 135 §2.

15. 1983 Code of Canon Law, c. 455.

16. See *Vos Estis Lux Mundi*, Art. 2: Reception of reports and data protection.

17. "Popular Perth Priest Denies Stealing Half a Million Dollars from Subiaco Church," WAtoday, November 6, 2019, https://www.watoday.com.au/national/western-australia/popular-perth-priest-denies-stealing-half-a-million-dollars-from-subiaco-church-20191106-p537z6.html.

18. 1983 Code of Canon Law, c. 10. "Only those laws are to be considered invalidating or incapacitating which expressly prescribe that an act is null or that a person is incapable."

Notes

19. 1983 Code of Canon Law, c. 134. "Ordinary can be local diocesan bishop, vicar general, diocesan administrator, apostolic administrator or major superior of a religious institute or society of apostolic life."

20. Josemaria Sanchis, in *Exegetical Commentary*, Vol. IV/l (Montreal: Wilson & Lafleur, 2004), 354.

21. In the *CCEO,* canon 1406 says a warning is the equivalent of a penal precept. Cf. F. Easton, in *A Practical Commentary to the Code of Canons of the Eastern Churches*, ed. J. Faris, J. Abbass (Montreal: Wilson and Lafleur, 2019), 2526–27.

22. 1983 Code of Canon Law, c. 1339 §3.

23. Patricia Duggan and Paul Gargaro, *A Simple Dictionary of Canon Law* (Philadelphia: Canon Law Books, 2005), 38.

24. Jose Pulickal, *A Dictionary of Canon Law* (Manila: Logos Publications, 2005), 312.

25. John Huels in *A Practical Commentary to the Code of Canons of the Eastern Churches*, ed. John Faris, vol. 2 (Montreal: Wilson & Lafleur, 2019), 2718.

26. G. Michiels, *De Delictis et poenis*, vol. LII, *De poenis in specie* (Rome, Typis Polyglottis Vaticanis, 1961), 447; quoted in Velasio de Paolis, "Penal Sanctions, Penal Remedies and Penances in Canon Law," in *The Penal Process*, 174.

27. Patricia Duggan and Paul Gargaro, *A Simple Dictionary of Canon Law*, 41.

28. 1983 Code of Canon Law, c. 134.

29. 1983 Code of Canon Law, c. 35.

30. 1983 Code of Canon Law, c. 1319. "§1. To the extent to which one can impose precepts by virtue of the power of governance in the external forum in accordance with the provisions of canons 48–58, to that extent can one also by precept threaten determined penalties, with the exception of perpetual expiatory penalties. §2. If, after the matter has been very carefully considered, a penal precept is to be imposed, what is established in canons 1317 and 1318 is to be observed."

31. 1983 Code of Canon Law, c. 49. "A singular precept is a decree which directly and legitimately enjoins a specific person or persons to do or omit something, especially in order to urge the observance of law."

32. De Paolis, in *Exegetical Commentary,* vol IV/l, 252.

33. 1983 Code of Canon Law, c. 36. "§1. An administrative act must be understood according to the proper meaning of the words and the common manner of speaking. In a case of doubt, those which refer to litigation, pertain to threatening or inflicting penalties, restrict the rights of a person, injure the acquired rights of others, or are contrary to a law which benefits private persons are subject to a strict interpretation; all others are subject to a broad interpretation. §2. An administrative act must not be extended to other cases besides those expressed."

34. 1983 Code of Canon Law, c. 1321 §1.

35. 1983 Code of Canon Law, cc. 1321–30.

36. 1983 Code of Canon Law, c. 50. "Before issuing a singular decree, an authority is to seek out the necessary information and proofs and, insofar as possible, to hear those whose rights can be injured."

37. 1983 Code of Canon Law, cc. 1737 and 1739.

38. 1983 Code of Canon Law, c. 51. "A decree is to be issued in writing, with the reasons at least summarily expressed if it is a decision."

39. 1983 Code of Canon Law, c. 52.

40. 1983 Code of Canon Law, c. 37. "An administrative act which regards the external forum must be put in writing. Furthermore, if it is given in commissariat form, the act of its execution must be put in writing."

41. 1983 Code of Canon Law, c. 54.

42. 1983 Code of Canon Law, cc. 1732–39.

43. 1983 Code of Canon Law, c. 56. "A decree is considered to have been made known if the one for whom it is destined has been properly summoned to receive or hear the decree but, without a just cause, did not appear or refused to sign."

44. Michael Moodie, SJ, commentary on canon 36, in *New Commentary on the Code of Canon Law*, ed. John P. Beal, James A. Coriden, and Thomas Green (Mahwah, NJ: Paulist Press, 2000), 113.

45. 1983 Code of Canon Law, c. 55. "Without prejudice to the prescripts of canons 37 and 51, when a very grave reason prevents the handing over of the written text of a decree, the decree is considered to have been made known if it is read to the person to whom it is destined in the presence of a notary or two witnesses. After a written record of what has occurred has been prepared, all those present must sign it." Canons 482–84 would indicate the chancellor would normally be involved.

46. 1983 Code of Canon Law, c. 58. "§1. A singular decree ceases to have force through legitimate revocation by competent authority as well as through cessation of the law for whose execution it was given. §2. A singular precept not imposed by a legitimate document ceases when the authority of the one who issued it expires."

47. Stephen Doktorczyk, *Persistent Disobedience to Church Authority: History, Analysis and Application of Canon 1371 no. 2* (Rome, Editrice Pontifica Universita Gregoriana, 2016), 286.

48. Doktorczyk, *Persistent Disobedience to Church Authority*, 264.

49. 1983 Code of Canon Law, c. 1347.

50. 1983 Code of Canon Law, c. 1339. "§3. The fact that there has been a warning or a correction must always be proven, at least from some document to be kept in the secret archive of the curia. §4. If on one or more occasions warnings or corrections have been made to someone to no effect, or if it is not possible to expect them to have any effect, the Ordinary is to issue a penal precept in which he sets out exactly what is to be done or avoided."

51. 1983 Code of Canon Law, c. 1321.

52. J. Arias in E. Caparros, M. Theriault, J. Thorn, eds., *Code of Canon Law Annotated* (Montreal: Wilson & LaFleur, 2004), 1029.

53. Velasio de Paolis, *De Sanctionibus*, quoted by Angel Marzoa, in Marzoa, Miras, Rodrigues-Ocana, *Exegetical Commentary*, vol. IV/1, 271.

54. *Exegetical Commentary*, vol. IV/l, 272; See *Communicationes* 8 (1976): 176.

55. David Price, "Penal Law Revisited for the '90's," Canon Law Society of Australia and New Zealand, *Proceedings of the Twenty-eighth Annual Conference*, Adelaide, 1994, 70.

56. DDF, *Vademecum*, 32–75.

57. 1983 Code of Canon Law, c. 1342. "§1. Whenever there are just reasons against the use of a judicial procedure, a penalty can be imposed or declared by means of an extra-judicial decree, observing canon 1720, especially in what concerns the right of defence and the moral certainty in the mind of the one issuing the decree, in accordance with the provision of can. 1608. Penal remedies and penances may in any case whatever be applied by a decree. §2. Perpetual penalties cannot be imposed or declared by means of a decree; nor can penalties which the law or precept establishing them forbids to be applied by decree. § 3. What the law or decree says of a judge in regard to the imposition or declaration of a penalty in a trial is to be applied also to a Superior who imposes or declares a penalty by an extra-judicial decree, unless it is otherwise clear, or unless there is question of provisions which concern only procedural matters."

58. Canon 1398.

59. Canon 695.

60. Canon 1321.

61. 1983 Code of Canon Law, c. 1341. "An ordinary is to take care to initiate a judicial or administrative process to impose or declare penalties only after he has ascertained that fraternal correction or rebuke or other means of pastoral solicitude cannot sufficiently repair the scandal, restore justice, reform the offender."

CHAPTER 7

1. 1983 Code of Canon Law, c. 1329 §2. For example, abortion is a crime according to canon 1398 that carries the penalty of a *latae sententiae* excommunication. Normally any abortion is going to involve the cooperation of several people, including the woman, a doctor, a nurse, and other people such as parents or boyfriends that pressure the woman to have the abortion.

2. Pope John Paul II, apostolic letter *Sacramentorum Sanctitatis Tutela*, April 30, 2001, in *AAS* 93 (2001): 737–39; see 1983 Code of Canon Law, c. 1378.

3. Fourth Lateran Council, no. 21, in Tanner, *Decrees of the Ecumenical Councils*, vol. 1, 245.

4. Thomas Aquinas, *Commentum in quattuor libros Sententiarum Petri Lombardi* (Parisiis: Sumptibus P. Lethelleux, 1947), 984.

5. R. Leone Linahen, *De Absolutione Complis in Peccato Turpi*, Canon Law Studies, no. 164 (Washington DC: Catholic University of America, 1942), 9.

6. Collectio Resollutionum Responsorumque S. Officio, no. 267, sub verbo "Confessarius," apud Analecta Ecclesiastica, III (1895) 80, in Linahen, *De Absolutione Complis in Peccato Turpi*, 9.

7. *Codicis Iuris Canonici Fontes*, cura Emi Petri Card Gasparri editi, vol. 7 (Rome: Typis Polyglottis Vaticanis, 1939), de causa, haec habent sub numero 734.

8. *Analecta Iuris Pontificii*, VII (1864), 752–55; De Smet, *De Absolutione Complicis et de Sollicitatione*, p. 12, nota I, quoted in Linahen, *De Absolutione Complis in Peccato Turpi*, 10–11.

9. Pope Benedict XIV, apostolic constitution, *Sacramentum Poenitentiae*, June 1, 1741, appendix V, in *Codex Iuris Canonici*, Pii X Pontificis Maximi iussu digestus, Benedict Papae XV auctoritate promulgatus, praefatione Petri Card. Gasparri et indice analytico-alphabetico auctus.

10. 1917 Code, c. 888 §1. "Priests in hearing confessions, shall remember that they sustain in their person equally judges and physicians, constituted by God, to look after the divine honor and the welfare of souls."

11. S. Poenit, March 18, 1912, and May 29, 1915, *AAS* VII, (1915): 282; T. Lincoln Bouscaren and Adam C. Ellis, *Canon Law: A Text and Commentary* (Milwaukee, WI: Bruce Publishing Company, 1957), 866ff. See also John A. Abbo and Jerome D. Hannan, *The Sacred Canons; A Concise Presentation of the Current Disciplinary Norms of the Church* (St. Louis: B. Herder Book Co., 1957).

12. See http://www.thefreedictionary.com/turpitude (accessed September 7, 2011).

13. Stanislaus Woywod, OFM, revised by Callistus Smith, *A Practical Commentary on the Code of Canon Law*, 556.

14. Pietro Palazzini, ed., "Accomplice," in *Dictionary of Moral Theology*, compiled under the direction of Francesco Cardinal Roberti, Pietro Palazzini, trans. Henry Yannone (Westminster, MD: The Newman Press, 1962), 21–22.

15. P. E. McKeever, "Penance, Sacrament of," in *New Catholic Encyclopedia*, ed. William McDonald, vol. XI, 83.

16. Palazzini, *Dictionary of Moral Theology*, 21.

17. 1917 Code, c. 2367 §1. "One absolving or pretending to absolve an accomplice in a sin of turpitude incurs by that fact the excommunication most especially reserved to the Apostolic See; likewise [he incurs this penalty] even [acting] in danger of death, if there is another priest, even though not approved for confessions, who could, without grave danger or infamy or scandal arising, hear the confession of the dying one, except in the case where the dying refuses to be confessed by the other."

18. 1917 Code, c. 2367 §2. "One does not escape the same excommunication who, absolving or pretending to absolve an accomplice who is implicated in [the crime of the priest], but who is not yet absolved [because he has not confessed the crime], but rather has so acted because the implicated confessor directly or indirectly induced him [to confess]."

19. S.C. Holy Office, November 16, 1934; *AAS* XXVI, 634; Bouscaren and Ellis, *Canon Law*, 912.

20. S.C. Holy Office, November 16, 1934; *AAS* XXVl, 634; *CLD*, vol. 2, 578; Bouscaren and Ellis, *Canon Law*, 912.

21. S.C. Holy Office, "Absolving Complex: Canon Interpreted," November 16, 1934, *CLD*, vol. 2, 578. This interpretation on November 16, 1934, from the Sacred Congregation of the Holy Office added the words "facto verbo cum Sanctissimo" to the doubt "inter inducentes, de quibus" in c. 2367 §2.

22. A. Vermeersch and J. Creusen, *Epitome iuris canonici*, vol. III, 6th ed., (Rome, Dessain, 1946), no. 570: "communis...sententia...censebat non contrahi excommunicationem quando sacerdos paenitentem persuaserat turpia inter se committenda non esse ullum vel saltem grave peccatum."

23. Velasio de Paolis in *Exegetical Commentary*, vol. IV/l, 497: Codicis 1. Adnumerandus etiam confessarius qui, sive intra, sive extra confessionem sacramentalem, alicui persuaserit in turpibus inter se patrandis aut nullum aut certe non grave inesse peccatum, eumque consequenter, de aliis tantum sibi postea confitentem, sacramentaliter absolvit vel fingit absolvere.

24. F. M. Cappello, *De Sacramentis*, vol. II, 7th ed., 388: mutat doctrinam antiquam, cum sit declaratione vere extensiva seu nova lex; ideoque addita verba facto verbo cum SS .mo.

25. 1917 Code, c. 2253. "Outside of danger of death. [the following] can absolve from....3. A censure reserved in law, he who constituted the censure or to whom it was reserved, [as well as] his successors or competent Superiors or delegates. Therefore from a censure reserved to a Bishop or Ordinary, any Ordinary can absolve his subjects, and a local ordinary [can absolve] travelers also; from one reserved to the Apostolic See, [besides it] those who have sought form it the power of absolving, whether generally if the censure is simply reserved, or specially if it is specially reserved, or finally most specially if it is most specially reserved, with due regard for the prescription of canon 2254."

26. 1917 Code, c. 2252. "Those constituted in danger of death can receive from a priest, without special faculties, absolution from any censure [*ab homine*] of man or from a censure most specially reserved to the Apostolic See, [but] are bound after recovering by the obligation of taking recourse under pain of reincidence to him who passed the censure, if it concerned a censure [*ab homine*] of man; [similarly] to the Sacred penitentiary or to a

bishop or another endowed with the faculty according to the norm of canon 2254 §1 if it was a censure of law; and they must obey his mandates."

27. James A. Coriden, *An Introduction to Canon Law* (Mahwah, NJ: Paulist Press, 1991), 36.

28. See *Communicationes* 10 (1978): 309ff. "In poena latae sententiae interdicti, vel si sit clericus, suspensionis, incurrit...qui, cum sacramentalem absolutionem dare valide nequeat, eam impertire se fingit vel sacramentalem confessionem audit."

29. *Communicationes* 15 (1983): 210.

30. L. Chiapetta, *Il Codice di Diritto Canonico* (Napoli: Edizioni Dehoniane, 1988), 510.

31. F. Nigro, commentary on canon 1378, in P.V. Pinto, ed., *Commento al Codice di Diritto Canonico* (Rome: Urbaniana University Press, 1985), 808–9.

32. *Catechism of the Catholic Church*, §1554: "Catholic doctrine, expressed in the liturgy, the Magisterium, and the constant practice of the Church, recognizes that there are two degrees of ministerial participation in the priesthood of Christ: the episcopacy and the presbyterate - the diaconate is intended to help and serve them. For this reason the term sacerdos in current usage denotes bishops and priests but not deacons." https://www.vatican.va/archive/ENG0015/__P4U.HTM.

33. De Paolis, *Exegetical Commentary*, vol. IV/l, 495.

34. De Paolis, *Exegetical Commentary*, vol. IV/l, 496.

35. See *Communicationes* 15 (1983): 210.

36. 1983 Code of Canon Law, c. 11. "Merely ecclesiastical laws bind those who have been baptized in the Catholic Church or received into it, possess the efficient use of reason, and, unless the law expressly provides otherwise, have completed seven years of age."

37. 1983 Code of Canon Law, c. 15 §1. "Ignorance or error about invalidating or disqualifying laws does not impede their effect unless it is expressly established otherwise."

38. Fernando Loza, commentary on canon 977, in *Exegetical Commentary*, vol. III/1, 798.

39. Loza, *Exegetical Commentary*, vol. III/1, 799.

40. J. McAreavey in G. Sheehy et al., eds., *The Canon Law: Letter and Spirit* (Collegeville, MN: The Liturgical Press, 1995), 533.

41. Schema Codicis de 1982, Pontificia Commissio Iuris Canonici Recognoscendo, *Codex Iuris Canonici: Schema novissimum iuxta placita Patrum Commissionis emendatum atque Summo Pontifici Praesentaum* (Rome: Typis Polyglottis Vaticanis, 1982).

42. 1983 Code of Canon Law, c. 988 §1. "A member of the Christian faithful is obliged to confess in kind and number all grave sins committed after baptism and not yet remitted directly through the keys of the Church nor acknowledged in individual confession, of which the person has knowledge after diligent examination of conscience."

43. J. Martin in *The Canon Law: Letter and Spirit*, 794.

44. Book VI, 2021. Canon 1379 §5: "A person who, apart from the cases mentioned in §§ 1–4 and in can. 1384, pretends to administer a sacrament is to be punished with a just penalty."

45. De Paolis, *Exegetical Commentary*, vol. IV/l, 499.

46. Pope John Paul II, apostolic letter, *Sacramentorum Sanctitatis Tutela*, 30 April 2001, in *AAS* 93 (2001): 737–39.

47. Congregation for the Doctrine of the Faith, Letter to the Bishops of the Catholic

Church and to the Ordinaries and Hierarchs regarding the modifications introduced in the *Normae de gravioribus delicits*.

48. Note that canon 1378 §1 became canon 1384 after the 2021 revision of Book VI.

CHAPTER 8

1. Congregation for the Doctrine of the Faith, "Glossary," http://www.vatican.va/resources/resources_glossary-terms_en.html (accessed September 10, 2011). The glossary does conclude by stating "these terms, which are subject to revision and update, are designed to assist in understanding; the terms provide an aid, but cannot substitute, careful study of canon law."

2. Pope John Paul II promulgated *Sacramentorum Sanctitatis Tutela*, April 30, 2001, *AAS* 93 (2001): 737–39, and the Congregation for the Doctrine of the Faith issued, "*Epistula ad totius Catholicae Ecclesiae Episcopos aliosque...de delictis gravioribus eidem Congregationi pro Doctrina Fidei reservatis*," May 18, 2001, *AAS* 93 (2001): 785–88. The CDF implementing norms were themselves modified in 2010. These modifications do not affect the topic of solicitation in confession. The revised norms are available online at http://www.vatican.va/resources/resources_norme_en.html.

3. Congregation for the Doctrine of the Faith, Letter, *Ad Exsequendam Ecclesiasticam Legem*, May 18, 2001, in *AAS* 93 (2001): 785–88, and *Normae Substantiales*, article 4; in Woestman, *Ecclesiastical Sanctions*, 300–309.

4. The Congregation for the Doctrine of the Faith is exclusively competent to deal with this particular case; see CDF, apostolic letter, *Sacramentorum Sanctitatis Tutela*, given motu proprio, *AAS* 93 (2001): 737–39; *Origins* 31 (2001–2002): 528–29.

5. Giovanni Mansi, *Sacrorum Conciliorum nova et amplissima collectio*, vol. XXIII (Paris: H. Welter, 1903), 33: "Item caveant sibi sacerdotes sub privatione honoris sui, ne sollicitent aliquam personam in confessione, quod et verbis fieri prohibemus, contrarium facientes excommunicamus."

6. Franz Wernz, *Ius canonicum. Ad codicis normam exactum opera P. Petri Vidal S.J.*, vol. 7, (Rome: Apud Aedes Universitatis Gregorianae, 1938), 566–67; Wernz, *Ius decretalium*, Prati, Ex Officina Libreria Giachetti, 1915, no. 469.

7. *Codicis Iuris Canonici Fontes*, cura Emi. Petri Card. Gasparri, editi, vol. 1 (Rome: Typis Polyglottis Vaticanis, 1923), 181; Abbo and Hannan, *The Sacred Canons*, 30.

8. *Codicis Iuris Canonici Fontes*, ed. Emi. Petri Card. Gasparri, vol. 1 (Rome: Typis Polyglottis Vaticanis, 1923), 384: "Omittitur residuum, quia ipsa Const. Est supra, n. 102. §3. Igitur, ut literae praedictae perpetuis futuris temporibus, et ubique locorum inviolabiliter observentur"; Abbo and Hannan, *The Sacred Canons*, 30.

9. *Codicis Iuris Canonici Fontes*, cura Emi. Petri Card. Gasparri, vol. 1, 385: "Mandantes omnibus Confessariis, ut suos poenitentes, quos noverint fuisse ab aliis, ut supra sollicitatos, moneant de obligatione denunciandi sollicitantes, seu ut praefertur, tractantes, Inquisitoribus, seu locorum Ordinariis praedictis: quod si hoc officium praetermiserint, vel poenitentes docuerint non teneri ad denunciandum Confessarios sollicitantes, seu tractantes, ut supra, iidem locorum Ordinarii, et Inquisitores illos pro modo culpae punire non negligant." Franz Wernz, *Ius canonicum. Ad codicis normam exactum opera P. Petri*

Vidal S.J., vol. 7 (Rome: Apud Aedes Universitatis Gregorianae, 1938), 566.

10. Pope Benedict XIV, apostolic constitution, *Sacramentum Poenitentiae*, June 1, 1741, appendix V, in *Codex iuris canonici*, Pii X Pontificis Maximi iussu digestus, Benedict Papae XV auctoritate promulgatus, praefatione Petri Card. Gasparri et indice analytico-alphabetico auctus, (Rome: Typis polyglottis Vaticanis, 1917).

11. Nicholas P. Cafardi, "The Scandal of Secrecy," *Commonweal*, July 21, 2010, https://www.commonwealmagazine.org/scandal-secrecy.

12. Pope Benedict XVI, *Substantive Norms on Graviora Delicta*, May 21, 2010, http://www.vatican.va/resources/resources_norme_en.html. Pope Benedict XVI reaffirmed this in 2010 explaining that "the norms issued in 1922 were an update, in light of the Code of Canon Law of 1917, of the Apostolic Constitution *Sacramentorum Poenitentiae* promulgated by Pope Benedict XIV in 1741."

13. See "Historical Introduction to the 2001 Norms," http://www.vatican.va/resources/resources_introd-storica_en.html.

14. See http://www.vatican.va/resources/resources_crimen-sollicitationis-1962_en.html.

15. Cafardi, "The Scandal of Secrecy."

16. The Holy Office has given a reply that there is no possibility of slight matter in sins against chastity especially in relation to solicitation. Cf. S.C. Holy Office, decree, February 11, 1661; apud Giraldi, *Expositio Iuris Pontificii iuxta Recentiorem Ecclesiae Disciplinam*, 3 vols. (Rome: 1829–1830), pars l, Lib. V, tit. 7, 632.

17. Abbo and Hannan, *The Sacred Canons*, 30.

18. See "Historical Introduction to the 2001 Norms."

19. As a parallel example of this, Monsignor Charles Scicluna states, "Between 1975 and 1985 I do not believe that any cases of paedophilia committed by priests were brought to the attention of our Congregation. Moreover, following the promulgation of the 1983 Code of Canon Law, there was a period of uncertainty as to which of the *delicta graviora* were reserved to the competency of this dicastery," http://www.vatican.va/resources/resources_mons-scicluna-2010_en.html (accessed October 31, 2011).

20. Archbishop Pompedda, "Observations of the Supreme Tribunal of the Apostolic Signatura," at the Meeting with Representatives of Some Episcopal Conferences Concerning Cases of Sexual Abuse Committed by Clergy, Vatican, April 4–7, 2000. The archbishop also noted from 1993 to 1998 that no penal trials were undertaken by tribunals in Australia, Canada, Ireland, New Zealand, and Scotland.

21. 1983 Code of Canon Law, c. 2368. "§1. Whoever commits the crime of solicitation mentioned in canon 904 is suspended from the celebration of Mass and from hearing sacramental confessions and even, for the gravity of the delict, is declared incapable of receiving them, is deprived of all benefices, dignities, active and passive voice, and is for all of these declared incapable, and in more serious cases is also subject to degradation. §2. But the faithful who knowingly omit to denounce him by whom they were solicited within one month against the prescription of canon 904 incur automatic excommunication reserved to no one, and shall not be absolved until after satisfying the obligation or seriously promising to satisfy it, Interdict is a censure by which the faithful, remaining in the communion of the Church, are prohibited those sacred things that are enumerated in the canons that follow."

22. Green, in *New Commentary*, 1591.

23. Igino Tarocchi, "Solicitation," in *Dictionary of Moral Theology*, compiled under the direction of Francesco Cardinal Roberti, Pietro Palazzini, trans. Henry Yannone (Westminster, MD: The Newman Press, 1962).

24. P. E. McKeever, "Penance, Sacrament of," in *New Catholic Encyclopedia*, ed. William McDonald, vol. XI, 83.

25. J. McAreavy, in Sheehy et al., *The Canon Law: Letter and Spirit*, 799.

26. Edward Peters, "When Bad Advice in Confession Becomes a Crime," in *Homiletic & Pastoral Review* (June 2011): 18–23.

27. Edward Peters, "When Bad Advice in Confession Becomes a Crime," 18–23.

28. J. P. Kimes, "Crimes against the Sacrament of Penance in the Two Codes," in *I delitti contro il sacramento della Penitenza riservati alla Congregazione per la Dottrina della Fede*, ed. C. Papale (Vatican City: Urbaniana University Press, 2016), 68.

29. 1983 Code of Canon Law, c. 18. "Laws which establish a penalty, restrict the free exercise of rights, or contain an exception from the law are subject to strict interpretation."

30. Green, *New Commentary*, 1591.

31. P. E. McKeever, "Penance, Sacrament of," in McDonald, *New Catholic Encyclopedia*, vol. Xl, 83.

32. Sacred Congregation of the Holy Office, Instruction, *Crimen Sollicitationis*, March 16, 1962, nos. 15, 16.

33. Sacred Congregation of the Holy Office, Instruction, *Crimen Sollicitationis*, no. 17.

34. Sacred Congregation of the Holy Office, Instruction, *Crimen Sollicitationis*, no. 18.

35. 1983 Code of Canon Law, cc. 983, 1378.

36. Sacred Congregation of the Holy Office, Instruction, *Crimen Sollicitationis*, 1962.

37. 1983 Code of Canon Law, c. 2363. "Whoever personally or through others falsely denounces to Superiors a confessor of the crime of solicitation by that fact incurs excommunication specially reserved to the Apostolic See, from which case he cannot be absolved until the false denunciation is retracted formally and the damages that might have flowed therefrom are repaired to the best of one's ability, and grave and long-standing penances are also imposed, with due regard for the prescription of Canon 894."

38. William H. Woestman, OMI, *Sacraments: Initiation, Penance, Anointing of the Sick, Commentary on Canons 840–1007* (Ottawa: Saint Paul University, 2004), 271.

39. Linus Neli, *Delicta Graviora: "More Grave Delicts" in the Catholic Church* (Bengaluru: ATC Publishers, 2018), 236.

40. Pope John Paul II, apostolic letter, *Sacramentorum sanctitatis tutela*, April 30, 2001, in *AAS* 93 (2001): 737–39.

41. Congregation for the Doctrine of the Faith, *Origins* 40, no. 10, (2010): 146–51.

42. Pope Benedict XVI, May 21, 2010, http://www.vatican.va/resources/resources_rel-modifiche_en.html.

43. Both this and the previous quote by Msgr. Charles J. Scicluna are taken from "The Procedure and Praxis of the Congregation for the Doctrine of the Faith regarding *Graviora Delicta*," http://www.vatican.va/resources/resources_mons-scicluna-graviora-delicta_en.html (accessed September 15, 2011).

44. Pope John Paul II, apostolic letter, *Sacramentorum Sanctitatis Tutela*, 737–39. Congregation for the Doctrine of the Faith, "A brief Introduction to the Modifications Made in the *Normae de Gravioribus Delictis*,

Reserved to the Congregation for the Doctrine of the Faith," May 21, 2010, no. 5.

45. Congregation for the Doctrine of the Faith, "A Brief Introduction to the Modifications Made in the *Normae de gravioribus delictis*," no. 6.

46. Linus, *Delicta Graviora*, 38.
47. Linus, *Delicta Graviora*, 38.
48. Linus, *Delicta Graviora*, 38–39.
49. Linus, *Delicta Graviora*, 39.

CHAPTER 9

1. See Karl Marx and Frederich Engels, *The Communist Manifesto*, https://www.marxists.org/archive/marx/works/1848/communist-manifesto.

2. "Programme," in W. Chamberlin, *Blueprint for World Congress* (Washington, DC: Human Events, 1946), 179; see also Richard J. Murphy, *The Canonico-Juridical Status of a Communist* (Washington, DC: Catholic University of America, 1959), 20.

3. Chamberlin, *Blueprint for World Congress*, 179; and Murphy, *The Canonico-Juridical Status*, 20.

4. Chamberlin, *Blueprint for World Congress*, 238; in Murphy, *The Canonico-Juridical Status*, 22.

5. Lenin, *Left Wing Communism* (New York: International Publishers, 1934), 138; quoted in Murphy, *The Canonico-Juridical Status*, 24.

6. Quoted in Chamberlin, *Blueprint for World Congress*, 181, and Murphy, *The Canonico-Juridical Status*, 20.

7. A. Michel, *Dividing the Church* (London: Sword of the Spirit, 1956), 9; quoted in Murphy, *The Canonico-Juridical Status*, 26.

8. Murphy, *The Canonico-Juridical Status*, 62.

9. Murphy, *The Canonico-Juridical Status*, 172.

10. Michael Chambon, "What Divides and Unites Chinese Christians," January 21, 2016, http://www.ucanews.com/news/-what-divides-and-unifies-chinese-christians/75016.

11. See Anthony E. Clark, "The Catholic Church in China: Historical Context and the Current Situation," *Catholic World Report*, March 9, 2018.

12. Philip Zhao Huaiyi; Simon Zhu Kaimin, SJ; Joseph Hu Ruoshan, CM; Melchior Sun Dezhen, CM; Odoric Cheng Hede, OFM; and Aloysius Chen Guodi, OFM.

13. Paul Mariani, "The First Six Chinese Bishops of Modern Times: A Study in Church Indigenization," *The Catholic Historical Review*, Summer 2014.

14. Mariani, "The First Six Chinese Bishops of Modern Times."

15. Yang Fenggang, "When Will China Become the World's Largest Christian Country?," *Slate*, sponsored by John Templeton Foundation, December 2, 2014.

16. Fenggang, "When Will China Become the World's Largest Christian Country?"

17. Sandro Magister, "Popeless Bishops: The Chinese Road to Schism" July 9, 2012, Chiesa Espressonline, http://www. http://chiesa.espresso.repubblica.it/articolo/1350284?eng=y.

18. Magister, "Popeless Bishops."

19. Magister, "Popeless Bishops."

20. "Chinese Authorities Take Down Catholic Church Cross," UCA News, February 26, 2016.

21. "China's Crackdown Continues as Christianity Thrives," UCA News, March 5, 2016, http://www.ucannews.com/news/chinas

-crackdown-continues-as-christianity-thrives/753...5/03/2016.

22. Yang, "When Will China Become the World's Largest Christian Country?"

23. Yang, "When Will China Become the World's Largest Christian Country?"

24. Yves Dam Van, "Vietnam PM Makes Last-Minute Comeback in Leadership Battle," AP News, January 24, 2016, https://apnews.com/article/5577b7c04d0b41e5bde74b9d79a1c3bb.

25. See Florence Beaugé, "Vietnam's Mix of Marxism and Capitalism Brings Economic Progress," *Guardian*, June 29, 2010, http://www.theguardian.com/world/2010/jun/29/vietnam-economy-growth-finance-success: "Twenty years ago, Vietnam was one of the poorest places in the world. Now it is among the middle-income countries and attracts donors, too, banking some $5bn a year in subsidies and loans from international agencies and Japan. Its ambition is to join the club of industrial nations by 2020. The Vietnamese economy is weathering the current global financial crisis because of consumer spending, exports and a substantial flow of foreign direct investment ($10bn to $11.5bn a year). In 2009 the growth rate was 5.3% (down from 7–8% in previous years), though not without a stimulus package, equal to 10% of gross domestic product, adding a little more to the budget deficit. This year Vietnam should keep up with the leaders in south-east Asia, at about 6.5% growth."

26. Vince Sherman, "Actually Existing Socialism in Vietnam," January 8, 2013; https://return2source.wordpress.com/2013/01/08/actually-existing-socialism-in-vietnam/; see "On the Road towards Capitalism," *The Economist*, March 24, 2012.

27. See Bill Hayton, *Vietnam: Rising Dragon* (New Haven, CT: Yale University Press, 2010).

28. Sherman, "Actually Existing Socialism in Vietnam."

29. "Vietnam Communist Party Chief Easily Wins Seat in Key Panel," Associated Press, January 26, 2016, https://www.voanews.com/a/vietnam-communist-party-chief-easily-wins-seat-on-key-panel/3163085.html.

30. Pope Pius XI, encyclical, *Divini Redemptoris*, November 9, 1846, no. 4, https://www.vatican.va/content/pius-xi/en/encyclicals/documents/hf_p-xi_enc_19370319_divini-redemptoris.html.

31. Pope Pius XI, encyclical, *Quanta Cura*, December 8, 1864, no. 4, https://www.papalencyclicals.net/pius09/p9quanta.htm.

32. Murphy, *Canonico-Juridical Status*, 49.

33. *Codex Iuris Canonici*, Pii X Pontificis Maximi iussu digestus, Benedict Papae XV auctoritate promulgatus, praefatione Petri Card. Gasparri et indice analytico-alphabetico auctus.

34. 1917 Code, c. 1325 §2. "After the reception of baptism, if anyone, retaining the name Christian, pertinaciously denies or doubts something to be believed from the truth of doctrine and Catholic faith, [such a one is] a heretic; if he completely turns away from the Christian faith, [such a one is] an apostate; if finally he refuses to be under the Supreme Pontiff or refuses communion with the members of the Church subject to him, he is schismatic."

35. Pope Pius XI, allocution, December 18, 1924, in *AAS* 16 (1924): 489–97.

36. Pope Pius XI, encyclical, *Quadragesimo Anno*, May 15, 1931, https://www.vatican.va/content/pius-xi/en/encyclicals/documents/hf_p-xi_enc_19310515_quadragesimo-anno.html.

37. Murphy, *Canonico-Juridical Status*, 51.

38. Pope Pius Xl, encyclical, *Divini Redemptoris*, *AAS* 29 (1937), November

9, 1846—*Fontes*, vol. II, no. 504, 65–106; translation in Murphy, *Canonico-Juridical Status*, 55.

39. Murphy, *Canonico-Juridical Status*, 58.

40. Sacred Congregation of the Holy Office, declaration, July 1, 1949; in *AAS* 41 (1949): 334; English translation in T. L. Bouscaren, *Canon Law Digest*, vol. 3 (Milwaukee: The Bruce. Publishing Co., 1955), 658–59.

41. Sacred Congregation of the Holy Office, declaration, August 11, 1949; in *AAS* 41 (1949): 427; English translation in Bouscaren, *CLD*, vol. 3, 407–8.

42. Sacred Congregation of the Holy Office, *Monitum*, July 28, 1950; in *AAS* 42 (1950): 553; English translation in Bouscaren, *CLD*, vol. 3, 660–61.

43. Matthaeus Conte a Coronata, *Institutiones Iuris Canonici*, vol. 4 (Taurini: Domus editorialis Marietti, 1936), 290.

44. Light suspicion is equivalent to rash judgment, vehement suspicion rests on effective signs, violent suspicion equates to moral certitude, cf. Murphy, *Canonico-Juridical Status*, 78.

45. Murphy, *Canonico-Juridical Status*, 79–80.

46. Murphy, *Canonico-Juridical Status*, 85.

47. A. Vermeersch, *De Prohibitione et Censura Librorum*, 2nd ed., Romae, 1898, 62; Hyginus Ganzi, "Nomen Dantes Communismo," *Periodica* 37 (1948): 102–18.

48. Murphy, *Canonico-Juridical Status*, 88–89.

49. Murphy, *Canonico-Juridical Status*, 109.

50. See *AAS* 26 (1934): 494; *CLD*, vol. 2, 286–87.

51. Maroto, "Annotationes Super Responsis Die 30 Iulii 1934 Datis a Pontif. Commissione Ad Codicis Canones Authentice Interpretandos," *Commentarium pro Religiosis*, 337–46; referred to by Murphy, *Canonico-Juridical Status*, 116.

52. Lenin, *Religion* (New York: International Publishers, 1933), 10; quoted in Murphy, *Canonico-Juridical Status*, 118.

53. *Fontes* III, no. 552, par. Ll, no. 4.

54. F. X. Wernz, *Ius Decretalium*, vol. VI, 63.

55. Coronata, Institutiones Iuris Canonici, 310; Murphy, *Canonico-Juridical Status*, 126.

56. 1917 Code, c. 2318 §1. "Publishers of the books of apostates, heretics and schismatics that propagate apostasy, heresy and schism incur by that face excommunication specially reserved to the Apostolic See upon the publication being released, and likewise those defending these books or other prohibited by name in apostolic letters, [as do those who] knowingly and without required permission read and retain them."

57. The response to Cardinal Ruffini's question is not in the Acta, but they are mentioned by Sirna in his "Annotationes ad Decretum S. Officii de Communismo," *Apollinaris* 22 (1949), 62, no. 8. They are also given by Palazzini, *Casus Conscientiae*, 3 vols., (Rome: Officium Libri Catholici, 1956), 11, *De Censuris*, 45; Murphy, *Canonico-Juridical Status*, 138–39.

58. Edward F. Condon, *Heresy by Association: The Canonical Prohibition of Freemasonry in History and in the Current Law* (Washington DC: Catholic University of America, 2015), 261–62.

59. Congregation for the Doctrine of the Faith, "*Complures episcopi*," July 18, 1974, in *CLD*, vol. 8, 1211.

60. Congregation for the Doctrine of the Faith, "Declaration on Masonic Associations," November 26, 1983, www.vatican.va.

61. 1983 Code of Canon Law, c. 1374. "A person who joins an association which plots against the Church is to be punished with a

just penalty; however, a person who promotes or directs an association of this kind is to be punished with an interdict." See http://www.vatican.va/archive/eng1104/__p53.htm.

62. 1983 Code of Canon Law, c. 1316. "Insofar as possible, diocesan bishops are to take care that if penal laws must be issued, they are uniform in the same city or region."

63. "God and State Draw Closer in Vietnam," February 7, 2011.

64. Andrea Gagliarducci, "Vietnam Likely the Model for Deal between China and Vatican," *Crux*, November 3, 2016.

65. See 1983 Code of Canon Law, cc. 1341 and 1342.

66. 1983 Code of Canon Law, c. 221. "§1. The Christian faithful can legitimately vindicate and defend the rights which they possess in the Church in the competent ecclesiastical forum according to the norm of law. §2. If they are summoned to a trial by a competent authority, the Christian faithful also have the right to be judged according to the prescripts of the law applied with equity. §3. The Christian faithful have the right not to be punished with canonical penalties except according to the norm of law."

67. 1983 Code of Canon Law, c. 1342. "§1. Whenever there are just reasons against the use of a judicial procedure, a penalty can be imposed or declared by means of an extra-judicial decree, observing canon 1720, especially in what concerns the right of defence and the moral certainty in the mind of the one issuing the decree, in accordance with the provision of canon 1608. Penal remedies and penances may in any case whatever be applied by a decree."

68. 1983 Code of Canon Law, c. 1342. "§3. What the law or decree says of a judge in regard to the imposition or declaration of a penalty in a trial is to be applied also to a Superior who imposes or declares a penalty by an extra-judicial decree, unless it is otherwise clear, or unless there is question of provisions which concern only procedural matters."

69. See 1983 Code of Canon Law, c. 1326.

70. 1983 Code of Canon Law, c. 18. "Laws which establish a penalty, restrict the free exercise of rights, or contain an exception from the law are subject to strict interpretation."

71. *Presbyterium Ordinis*, 6.

72. 1983 Code of Canon Law, c. 1339. "§4. If on one or more occasions warnings or corrections have been made to someone to no effect, or if it is not possible to expect them to have any effect, the Ordinary is to issue a penal precept in which he sets out exactly what is to be done or avoided. §5. If the gravity of the case so requires, and especially in a case where someone is in danger of relapsing into an offence, the Ordinary is also to subject the offender, over and above the penalties imposed according to the provision of the law or declared by sentence or decree, to a measure of vigilance determined by means of a singular decree."

73. George Weigel, quoted by John Thavis, in "US Author Cites New Evidence of Communism's 'War' with the Church," Catholic News, January 13, 2011.

74. Thavis, "US Author Cites New Evidence."

75. Thavis, "US Author Cites New Evidence."

76. "In Interview, Pope Offers Encouraging Words to Beijing," UCA News, February 3, 2016.

77. See Fonti Ricciane, ed., Pasqulae M. D'Ella, SJ, vol. 2, (Rome 1949), no. 617, 152; Pope John Paul II, "Message to Matteo Ricci convention," no. 4.

78. Pope Benedict XVI, "Letter to Chinese Catholics," June 30, 2007, in *Origins* 37 (2007), no. 10, 147.

79. Pope Benedict XVI, "Letter to Chinese Catholics," no. 153.
80. Pope Benedict XVI, "Letter to Chinese Catholics," no. 151.
81. Pope Benedict XVI, "Letter to Chinese Catholics," no. 151.
82. 1983 Code of Canon Law, c. 1387. "A bishop who consecrates someone a bishop without a pontifical mandate and the person who receives the consecration from him incur a latae sententiae excommunication reserved to the Apostolic See."
83. Pope Benedict XVI, "Letter to Chinese Catholics," nos. 10, 154.
84. Pope Benedict XVI, "Letter to Chinese Catholics," no. 154.
85. Jeroom Heyndrickx, "Vatican Dialogue with China Buoyed by Pope's Remarks," UCA News, February 5, 2016, http://www.ucanews.com/news/vatican-dialogue-with-china-buoyed-by-popes-remarks/75149.
86. Heyndrickx, "Vatican Dialogue with China."
87. Heyndrickx, "Vatican Dialogue with China."
88. Heyndrickx, "Vatican Dialogue with China."
89. Heyndrickx, "Vatican Dialogue with China."
90. "China, Vatican Negotiate further on Bishop Appointments," UCA News, February 3, 2016.

CHAPTER 10

1. Henry Black, *Black's Law Dictionary* (St. Paul, MN: West Publishing Co., 1983), 477.
2. "Pope Francis Begins Meetings with Chilean Clerical Abuse Victims," Catholic News Agency, June 2, 2018, https://www.catholicnewsagency.com/news/pope-francis-begins-meetings-with-chilean-clerical-abuse-victims-79074.
3. See David Cito, "La Pérdida del estado clerical ex officio ante las actuals urgencias pastorals," *Ius Canonicum* 51 (2011): 225–26.
4. A. Borras, *Exegetical Commentary*, vol. IV/1, 425.
5. Brian Austin, "Due Process of Law and the USCCB Essential Norms," *Studia Canonica* 51 (2017): 70–71.
6. Valere Nkouaya Mbandji, "La Prescription Canonique et les delicts commis par les Clercs," Paper to the Canadian Canon Law Society 52nd Annual Convention 2017.
7. Austin, "Due Process of Law," 66.
8. Mbandji, "La Prescription Canonique"; Austin, "Due Process of Law," 70–71.
9. Mbandji, "La Prescription Canonique"; F. X. Wernz and P. Vidal, *Ius Canonicum*, vol. 6 (Rome: Apud aedes Universitatis Gregorianae, 1927), 315–16: "The foundation of prescription of the criminal action, especially the reason is placed: a) in it the lapse of time the memory of the crime reduces more and more, and with it the condemnation of society that the criminal and penal action intended to address; with the result that in the Church in many cases, the taking of criminal action after a long period of time induces scandal and wonderment; b) another reason is that after a long period of time the proof of the crime and the defence of the accused are presented with a significant difficulty; as well as the public authority has the danger of condemning and innocent man, because the passage of time removes significant proofs."
10. Kenneth Boccafola, "The Special Penal Norms of the United States and Their Application," in Dugan, *The Penal Process*, 269–70.

11. Thomas Green, "Delicts and Penalties in General [cc.1311–1363]," in *New Commentary*, 1573.

12. John P. Beal, "Hiding in the Thickets of the Law: Canonical Reflections on Some Disturbing Aspects of the Dallas Charter," *America* 187 (October 7, 2002): 18.

13. Holy See, "Observations of the Holy See with Reference to the Response of the Australian Catholic Bishops' Conference to the Recommendations of the Royal Commission," February 26, 2020, no. 484.110, https://www.catholic.org.au/images/Observations_of_the_Holy_See_to_the_Recommendations_of_the_Royal_Commission.pdf; *in dubio pro re* means "when in doubt, in favor of the defendant."

14. Thomas Green, "Sanctions in the Church" in Coriden, Green, and Heintschel, *The Code of Canon Law: A Text and Commentary*, 919.

15. Nicholas Cafardi, *Before Dallas: The US Bishops' Response to Clergy Sexual Abuse of Children* (Mahwah, NJ: Paulist Press, 2008), 30.

16. John Paul II, motu proprio, *Sacramentorum Sanctitatis Tutela*, April 30, 2001, https://www.vatican.va. Usually, an instruction would not be law, but an explanation of the law for a more precise application (see c. 34).

17. Congregation for the Doctrine of the Faith, Letter *Ad Exsequendam*, May 18, 2001, *AAS* 93 (2001), 785–86.

18. Cafardi, *Before Dallas*, 30–31. Cafardi proposed what he thought could have been a solution: "While the statute (i.e. canon 1362 §1, 2) may have applied in canonical penal prosecution that remained at the diocesan level, perhaps all that had to be done to avoid the statute was for the diocese to refer the crime to the Holy Office (now the Congregation for the Doctrine of the Faith) for prosecution. One the crime was referred or reported, the reserved jurisdiction of the Congregation would have become applicable and prescription did not run against those crimes reserved to the Holy Office (Congregation for the Doctrine of the Faith."

19. John Beal, "To Be or Not to Be, That Is the Question: The Rights of the Accused in the Canonical Penal Process," in *CLSA Proceedings* 53 (1991): 82.

20. Juan Arrieta, "Cardinal Ratzinger's Influence on the Revision of the Canonical Penal Law System," in *Origins* 40 (2010): 496.

21. See 1983 Code of Canon Law, c. 1362 §1.

22. See 1983 Code of Canon Law, c. 1362. See also John Kozlowski, OP, "Understanding the Ius Vigens of the Mandatory Dismissal Process," *The Jurist* 75, no. 2 (2015): 403.

23. Juan Arrieta, "Cardinal Ratzinger and the Revision of the Canonical Penal System: A Crucial Role," http://www.vatican.va/resources/resources_arrieta-20101202_en.html.

24. Arrieta, "Cardinal Ratzinger and the Revision of the Canonical Penal System."

25. Arrieta, "Cardinal Ratzinger and the Revision of the Canonical Penal System."

26. Pope John Paul II, apostolic constitution on the Roman curia, *Pastor Bonus*, June 28, 1988, https://www.vatican.va/content/john-paul-ii/en/apost_constitutions/documents/hf_jp-ii_apc_19880628_pastor-bonus.html.

27. Pope Paul VI, apostolic constitution *Regimini Ecclesiae Universae*, August 15, 1967, http://w2.vatican.va/content/paul-vi/la/apost_constitutions/documents/hf_p-vi_apc_19670815_regimini-ecclesiae-universae.html.

28. Canon Law Society of America Newsletter, quoted in Thomas Doyle, OP, "The 1922 Instruction and the 1962 Instruction *Crimen*

Sollicitationis," promulgated by the Vatican, October 3, 2008, http://www.awrsipe.com/doyle/2008/2008-10-03-commentary%20on%201922%20and%201962%20documents.pdf.

29. Woestman, *Ecclesiastical Sanctions and the Penal Process*, 270–71.

30. Congregation for the Doctrine of the Faith, "Circular Letter to help Episcopal Conferences Prepare Guidelines for the Treatment of Cases of Sexual Abuse of Minors by Clerics," May 3, 2011, http://www.vatican.va/roman_curia/congregations/cfaith/documents/rc_con_cfaith_doc_20110503_abuso-minori_it.html.

31. Msgr. Charles Scicluna, "The Procedure and Praxis of the Congregation for the Doctrine of the Faith regarding *Graviora Delicta*," http://www.vatican.va/resources/resources_mons-scicluna-graviora-delicta_en.html.

32. Msgr. Charles Scicluna, "Sexual Abuse of children and Young People by Priests and Religious: Description of the Problem from a Church perspective," in *Sexual Abuse in the Catholic Church: Scientific and Legal Perspectives*, ed. R.K. Hanson et al. (Vatican City: Libreria Editrice Vaticana, 2003), 19.

33. Congregation for the Doctrine of the Faith, "Circular Letter to Assist Episcopal Conferences in Developing Guidelines for Dealing with Cases of Sexual Abuses of Minors Perpetrated by Clerics," May 3, 2011, http://www.vatican.va/roman_curia/congregations/cfaith/documents/rc_con_cfaith_doc_20110503_abuso-minori_en.html.

34. Congregation for the Doctrine of the Faith, Art. 4, 1, April 30, 2001, in Woestman, *Ecclesiastical Sanctions*, 304–5.

35. Scicluna, "Sexual Abuse," 239. Quoted in Kozlowski. "Understanding the *Ius Vigens*,"422.

36. John Kozlowski, "Understanding the *Ius Vigens*," 422.

37. See C. G. Renati, "Prescription and Derogation from Prescription in Sexual Abuse of Minors Cases," *The Jurist* 67 (2007): 503; and P. Brown, "Prescription and Statutes of Limitation," *Proceedings of the Canon Law Society of America* 70 (2008): 384.

38. Renati, "Prescription and Derogation," 505.

39. Thomas Green, "Clerical Sexual Abuse of Minors: Some Canonical Reflections," *The Jurist* 63 (2003): 417; and Ladislas Orsy, "Bishops' Norms: Commentary and Evaluation," *Boston College Law Review* 44 (2002–2003): 1015–16.

40. Austin, "Due Process of Law," 72.

41. Article 11, https://www.ohchr.org/EN/UDHR/Documents/UDHR_Translations/eng.pdf.

42. Austin, "Due Process of Law," 73.

43. Renati, "Prescription and Derogation," 507.

44. Pope John Paul II *motu proprio Sacramentorum Sanctitatis Tutela*.

45. Pope John Paul II *motu proprio Sacramentorum sanctitatis tutela*.

46. Austin, "Due Process of Law," 74.

47. Francis Morrisey, OMI, Lecture Notes: "Penal Law and Jurisprudence, Faculty of Canon Law," Faculty of Canon Law, Saint Paul University, Ottawa, 2017–2018, 52–53: "Taking into account the time passed and considering that the presumed delicts are already prescribed according to the norm of canon 1703, no. 2 CIC 1917 and furthermore given the advanced age of the above-named brother, this Congregation does not hold that there is sufficient reason to derogate from prescription. Therefore, it is not permissible

to commence any penal action against 'X.' However, the public exercise of sacred orders of the brother can be limited by disciplinary means. If it is opportune and necessary you could impose on the brother a precept according to canons 49–51, 1319 and 1339 CIC citing canon 1371 no. 2 warning that the violation of the same would carry the imposition of a punishment. Should a precept emanate, I ask you to ensure a copy of the aforementioned precept comes to this Dicastery signed by the brother at the moment of his notification."

48. Morrisey, Lecture Notes: "Penal Law and Jurisprudence," 52–53.

49. Morrisey, Lecture Notes: "Penal Law and Jurisprudence," 52–53.

50. Morrisey, Lecture Notes: "Penal Law and Jurisprudence," 52.

51. See 1983 Code of Canon Law, c. 1362 §1 and §2.

52. The faculty to derogate from prescription was incorporated into the revised edition of *Sacramentorum Sanctitatis Tutela* on May 21, 2010. See Art. 7. "§1. A criminal action for delicts reserved to the Congregation for the Doctrine of the Faith is extinguished by prescription after twenty years, with due regard to the right of the Congregation for the Doctrine of the Faith to derogate from prescription in individual cases. §2. Prescription runs according to the norm of can. 1362 of the Code of Canon Law and canon 1152 §3 of the Code of Canons of the Eastern Churches."

53. Congregation for the Doctrine of the Faith, "Circular Letter."

54. Commonwealth of Australia, "Royal Commission into Institutional Responses to Child Sex Abuses. Final Report: Religious Institutions," vol. 16, Book 1 (2017), 518; https://www.childabuseroyalcommission.gov.au/sites/default/files/final_report_-_volume_16_religious_institutions_book_1.pdf.

55. Commonwealth of Australia, "Final Report: Religious Institutions," 519.

CHAPTER 11

1. Hugh Laracy. "Douglas, Francis Vernon—Biography," in *Te Ara: The Encyclopedia of New Zealand*, the Ministry for Culture and Heritage of the New Zealand Government, updated September 1, 2010, http://www.TeAra.govt.nz/en/biographies/5d23/1. Accessed 1 September 2011; see also Patricia Brooks, *With No Regrets: The Story of Francis Vernon Douglas* (Quezon City: Claretian Publications, 1998). The Francis Douglas Memorial College in New Plymouth is named after him.

2. Gregory Zubacz, *The Seal of Confession and Canadian Law* (Montreal: Wilson & Lafleur Ltée, 2009), 1.

3. V. de Paolis and D. Cito, *Sanctions in the Church: Commentary on the Code of Canon Law. Book VI* (Vatican City, Urbaniana University Press, 2000), 345; in "Note of the Apostolic Penitentiary on the Importance of the Internal Forum and the Inviolability of the Sacramental Seal," July 1, 2019, http://press.vatican.va/content/salastampa/it/bollettino/pubblico/2019/07/01/0565/01171.html.

4. Holy See, "Glossary of Terms," http://www.vatican.va/resources/resources_glossary-terms_en.html (accessed September 12, 2011).

5. Fourth Lateran Council, c. 21, in Tanner, *Decrees of the Ecumenical Councils*, vol. 1, 245.

6. St. Thomas Aquinas, *Summa, supple.*, q.11 a.1.

7. "To express this truth, the Church has always taught that priests, in the celebration of the sacraments, act '*in persona Christi capitis*,' that is, in the very person of Christ the head: 'Christ allows us to use his "I," we speak in the "I" of Christ, Christ "pulls into himself" and allows us to unite, unites us with his "I."…It is this union with his "I" that is realized in the words of consecration. Even in the "I absolve you"—because none of us could absolve from sins—it is the "I" of Christ, of God, who alone can absolve.'" See "Note of the Apostolic Penitentiary."

8. See Kennedy, *State Protection of Confessional Secrecy in the United States of America*, 22. St. Thomas Aquinas, *Sent*. IV, d. XXI, q. LII, a. 1.

9. St. Thomas Aquinas, *Sent*. IV, d. XXI, q. LII, a. L, q. 3, s. 2.

10. Pope Innocent III, Sermo I in consecratione pontficis, PL. 217:625–50.

11. Fernando Loza, *Exegetical Commentary* III/l, 821. This distinction was discussed and affirmed during the revision of the Code. See *Communicationes* 31 (1999): 272: "Rev. mus Secretarius ad. Proponit ut in par. 1 affirmetur obligation servandi sigillum, quo etiam interpres ligatur; ut in par. 2 affirmetur obligatio ad secretum inviolabile servandum, quo omnes tenentur ad quos quo modo notitia confessionis perveneri. Petit ipse Emmus Praeses utrum distinction facienda sit necne inter interpretem et alios. Aestimat Rev. mus primus Consultor distinctionem hanc esse faciendam, sed in eadem par. 2. Consentiunt omnes ut distinction fiat."

12. See New Version of Book VI Code of Canon Law (2021), c. 1386, http://www.vatican.va/archive/ENG1104/__P3F.HTM.

13. Linus, *Delicta Graviora*, 40.

14. New Version of Book VI Code of Canon Law (2021), c. 1386. "§1. A confessor who directly violates the sacramental seal incurs a *latae sententiae* excommunication reserved to the Apostolic See; he who does so only indirectly is to be punished according to the gravity of the offence. prohibitions and deprivations; in the more serious cases he is to be dismissed from the clerical state."

15. Pope John Paul II, *Sacramentorum Sanctitatis Tutela*, Art. 3, no. 3.

16. Ed Langlois, "Confession Tape Coils to Bite as Defense, Prosecution Prepare for Murder Trial," *Catholic Sentinel*, March 5, 1988, http://www.catholicsentinel.org/main.asp?SectionID=2&SubSectionID=35&ArticleID=2653.

17. Scicluna, "The Procedure and Praxis of the Congregation for the Doctrine of the Faith regarding *Graviora Delicta*," http://www.vatican.va/resources/resources_mons-scicluna-graviora-delicta_en.html.

18. Pope John Paul II, "Substantive Norms," Art. 4 §2, http://www.vatican.va/resources/resources_norme_en.html.

19. Holy See, "Glossary of Terms," http://www.vatican.va/resources/resources_glossary-terms_en.html.

20. Zubacz, *The Seal of Confession and Canadian Law*, 51.

21. See Apostolic Penitentiary, Letter, *Pro Memoria*, October 24, 1983, in *CLD*, vol. 11, 49–52.

22. See commentary by Juan Arias in E. Caparros et al., *Code of Canon Law Annotated*, 1078.

23. Holy Office, Instruction on the Seal of Confession, June 9, 1915, *CLD*, vol. 1, 414.

24. Pope Innocent XI, decree, November 18, 1862 (Denzinger-Schonmetzer, no. 2195), translated in Ian Waters, "The Seal of Confession," *The Australasian Catholic Record* 94, no. 3 (2017): 330–43: "Is it lawful to use knowledge obtained in confession, provided it is done without direct or indirect revelation, and without burden upon the penitent,

unless some greater evil follows from its non-use, in comparison with which the first would rightly be held of little account, an explanation or limitation then being added, that it is to be understood concerning the use of knowledge obtained from confession with burden to the penitent, any revelation whatsoever being excluded, and even in the case in which a much greater burden to the same penitent would follow from its non-use? *Reply*. The stated proposition, even with the aforesaid explanation or limitation, must be altogether prohibited, inasmuch as it admits the use of the said knowledge with burden upon the penitent."

25. Apostolic Penitentiary, "Note of the Apostolic Penitentiary," July 1, 2019.

26. Dicastery for the Doctrine of Faith, "*Vademecum*: On Certain Points of Procedure in Treating Cases of Sexual Abuse of Minors Committed by Clerics," June 5, 2022, https://www.vatican.va/roman_curia/congregations/cfaith/documents/rc_con_cfaith_doc_20200716_vademecum-casi-abuso_en.html.

27. Hannah Brockhaus, "Australian Court Finds Archbishop Wilson Guilty of Concealing Abuse," Catholic News Service, May 22, 2018, https://www.catholicnewsagency.com/news/australian-court-finds-archbishop-wilson-guilty-of-concealing-abuse-66003. "The second victim said he had told Wilson of the abuse in the confessional in 1976, but that Wilson had dismissed the boy with a penance, saying that he was lying. Wilson said he would never tell someone in the confessional that they were untruthful, and that he did not remember having seen the boy at all in 1976. Fletcher was convicted of nine counts of sexual abuse and was jailed in 2006. He died of a stroke within the year. Wilson said he had no previous suspicions about the integrity of Fletcher's character," The convictions were overturned on appeal.

28. Holy See, Letter: "Observations of the Holy See with Reference to the Response of the Australian Catholic Bishops' Conference to the Recommendations of the Royal Commission," February 26, 2020, N. 484.110, https://www.catholic.org.au/images/Observations_of_the_Holy_See_to_the_Recommendations_of_the_Royal_Commission.pdf.

29. 1983 Code of Canon Law, c. 979. "In posing questions, the priest is to proceed with prudence and discretion, attentive to the condition and age of the penitent, and is to refrain from asking the name of an accomplice."

30. Holy Office, Decree Condemning Sixty-Five Propositions, March 2, 1679, (Denzinger, no. 2164). quoted in Ian Waters, "The Seal of Confession," *The Australasian Catholic Record*, 340. Proposition number 60 stated, "The penitent who has the habit of sinning against the law of God, of nature, or of the Church, even if there appears no hope of amendment, is not to be denied absolution or to be put off, provided he professes orally that he is sorry and proposes amendment."

31. Lucie Morris-Marr, "Priest Who Confessed to Abuse 1500 Times 'Proves Need for Change," *The New Daily*, June 14, 2018, https://thenewdaily.com.au/news/national/2018/06/14/confession-child-abuse-royal-commission/.

32. Nicolas Vaux-Montagny, "Church Covered for Predator Priest," Crux, January 20, 2020, https://cruxnow.com/church-in-europe/2020/01/french-trial-exposes-how-church-covered-for-predator-priest/. "Aside from church superiors, Preynat said he also systematically spoke about his behaviour in the confessional. 'I always confessed my faults,' he said. 'Every time the confessor gave me absolution and urged me not to start again. A month later, I'd start again.'"

33. 1983 Code of Canon Law, c. 978. "§1. In hearing confessions the priest is to remem-

ber that he is equally a judge and a physician and has been established by God as a minister of divine justice and mercy, so that he has regard for the divine honour and the salvation of souls. §2. In administering the sacrament, the confessor as a minister of the Church is to adhere faithfully to the doctrine of the magisterium and the norms issued by competent authority." See also 1983 Code of Canon Law, c. 980. "If the confessor has no doubt about the disposition of the penitent, and the penitent seeks absolution, absolution is to be neither refused nor deferred."

34. See Apostolic Penitentiary, "Note of the Apostolic Penitentiary," July 1, 2019.

35. Holy See, Letter: "Observations of the Holy See with Reference to the Response of the Australian Catholic Bishops' Conference to the Recommendations of the Royal Commission."

36. Apostolic Penitentiary, "Note of the Apostolic Penitentiary."

37. Apostolic Penitentiary, "Note of the Apostolic Penitentiary."

38. Linus, *Delicta Graviora*, 41; see also G. P. Montini, *La tutela Penale*, 226–27.

CHAPTER 12

1. Laurie Goodstein, "Vatican Declined to Defrock U.S. Priest Who Abused Boys," March 24, 2010, http://www.nytimes.com/2010/03/25/world/europe/25vatican.html?pagewanted=1.

2. Tony Wall, "Catholic Priest Defrocked after Affair in the US Now in Charge of Auckland Parish," March 11, 2018, https://www.stuff.co.nz/national/102066087/a-catholic-priest-defrocked-after-an-affair-in-the-us-is-in-charge-of-a-parish-in-auckland.

3. Charles Augustine, OSB, *A Commentary on the New Code of Canon Law, Penalties*, vol. 8 (Canons 2298–2305) (St. Louis: B. Herder Book Co., 1918), 259–62.

4. John A. Alesandro, "A Study of Canon Law: Dismissal from the Clerical State in Cases of Sexual Misconduct," *The Catholic Lawyer* 36, no. 3 (2017): 259; John Beal, "Doing What One Can: Canon Law and Clerical Sexual Misconduct," *The Jurist* 52 (1992): 642, 647.

5. 1983 Code of Canon Law, c. 976. "Even though a priest lacks the faculty to hear confessions, he absolves validly and licitly any penitents whatsoever in danger of death from any censures and sins, even if an approved priest is present."

6. Polycarp, "Letter to the Philippians," in *Sexual Abuse in the Catholic Church: Scientific and Legal Perspectives*, ed. R. Hanson, F. Pfafflin, and M. Lutz (Vatican City: Libreria Editrice Vaticana, 2004), 14.

7. Nicholas Cafardi, *Before Dallas* (Mahwah, NJ: Paulist Press, 2008), 2.

8. Stephen Rossetti, *A Tragic Grace: The Catholic Church and Child Sexual Abuse* (Collegeville, MN: The Liturgical Press, 1996), 104.

9. See "Council of Nicaea," canon 9, in Christian Cochini, SJ, *The Apostolic Origins of Priestly Celibacy* (San Francisco: Ignatius Press, 1981), 336.

10. J. McNeil and Helena Gamer, *Medieval Handbooks of Penance: A Translation of the Principal "Libri Poenitentiales" and Selections from Related Documents* (New York: Columbia University, 1990), 226; quoted in Cafardi, *Before Dallas*, 3.

11. In his *Concordantia Discordantium Canonum*, Gratian classifies sexual acts contrary to nature, including pedophile activity as crimes in canon law (no. 11).

12. Cafardi, *Before Dallas*, 3.

13. Peter Damian, "Letter 13, chapter 10," quoted in Cafardi, *Before Dallas*, 3.

14. Hanson et al., *Sexual Abuse*, 14.

15. Hanson et al., *Sexual Abuse*, 15.

16. Hanson et al., *Sexual Abuse*, 15.

17. H. J. Schroeder, OP, "Council of Trent 13th Session, Decree on Reformation," in *Canons and Decrees of the Council of Trent*, 83: "Since ecclesiastics are sometimes guilty of crimes so grave that on account of their shocking wickedness they have to be deposed from sacred orders and handed over to the secular court…it is ordained and decreed that it shall be lawful for a bishop by himself… even without the presence of other bishops, to proceed against a cleric."

18. "Council of Trent," in Tanner, *Decrees of the Ecumenical Councils*, vol. 2, 700.

19. "Council of Trent," in Tanner, *Decrees of the Ecumenical Councils*, vol. 2, 700.

20. Richard Sherr, "A Canon, a Choirboy, and Homosexuality in Late Sixteenth-Century Italy: A Case Study," *Journal of Homosexuality* 21, no. 3 (1991): 1–22; See also Rossetti, *A Tragic Grace*, 104.

21. See Stewart Lamont, "Life as a Galley Slave," *Christianity Today* 46 (1995), https://www.christianitytoday.com/history/issues/issue-46/life-as-galley-slave.html. Being sentenced as a galley slave to row ships was the next most severe punishment after execution. He was shackled to his seat, where he ate, slept, and toileted until he died or was near death.

22. Sacred Congregation for the Council, June 8 and July 6, 1726, Gasparri, *Fontes*, vol. V, 763–64. See James Provost, "Offences against the Sixth Commandment: Toward a Canonical Analysis of Canon 1395," *The Jurist* 55 (1995): 632–63.

23. 1917 Code of Canon Law, c. 107.

24. 1917 Code of Canon Law, cc. 108, 212.

25. Augustine, *Commentary on the 1917 Code, Ecclesiastical Persons* (Canons 211–214) vol. 2, 197.

26. 1917 Code of Canon Law, c. 211 §2.

27. 1917 Code of Canon Law, c. 132 §2.

28. 1917 Code of Canon Law, c. 136 §3.

29. 1917 Code of Canon Law, c. 141 §2.

30. 1917 Code of Canon Law, c. 213.

31. 1917 Code of Canon Law, c. 120 §1.

32. 1917 Code of Canon Law, c. 119.

33. 1917 Code of Canon Law, c. 121.

34. Sacred Congregation for the Sacraments, decree, "*Regulae servandae in Processibus super nullitate sacrae ordinationis*," July 9, 1931: *AAS* 23 (1931), 457; English translation in *Canon Law Digest*, vol. 1, 812–33.

35. Sacred Congregation for the Sacraments, instruction, *Ad Reverendissimos Locorum Ordinarios de Scrutinio Alumnorum Peragenda antequam ad Ordines Provoveantur*, December 27, 1930, *AAS* 23 (1931), 126. English translation in *CLD*, vol. 1, 470–71: "Others there are who have received minor and sacred orders in good faith, but before they reach the priesthood realise that they are unable to bear the burdens of sacred ordination, or else by that time have become entangled in vicious habits or worldly ways: in these the want of a holy vocation will be more easily and clearly discovered, and they themselves will ask to be relieved of their miserable condition."

36. Javier De Otaduy, "The Loss of the Clerical State," *Exegetical Commentary*, vol. II/1, 399.

37. William Woestman, OMI, *The Sacrament of Orders and the Clerical State: A Commentary on the Code of Canon Law*, 3rd ed., revised and updated, (Ottawa: Saint Paul University, 2006, 213.

38. Abbo and Hannan, *The Sacred Canons*, vol. 1, 268.

39. 1917 Code of Canon Law, c. 120 §2. "The Ordinary, however, especially when a lay person is the petitioner, will not deny this permission except for a just and grave causes, all the more so when he was unable to bring about a resolution of the controversy between the parties."

40. Secretariat of State, Concordat between the Holy See and German Reich, July 20, 1933: Art. 33.

41. Augustine, *Commentary on the 1917 Code, Ecclesiastical Persons* (Canon 120) vol. 2, 64. Cf. M. Conte a Coronata, *Institutiones Iuris Canonici*, vol. I, 209–11.

42. Rodger J. Austin, "Report on Canon Law Submitted to the Royal Commission into Institutional Responses to Child Sexual Abuse," *The Canonist* 8, no. 2 (2017): 303.

43. 1917 Code of Canon Law, c. 2195 §1.

44. See 1917 Code of Canon Law, c. 2305.

45. See 1917 Code of Canon Law, c. 2305.

46. See 1917 Code of Canon Law, c. 2305 §2.

47. Joseph Diermeier, "Loss of the Clerical State: Specific Focus on Dismissal from the Clerical State" (JCL Thesis, The Catholic University of America, 2010), 11–12.

48. See 1917 Code of Canon Law, c. 1576 §1, no. 2.

49. See Sacred Congregation of the Holy Office, Instruction, *Crimen Sollicitationis*, "On the Manner of Proceeding in Cases Involving the Crime of Solicitation," 71: "The term *crimen pessimum* [the foulest crime] is here understood to mean any external obscene act, gravely sinful, perpetrated or attempted by a cleric in any way whatsoever with a person of his own sex." See http://www.vatican.va/resources/resources_crimen-sollicitationis-1962_en.html.

50. *Crimen Sollicitationis*, 72.

51. *Crimen Sollicitationis*, 61.

52. *Crimen Sollicitationis*, 62.

53. Sacred Congregation of the Holy Office, *Reduction to the Lay State*: *Norms*, February 2, 1964, in *CLD*, vol.7, 1002–15.

54. Vatican II, Dogmatic Constitution on the Church, *Lumen Gentium* 32, https://www.vatican.va/archive/hist_councils/ii_vatican_council/documents/vat-ii_const_19641121_lumen-gentium_en.html.

55. *Lumen Gentium* 39.

56. Congregation for the Doctrine of the Faith, *Declaration Regarding the Interpretation of Certain Provisions Which Were Established by the Norms of 13 January 1971*, in *CLD*, vol. 7, 121–24.

57. Sacred Congregation for the Doctrine of the Faith, circular letter, *Litteris Encyclicis*, January 13, 1971, *AAS* 63 (1971), 310: English translation in *Canon Law Digest*, vol. 7, 119.

58. Pope Paul VI, apostolic letter, *Ministeria quaedam*, August 15, 1972, https://www.vatican.va/content/paul-vi/la/motu_proprio/documents/hf_p-vi_motu-proprio_19720815_ministeria-quaedam.html; Pope Paul VI, apostolic letter, *Ad Pascendum*, August 15, 1972, *AAS* 64 (1972), 534–540; English translation in *CLD*, vol. 7, 690–698.

59. Tomas Rincon, "Sacred Ministers or Clerics," in *Code of Canon Law Annotated*, ed. Ernest Caparros et al. (Montreal: Wilson & Lafleur Ltée, 2004), 187.

60. Synod of Bishops 1967, "Principia quae Codicis iuris canonici recognitionem dirigant," in *Communicationes* I (1969): 77–85, English translation by Roger Schoenbechler in Hite et al., *Readings, Cases, Materials in Canon Law: A Textbook for Ministerial Students*, 70–78.

61. Pontifica Commissio Codici Iuris Recognoscendo, *Schema Documenti quo Disciplina Sanctionum seu Poenarum in Ecclesia*

Latina denuo Ordinatur (Vatican City: Typis Polyglottis Vaticanis, 1973).

62. James Provost, "Revision of Book VI of the Code of Canon Law," in *Studia Canonica* 9 (1975): 135.

63. Thomas Green, "Penal Law: A Review of Selected Themes," *The Jurist* 50 (1990): 228.

64. 1983 Code of Canon Law, c. 277 §1. "Clerics are obliged to observe perfect and perpetual continence for the sake of the Kingdom of heaven, and are therefore bound to celibacy. Celibacy is a special gift of God by which sacred ministers can more easily remain close to Christ with an undivided heart, and can dedicate themselves more freely to the service of God and their neighbor."

65. The Congregation for Divine Worship and the Discipline of the Sacraments revised the norms to be observed for the declaration of nullity of ordination on October 26, 2001.

66. 1983 Code of Canon Law, cc. 1331–33.

67. 1983 Code of Canon Law, c. 1317. "Penalties are to be established only insofar as they are truly necessary to provide more suitably for ecclesiastical discipline. Particular law, however, cannot establish a penalty of dismissal from the clerical state."

68. 1983 Code of Canon Law, c. 1314. "Generally, a penalty is *ferendae sententiae*, so that it does not bind the guilty party until after it has been imposed; if the law or precept expressly establishes it, however, a penalty is *latae sententiae*, so that it is incurred ipso facto when the delict is committed."

69. Woestman, *The Sacrament of Orders*, 213.

70. De Otaduy, "The Loss of the Clerical State," 401.

71. Alesandro, "A Study of Canon Law," 271–72.

72. The decree of dismissal states, "a. A priest who has been dismissed automatically loses the rights proper to the clerical state, and also all dignities and ecclesiastical offices; he is no longer bound by other obligations connected with the clerical state; b. He remains excluded from the exercise of sacred ministry, except for those matters contained in canon 976 and canon 986 §2 of the Code of Canon Law, and therefore may not give the homily, nor hold an executive office (*officium directium*) in the pastoral field, nor exercise the role of parish administrator; c. Furthermore, he may not carry out any role in Seminaries or equivalent institutes. In other institutes of studies of a higher level, which in any way depend on ecclesiastical authority, he may not carry out an executive role or an office of teaching; d. In other institutes of studies of a higher level, which in any way depend on ecclesiastical authority, he may not carry out an executive role or an office of teaching; e. In other institutes of studies of a higher level not dependent on ecclesiastical authority he may not teach any theological discipline; e. In institutes of studies of a lower level depending on ecclesiastical authority he may not carry out either an executive role or a teaching role. The same rule binds any priest dismissed and dispensed in teaching religion in institutes of the same kind not depending on ecclesiastical authority." See Congregation for the Doctrine of the Faith, decree, John Nestor, October 17, 2008, https://www.childabuseroyalcommission.gov.au/sites/default/files/CTJH.001.12001.0060.pdf.

73. Alesandro, "A Study of Canon Law," 264–69.

74. Pope John Paul II, Rescript, April 25, 1994, in *Roman Replies,* 1994, 20–21.

75. Congregation for the Doctrine of the Faith, "Letter from Prefect of the Congregation to Bishops, Ordinaries and Hierarchs,"

May 21, 2010, with the revised *Substantive Norms*, http://www.vatican.va/resources/resources_norme_en.html.

76. CDF, "Letter from Prefect of the Congregation to Bishops, Ordinaries and Hierarchs," Art. 2 §1. "The delicts against the faith referred to in art. 1 are heresy, apostasy and schism according to the norm of canon 751 and 1364 of the Code of Canon Law, and canon 1436 and 1437 of the Code of Canons of the Eastern Churches."

77. CDF, "Letter from Prefect of the Congregation to Bishops, Ordinaries and Hierarchs," Art. 6 §1. "The more grave delicts against morals which are reserved to the Congregation for the Doctrine of the Faith are: 1° the delict against the sixth commandment of the Decalogue committed by a cleric with a minor below the age of eighteen years; in this case, a person who habitually lacks the use of reason is to be considered equivalent to a minor. 2° the acquisition, possession, or distribution by a cleric of pornographic images of minors under the age of fourteen, for purposes of sexual gratification, by whatever means or using whatever technology; §2. A cleric who commits the delicts mentioned above in §1 is to be punished according to the gravity of his crime, not excluding dismissal or deposition."

78. CDF, "Letter from Prefect of the Congregation to Bishops, Ordinaries and Hierarchs," Art. 4. §1. "5° the direct and indirect violation of the sacramental seal, mentioned in canon 1388 §1 of the Code of Canon Law, and in canon 1456 §1 of the Code of Canons of the Eastern Churches."

79. CDF, "Letter from Prefect of the Congregation to Bishops, Ordinaries and Hierarchs," Art. 4 §2. "With due regard for §1, no. 5, also reserved to the Congregation for the Doctrine of the Faith is the more grave delict which consists in the recording, by whatever technical means, or in the malicious diffusion through communications media, of what is said in sacramental confession, whether true or false, by the confessor or the penitent. Anyone who commits such a delict is to be punished according to the gravity of the crime, not excluding, if he be a cleric, dismissal or deposition."

80. CDF, "Letter from Prefect of the Congregation to Bishops, Ordinaries and Hierarchs," Art. 4 §1. "4° the solicitation to a sin against the sixth commandment of the Decalogue in the act, on the occasion, or under the pretext of confession, as mentioned in canon 1387 of the Code of Canon Law, and in canon 1458 of the Code of Canons of the Eastern Churches, if it is directed to sinning with the confessor himself."

81. CDF, "Letter from Prefect of the Congregation to Bishops, Ordinaries and Hierarchs," Art. 4 §1. "1° the absolution of an accomplice in a sin against the sixth commandment of the Decalogue, mentioned in canon 1378 §1 of the Code of Canon Law, and in canon 1457 of the Code of Canons of the Eastern Churches."

82. CDF, "Letter from Prefect of the Congregation to Bishops, Ordinaries and Hierarchs," Art. 3 §2. "Also reserved to the Congregation for the Doctrine of the Faith is the delict which consists in the consecration for a sacrilegious purpose of one matter without the other or even of both, either within or outside of the eucharistic celebration. One who has perpetrated this delict is to be punished according to the gravity of the crime, not excluding dismissal or deposition."

83. CDF, "Letter from Prefect of the Congregation to Bishops, Ordinaries and Hierarchs," Art. 3 §1. "1° the taking or retaining for a sacrilegious purpose or the throwing away of the consecrated species, as mentioned in canon 1382 of the Code of Canon Law, and

in canon 1442 of the Code of Canons of the Eastern Churches."

84. CDF, "Letter from Prefect of the Congregation to Bishops, Ordinaries and Hierarchs," Art. 3 §1. "2° attempting the liturgical action of the Eucharistic Sacrifice spoken of in canon 1378 §2, no. 1, of the Code of Canon Law."

85. CDF, "Letter from Prefect of the Congregation to Bishops, Ordinaries and Hierarchs," Art. 3 §1. "3° the simulation of the same, spoken of in canon 1379 of the Code of Canon Law and in canon 1443 of the Code of Canons of the Eastern Churches."

86. CDF, "Letter from Prefect of the Congregation to Bishops, Ordinaries and Hierarchs," Art. 3 §1. "4° the concelebration of the Eucharistic Sacrifice prohibited in canon 908 of the Code of Canon Law, and in canon 702 of the Code of Canons of the Eastern Churches, spoken of in canon 1381 of the Code of Canon Law, and in canon 1440 of the Code of Canons of the Eastern Churches, with ministers of ecclesial communities which do not have apostolic succession and do not acknowledge the sacramental dignity of priestly ordination."

87. CDF, "Letter from Prefect of the Congregation to Bishops, Ordinaries and Hierarchs," Art. 4 §1. "3° simulated sacramental absolution, mentioned in canon 1379 of the Code of Canon Law, and in canon 1443 of the Code of Canons of the Eastern Churches; 2° attempted sacramental absolution or the prohibited hearing of confession, mentioned in canon 1379 §1, 2° of the Code of Canon Law."

88. CDF, "Letter from Prefect of the Congregation to Bishops, Ordinaries and Hierarchs," Art. 5 "The more grave delict of the attempted sacred ordination of a woman is also reserved to the Congregation for the Doctrine of the Faith: 1° With due regard for canon 1379 §3 of the Code of Canon Law, both the one who attempts to confer sacred ordination on a woman, and she who attempts to receive sacred ordination, incurs a *latae sententiae* excommunication reserved to the Apostolic See.....3° If the guilty party is a cleric he may be punished by dismissal or deposition."

89. Congregation for the Doctrine of the Faith, A Brief Introduction to the Modifications Made in the *Normae de gravioribus delictis*, reserved to the Congregation of the Doctrine of the Faith, from William Cardinal Levada Prefect May 21, 2010, http://www.vatican.va/resources/resources_norme_en.html.

90. Congregation for the Evangelization of Peoples, "Letter to Pontifical Representatives," June 3, 1997, Prot. No. 2154/97, in Woestman, *The Sacrament of Orders*, 214; *Canon Law Digest*, vol. 14, 235–37.

91. Later, a very similar faculty was granted to the Congregation for Clergy. See Congregation for Clergy, circular letter, April 18, 2009, Prot. No. 2009/0556, in John Renken, *The Penal Law of the Roman Catholic Church: Commentary on canons 1311–1399 and 1717–1731 and Other Sources of Penal Law* (Ottawa: Saint Paul University, 2015), 491–99.

92. Congregation for the Evangelization of Peoples, "Letter to Pontifical Representatives," in Woestman, *The Sacrament of Orders*, 214. The bishop had to have already suspended the priest, imposed the penalty of residing in another place, and the priest had to have shown no signs of reforming.

93. 1983 Code of Canon Law, c. 292. "A cleric who loses the clerical state according to the norm of law loses with it the rights proper to the clerical state and is no longer bound by any obligations of the clerical state, without prejudice to the prescript of canon 291. He is prohibited from exercising the power of

orders, without prejudice to the prescript of canon 976. By the loss of the clerical state, he is deprived of all offices, functions, and any delegated power. Canon 976. Even though a priest lacks the faculty to hear confessions, he absolves validly and licitly any penitents whatsoever in danger of death from any censures and sins, even if an approved priest is present."

94. Congregation for the Evangelization of Peoples, "Circular Letter," Prot. No. 0579/09, in Renken, *The Penal Law*, 485. Similar faculties were granted to the Congregation for the Clergy on January 30, 2009.

95. The same faculty is also applied to a cleric who is guilty of attempted marriage and, though duly admonished by the competent ordinary, refuses to mend his ways and continues his irregular and scandalous life (see 1983 Code of Canon Law, c. 1394 §1).

96. See 1983 Code of Canon Law, c. 1395.

97. 1983 Code of Canon Law, c. 1392; Congregation for the Clergy, "Circular Letter," Prot. No. 2009 0556, in Renken, *The Penal Law*, 496. "The special faculty to handle cases of clerics, who having freely abandoned the ministry for a period of more than five consecutive years and who, after careful verification of the facts insofar as this is possible, persist in such freely chosen and illicit absence from the ministry; taking this situation into account, to declare then their dismissal from the clerical state, with dispensation from the obligations consequent to ordination, including that of celibacy."

98. To proceed administratively and bring to the approval *in forma specifica* and decision of the Holy Father cases regarding the dismissal *in poenam* from the clerical status of those clerics who are found guilty of the offenses in canon 1395 (concubinage and other serious scandals), without prejudice to the exclusive competence of the Congregation for the Doctrine of the Faith regarding cases of pedophilia.

99. Congregation for the Evangelization of Peoples, "Circular Letter," in Renken, *The Penal Law*, 485.

100. Congregation for the Clergy, in Renken, *The Penal Law*, 495–96.

101. Ronny Jenkins, "Memorandum to Cardinal George OMI," May 26, 2009.

102. If a complaint proven with moral certainty concerns a religious brother or sister, the provincial/major superior shall follow the Constitutions to dismiss the religious brother or sister in an administrative process following canon 695.

103. Alesandro, *A Study of Canon Law*, 275.

104. Thomas Green, "Penal Law: A Review," 229, notes that "with this penalty the primary emphasis is repairing scandal and restoring community order. It cannot be incurred automatically. The legislator also does not allow the penalty to be imposed administratively, but since 2001 the Congregation for the Doctrine of the Faith has allowed this penalty to be imposed by an extrajudicial process. Also, the law prefers the judicial process be used (Canons 221 and 1718 §1, no. 3.)."

105. Following the 1983 Code of Canon Law, canons 1400 to 1500 on trials in general and canons 1501 to 1670 on ordinary contentious trials.

106. DDF, *Vademecum*, 84.

107. See Judith Hahn, "Guilt, Innocence, and Remaining Doubts: Some Considerations on the Catholic Three-Verdict System of Deciding Cases of Sexual Abuse," *Oxford Journal of Law and Religion* 10 (2021).

108. A bishop can be removed from office. See Pope Francis, *motu proprio*, *As a Loving Mother*, June 4, 2016; https://w2.vatican.va/content/francesco/en/apost

_letters/documents/papa-francesco_lettera-ap_20160604_come-una-madre-amorevole.html. The Vatican's Apostolic Tribunal of the Congregation for the Doctrine of the Faith, which was composed of five judges, found Apuron guilty of charges and imposed penalties on him including "privation of office and prohibition of residence in the Archdiocese of Agana." https://www.guampdn.com/story/news/2018/03/19/guam-archbishop-byrnes-speaks-vaticans-guilty-verdict-apuron/437020002/.

109. Archbishop Milingowas was excommunicated by Pope Benedict XVI for ordaining four bishops without a pontifical mandate. When he ordained more bishops, Pope Benedict dismissed Archbishop Milingowas from the clerical state on December 17, 2009.

110. Ronny Jenkins, "Memorandum to Cardinal George OMI," May 26, 2009.

111. Book VI, 2021, Canon 1342 §1. "Whenever there are just reasons against the use of a judicial procedure, a penalty can be imposed or declared by means of an extra-judicial decree, observing canon 1720, especially in what concerns the right of defence and the moral certainty in the mind of the one issuing the decree, in accordance with the provision of can. 1608. Penal remedies and penances may in any case whatever be applied by a decree."

112. Book VI, 2021, Canon 1311 §2.

113. Pope Benedict XVI, "Pastoral Letter of the Holy Father Pope Benedict XVI to the Catholics of Ireland," March 19, 2010, no. 11. https://www.vatican.va/content/benedict-xvi/en/letters/2010/documents/hf_ben-xvi_let_20100319_church-ireland.html. See also Alesandro, *A Study of Canon Law*, 299–300.

SELECTED BIBLIOGRAPHY

VATICAN DOCUMENTS

Apostolic Penitentiary. "Note of the Apostolic Penitentiary on the Importance of the Internal Forum and the Inviolability of the Sacramental Seal." June 29, 2019. https://www.vatican.va/roman_curia/tribunals/apost_penit/documents/rc_trib_appen_pro_20190629_forointerno_en.html.

Code of Canon Law 1983. Vatican City: Libreria Editrice Vaticana, 1983. Accessible at http://www.vatican.va/archive/ENG1104/_INDEX.HTM.

Congregation for the Doctrine of the Faith "*Sacramentorum Sanctitatis Tutela*: Revised Norms on Dealing with Clerical Sex Abuse of Minors and Other Grave Offenses." *Origins* 40 (2010): 146–51. See also https://www.vatican.va/resources/resources_introd-storica_en.html.

Dicastery for the Doctrine of the Faith. "*Vademecum*: On Certain Points of Procedure in Treating Cases of Sexual Abuse of Minors Committed by Clerics." June 5, 2022. http://www.vatican.va/roman_curia/congregations/cfaith/documents/rc_con_cfaith_doc_20200716_vademecum-casi-abuso_en.html.

Francis, Pope. "Address of His Holiness Pope Francis Commemorating the 50th Anniversary of the Institution of the Synod of Bishops." October 17, 2015.

———. Apostolic Letter issued *motu proprio*, "As a Loving Mother." June 4, 2016.

———. Apostolic Letter issued *motu proprio*, *Vos Estis Lux Mundi*. May 7, 2019.

———. Apostolic Exhortation, *Evangelii Gaudium*. November 24, 2013. http://www.vatican.va/content/francesco/en/apost_exhortations/documents/papa-francesco_esortazione-ap_20131124_evangelii-gaudium.html.

———. Apostolic Exhortation, *Gaudete et Exsultate*. March 19, 2018.

———. "Christmas Greetings to the Roman Curia, Address by His Holiness Pope Francis." December 21, 2019.

———. Encyclical Letter, *Laudato Si'*. May 24, 2015.

———. "Letter of His Holiness Pope Francis to the People of God." August 20, 2018.

———. Rescript, "Some Amendments to the Normae de Gravioribus Delictis." December 3, 2019.

International Theological Commission. "Synodality in the Life and Mission of the Church." 2018. http://www.vatican.va/roman_curia/congregations/cfaith/cti

_documents/rc_cti_20180302_sinodalita_en.html.

John XXIII, Pope. Instruction, *Crimen Sollicitationis*, 1962. http://www.vatican.va/resources/resources_crimen-Sollicitationis-1962_en.html.

John Paul II, Pope. "Address to the Cardinals of the United States," *Origins* 31 (2001–2002): 759.

———. Apostolic Letter issued *motu proprio*, *Sacramentorum Sanctitatis Tutela*, 2001.

———. "Discourse to the Tribunal of the Holy Roman Rota." In *Teachings of John Paul II*, II/1 (1979), 411–12.

———. *Dominum et Vivificantem*. On the Holy Spirit in the Life of the Church and the World. May 19, 1986.

———. Post-synodal Apostolic Exhortation, *Pastores Dabo Vobis*. March 15, 1992.

———. Post-synodal Apostolic Exhortation, *Pastores Gregis*. October 16, 2003.

Paul VI, Pope. Apostolic Letter issued *motu proprio*, *Ecclesiae Sanctae*. August 6, 1966. http://www.vatican.va/content/paul-vi/en/motu_proprio/documents/hf_p-vi_motu-proprio_19660806_ecclesiae-sanctae.html.

BOOKS

Abbo, J. A., and Hannan, J. *The Sacred Canons: A Concise Presentation of the Current Disciplinary Norms of the Church*. 2nd ed. 2 vols. St. Louis: B. Herder Book Co., 1960.

Akpoghiran, Peter. *The Catholic Formulary*. 6 vols. New Orleans: Guadalupe Book Publishers, 2014.

Armstrong, Christopher. *A Critical Appraisal of Latae Sententiae Penalties in the 1983 Code of Canon Law*. Canon Law Studies 548. Washington, DC: Catholic University of America, 1996.

Bartchak, Mark. *Responsibility for Providing Spiritual Formation in Diocesan Seminaries according to the 1983 Code of Canon Law, with special reference to the United States*. Washington, DC: Catholic University of America, 1992.

Beal, John P., James A. Coriden, and Thomas J. Green, eds. *New Commentary on the Code of Canon Law*. Mahwah, NJ: Paulist, 2000.

Black, Henry. *Black's Law Dictionary*. St. Paul, MN: West Publishing Co., 1983.

Bouscaren, T. Lincoln, and Adam C. Ellis. *Canon Law: A Text and Commentary*. Milwaukee: Bruce, 1957.

Cafardi, Nicholas. *Before Dallas*. Mahwah, NJ: Paulist Press, 2008.

Calvo, Randolf, and Nevin Klinger, eds. *Clergy Procedural Handbook*. Washington, DC: Canon Law Society of America, 1992.

Caparros, Ernest, ed. *Exegetical Commentary on the Code of Canon Law*. 8 vols. Montreal: Wilson and Lafleur, 2004.

Caparros, Ernest, Michel Theriault, and Jean Thorn, eds. *Code of Canon Law Annotated*. 2nd ed. Montreal: Wilson and Lafleur, 2004.

Cappello, Felix. *Summa Iuris Canonici*. 5 vols. Rome: Apud aedes Universitatis Gregorianae, 1951.

———. *Tractatus Canonico-Moralis De Sacramentis*. 2 vols. Taurini-Romae: Marietti, 1947.

Carr, John. *The Suspension of a Cleric by the Administrative Procedure according to the 1983 Code of Canon Law*. Ottawa: Saint Paul University, 1989.

Selected Bibliography

Catechism of the Catholic Church: Revised in Accordance with the Official Latin Text. Vatican City: Libreria Editrice Vaticana, 1997.

Catholic Church England and Wales. "Catholic Safeguarding Advisory Service (CSAS) Procedures Manual." http://www.csasprocedures.uk.net.

Cholij, Roman. *Clerical Celibacy in East and West.* Herefordshire, UK: Fowler Wright Books, 1989.

Codex Iuris Canonici (1917). Rome: Typis Polyglottis Vaticanis, 1917. Translated by Edward Peters and published as *The 1917 or Pio-Benedictine Code of Canon Law.* San Francisco: Ignatius, 2001.

Cogan, Pat, ed. *Sacerdotes iuris.* Ottawa: Saint Paul University, 2005.

Condon, Edward. *Heresy by Association: The Canonical Prohibition of Freemasonry in History and in the Current Law.* Washington, DC: Catholic University of America, 2015.

Coriden, J. A., T. J. Green, and D. E. Heintschel, eds. *The Code of Canon Law: A Text and Commentary.* Mahwah, NJ: Paulist, 1985.

Coronata, M. Conte a. *Institutiones Iuris Canonici.* 5 vols. Rome: Domus Editorialis Marietti, 1944.

Cuschieri, A. *The Sacrament of Reconciliation: A Theological and Canonical Treatise.* Lanham, MD: University Press of America, 1992.

Daly, Brendan. *Canon Law in Action.* Sydney: Saint Paul Publications, 2015.

Daniel, William, trans. *Ministerium Iustitiae: Jurisprudence of the Supreme Tribunal of the Apostolic Signatura.* Montreal: Wilson & Lafleur, 2011.

De Paolis, V., and D. Cito, *Le sanzione Nella Chiesa. Commento al Codice di Diritto Canonico Libro VI.* Vatican City: Urbaniana University Press, 2001.

Diermeier, Joseph. "Loss of the Clerical State: Specific Focus on Dismissal from the Clerical State." JCL thesis, The Catholic University of America, 2010.

Doktorczyk, Stephen. *Persistent Disobedience to Church Authority: History, Analysis and Application of Canon 1371 no. 2.* Rome: Editrice Pontifica Universita Gregoriana, 2016.

Dublin Archdiocese Commission of Investigation. "2009 Commission of Investigation Report into the Catholic Archdiocese of Dublin" (Murphy Report). Accessed February 13, 2020. http://www.justice.ie/en/JELR/Pages/Dublin_Archdiocese_Commission_of_Investigation.

Dugan, Patricia, ed. *The Penal Process and the Protection of Rights in Canon Law: Proceedings of a Conference Held at the Pontifical University of the Holy Cross.* Rome, March 25–26, 2004. Montreal: Wilson and Lafleur, 2005.

Dugan, P., P. Gargaro, P., and V. Vondenberger. *Canon Law 101, Penal Law, Priest Problems and Legal Issues.* Philadelphia: Canon Law Books, 2017.

Fagothey, Austin. *Right and Reason: Ethics in Theory and Practice.* Saint Louis: C. V. Mosby, 1967.

Gillon, Chris, and Damian Grace. *Reckoning: The Catholic Church and Child Sexual Abuse.* Adelaide: ATF Press, 2014.

Glynn, John. *The Promotor of Justice: His Rights and Duties.* Canon Law Studies 101. Washington, DC: Catholic University of America, 1936.

Gray, Jason. *The Evolution of the Promoter of the Faith in Causes of Beatification and Canonization: A Study of the Law of 1917 and 1983.* Rome: Lateran University,

2015. http://www.jgray.org/docs/Promotor_Fidei_lulu.pdf.

Grocholewski, Z., and V. Carcel Orti, eds. *Dilexit iustitiam*. Vatican City: Libreria Editrice Vaticana, 1984.

Hannan, P. *The Canonical Concept of "Congrua Sustentatio'" for the Secular Clergy*. Canon Law Studies 302. Washington, DC: Catholic University of America, 1950.

Hanson, R., F. Pfafflin, and M. Lutz, eds. *Sexual Abuse in the Catholic Church: Scientific and Legal Perspectives*. Vatican City: Libreria Editrice Vaticana, 2004.

Hite, J., et al., eds. *Readings, Cases, Materials in Canon Law*. Collegeville, MN: Liturgical Press, 1986.

Huels, J. *The Pastoral Companion: A Canon Law Handbook for Catholic Ministry*. Illinois: Franciscan, 1995.

Huser, R. J. *The Crime of Abortion in Canon Law*. Washington, DC: Catholic University of America, 1942.

International Commission on English in the Liturgy. *The Rites of the Catholic Church*. 2 vols. Collegeville, MN: Liturgical Press, 1990.

Kennedy, Robert. *State Protection of Confessional Secrecy in the United States of America*. Rome: Pontificia Universitas Lateranensis, 1975.

Kurtscheid, Bertrand. *A History of the Seal of Confession*. Translated by F. Marks. London: Herder, 1927.

Limbourn, Brian. *The Sacrament of Reconciliation and General Absolution*. Ottawa: Saint Paul University, 2002.

Ludicke, Kalus and Ronny Jenkins. *Dignitas Connubii: Norms and Commentary*. Washington, DC: Catholic University of America, 2006.

Martini, Carlo. *Prêtres, Quelques Années Après: Méditations sur le Ministère Presbytéral*. Translated from Italian into French by Francois Vial. Paris, Cerf, 1992.

McBride, James. *Incardination and Excardination of Seculars: An Historical Synopsis and Commentary*. Canon Law Studies 145. Washington, DC: Catholic University of America, 1941.

Miller, D., and Donna and Eileen Jaramillo, eds. *Procedural Handbook for Institutes of Consecrated Life and Societies of Apostolic Life*. Washington, DC: Canon Law Society of America, 2021.

Min, Nereus Tun. "The Diocesan Bishop's Concern for Clerical Celibacy in the Light of Canon 277 §3: Bishops of Myanmar and Priestly Celibacy." Doctoral thesis. Pontificia Universitas Urbaniana, 2001.

Morrissey, Robert. *Abortion and the Excommunication of Canon 1398 in the 1983 Code of Canon Law*. Washington, DC: Catholic University of America, 1992.

Murphy, Richard, *The Canonico-Juridical Status of a Communist*. Washington, DC: Catholic University of America, 1959.

National Conference of Catholic Bishops (United States of America). *Norms for Priestly Formation*. 2 vols. Washington, DC: National Conference of Catholic Bishops, 1992.

Neli, Linus. *Delicta Graviora: "More Grave Delicts" in the Catholic Church*. Bengaluru: ATC Publishers, 2018.

New Zealand Catholic Bishops' Conference. *Programme for Priestly Formation*. Wellington: New Zealand Catholic Bishops' Conference, 2004.

Noldin, H, and A. Schmitt. *Summa Theologiae Moralis*. Oeniponte: Typis et Sumptibus Feliciani Rauch, 1955.

Olattupuram, Thomas. *The Vow of Poverty in Religious Life: Canon 600*. Rome: Pontificia Universitatas Lateranensis, 2006.

O'Neill, Kevin, and Peter Black. *Life, Death, and Catholic Medical Choices*. Missouri: Ligouri, 2011.

Palmer, Paul. *Sacraments and Forgiveness: History and Doctrinal Development of Penance, Extreme Unction and Indulgences*. 2 vols. London: Darton, Longman and Todd, 1960.

Papale, C. "Il Delitto contro il sacramento della penitenza riservati alla congregazione per la Dottrina della fide." *Quaderni Ius Missionale* 7 (2016).

———. *Il Delitto contro il sacramento dell'eucaristia riservati alla congregazione per la dottrina della fede*. Vatican City: Urbaniana University Press, 2017.

———. *Il processo penale canonico: commento al Codice di Dirritto Canonico, Libro VII*. 2nd ed. Vatican City: Urbaniana University Press, 2012.

Peters, Edward, ed. *Incrementa in Progressu 1983 Codicis Iuris Canonici*. Montreal: Wilson and Lafleur, 2005.

Pontificia Commissio Codici Iuris Canonici Recognoscendo. *Relatio complectens synthesim animadversionum ab Em. mis. atque Exc. mis. Patribus Commissionis ad ultimum schema Codici Iuris Canonici Exhibitarum, cum responsionibus a Secretaria et Consultoribus datis*. Vatican City: Typis Polyglottis Vaticanis, 1981.

Price, David. "Penal Law Revisited for the '90s." In *Proceedings of the Twenty-Eighth Annual Conference*, 60–77. Adelaide: Canon Law Society of Australia and New Zealand, 1994.

Ratzinger, Joseph. *Salt of the Earth: The Church at the End of the Millennium*. Translated by Adrian Walker. San Francisco: Ignatius, 1997.

Renken, John, *The Penal Law of the Roman Catholic Church: Commentary on canons 1311–1399 and 1717–1731 and Other Sources of Penal Law*. Ottawa: Saint Paul University, 2015.

Roberti, Cardinal Francesco, and Pietro Palazzini, eds. Translated by Henry Yannone. *Dictionary of Moral Theology*. Westminster, PA: The Newman Press, 1962.

Rossetti, Stephen. *A Tragic Grace: The Catholic Church and Child Sexual Abuse*. Collegeville, MN: The Liturgical Press, 1996.

Schneider, Francis J. *Obedience to the Diocesan Bishop by the Diocesan Priest in the 1983 Code of Canon Law*. Canon Law Studies 533. Washington, DC: Catholic University of America, 1990.

Schwartz, John. *The Obligation of Accepting Ecclesiastical Appointments (Canon 128)*. Canon Law Studies 6. Washington, DC: Catholic University of America, 1948.

Secretariat for Priestly Life and Ministry. *Priests for a New Millennium*. Washington, DC: United States Conference of Catholic Bishops, 2000.

Sheehan, Joseph. *The Obligations of Respect and Obedience of Clerics toward Their Ordinary (Canon 127)*. Canon Law Studies 344. Washington, DC: Catholic University of America, 1954.

Sheehy, G., et al., eds. *The Canon Law: Letter and Spirit*. Collegeville, MN: The Liturgical Press, 1995.

Stickler, Alphons. *The Case for Clerical Celibacy: Its Historical Development and Theological Foundations*. Translated by Brian Ferme. San Francisco, Ignatius, 1995.

Tanner, Norman P., ed. *Decrees of the Ecumenical Councils*. 2 vols. Washington, DC: Sheed and Ward, 1990.

Thompson, A. Keith. *Religious Confession Privilege and the Common Law*. Leiden: Martinus Nijhoff, 2011.

Tillard, Jean-Marie. *Dilemmas of Modern Religious Life.* Wilmington, NC: Michael Glazier, 1984.

United States Catholic Bishops Conference. "Essential Norms for Diocesan/Eparchial Policies Dealing with Allegations of Sexual Abuse of Minors by Priests or Deacons." *Origins* 32, no. 25 (2002): 415ff. http://www.usccb.org/issues-and-action/child-and-youth-protection/upload/Charter-for-the-Protection-of-Children-and-Young-People-revised-2011.pdf.

Vogels, Heinz. *Celibacy: Gift or Law? A Critical Investigation.* London: Burns and Oates, 1992.

Vondenberger, Victoria, RSM. "The Promoter of Justice." In *Canon Law 101: Penal Law, Priest Problems and Legal Issues*, ed. P. Dugan, P. Gargaro, and V. Vondenberger. Philadelphia: Canon Law Books, 2017.

Wernz, Francisco, and Pietro Vidal. *Ius Canonicum.* 7 vols. Rome, Apud Aedes Universitatis Gregorianiae, 1943.

Wijlens, Myriam. *Sharing the Eucharist: A Theological Evaluation of the Post Conciliar Legislation.* New York: University Press of America, 2000.

Woestman, William H. *Ecclesiastical Sanctions and the Penal Process.* Ottawa: Saint Paul University, 2000.

———. *The Sacrament of Orders and the Clerical State.* Ottawa: Saint Paul University, 1999.

———. *Sacraments: Initiation, Penance, Anointing of the Sick.* Ottawa: Saint Paul University, 1992.

Zubacz, Gregory. *The Seal of Confession and Canadian Law.* Montreal: Wilson and Lafleur, 2009.

ARTICLES

Alesandro, John. "A Study of Canon Law: Dismissal from the Clerical State in Cases of Sexual Misconduct." *The Catholic Lawyer* 36, no. 3 (2017): 257–300.

Arrieta, Juan, "Cardinal Ratzinger and the Revision of the Canonical Penal System: A Crucial Role." http://www.vatican.va/resources/resources_arrieta-20101202_en.html.

Austin, Rodger. "Submission on Canon Law to the Royal Commission into Institutional Responses to Child Sexual Abuse in Australia." *The Canonist* 8, no. 2 (2017): 276–328.

Beal, John, "Administrative Leave: Canon 1722 Revisited." *Studia Canonica* 27 (1993): 293–320.

———. "Too Good to Be True? A Response to Professor Woestman on the Interpretation of Canons 1041, 1° and 1044 §2, 2°." *Monitor Ecclesiasticus* 121 (1996): 431–63.

Brewer, Dexter. "The Right of a Penitent to Release the Confessor from the Seal: Considerations in Canon Law and American Law." *The Jurist* 54 (1994).

Brundage, Thomas. "The Promotor [sic] of Justice in the 1983 Code of Canon Law." Washington, DC: Catholic University of America, 2005.

Catholic Church England and Wales. "Catholic Safeguarding Advisory Service (CSAS): Procedures Manual." http://www.csasprocedures.uk.net.

Ghirlanda, Gianfranco. "The Significance of the Apostolic Constitution Anglicanorum Coetibus." http://www.catholicculture.org/culture/library/view.cfm?recnum=9178.

Green, Thomas. "Penal Law: A Review of Selected Themes." *The Jurist* 50 (1990).

Huels, John. "Denial of a Sacrament without Due Process." In CLSA Advisory Opinions 1984–1993, 236–38. Washington, DC: Canon Law Society of America, 1995.

International Theological Commission. Report, "Penance and Reconciliation." *Origins* 13 (1984): 513–24.

Jehaut, Rikardus. "Loss of the Clerical State by a Rescript of Dispensation: Procedural Norms and Responsibilities of the Diocesan Bishop." *The Canonist* 9, no. 2 (2018): 177–203.

Jenkins, R. E. "Clerical Sexual Abuse as an Irregularity." *Periodica* 94 (2005): 275–340.

Kozlowski, John, OP. "Understanding the *Ius Vigens* of the Mandatory Dismissal Process." *The Jurist* 75 (2015): 387–427.

Lohse, Edwards. "The Origin and Nature of the Suspension *ad cautelam* of Article 4 of the 1980 Normae Procedurales for Dispensations from Celibacy." *Periodica* 95 (2006).

Mascord, Brian. "When in Rome: A Letter from Bishop Brian as He Prepares for Ad Limina Visit." *Catholic Education Diocese of Wollongong News*. June 10, 2019. https://www.dow.catholic.edu.au. Accessed February 13, 2020.

Mbandji, Valere Nkouaya. "La Prescription Canonique et les delicts commis par les Clercs." Paper to the Canadian Canon Law Society 52nd Annual Convention 2017.

Mendonça, Augustine. "The Bishop as the Mirror of Justice and Equity in the Particular Church: Some Practical Reflections on Episcopal Ministry." *Canonical Studies* (2002): 28.

Morrisey, Francis. "Denial of a Sacrament without Due Process." CLSA Advisory Opinions 1984–1993, 240–41. Washington, DC: Canon Law Society of America, 1995.

———. "Violations of Canon 277 (with an Adult): Appropriate and Just Responses." *The Canonist* 1, no. 2 (2010): 55–67.

The National Review Board for the Protection of Children and Young People 2004. "A Report on the Crisis in the Catholic Church in the United States." Accessed February 13, 2020. http://www.usccb.org/issues-and-action/child-and-youth-protection/upload/National-Review-Board-Report-2004.pdf.

Provost, James. "Offences against the Sixth Commandment: Toward a Canonical Analysis of Canon 1395." *The Jurist* 55 (1995): 632–63.

———. "Some Canonical Considerations on Closing Parishes." *The Jurist* 53 (1993): 362–70.

Rainer, Eligius. *Suspension of Clerics: An Historical Synopsis and Commentary*. Canon Law Studies 111. Washington, DC: The Catholic University of America, 1937.

Reynolds, J. 2019, "Pope Francis Makes It Mandatory for Clergy to Report Sex Abuse." BBC News. May 9, 2019. Accessed February 13, 2020. https://www.bbc.com.

"Royal Commission into Institutional Responses to Child Sexual Abuse 2017." Final Report, volume 16, Religious Institutions: Book 2. Accessed February 13, 2020. https://www.childabuseroyalcommission.gov.au/sites/default/files/final_report_-_volume_16_religious_institutions_book_2.pdf.

"Royal Commission into Misconduct in the Banking, Superannuation and Financial Services Industry 2019." Final Report, Volume 1. Accessed February 13, 2020. https://www.royalcommission.gov.au/sites/default/files/2019-02/fsrc-volume-1-final-report.pdf.

Rzeznik, Thomas. "The Church in the Changing City: Parochial Restructuring in the Archdiocese of Philadelphia in Historical Perspective." *U.S. Catholic Historian* 24, no. 4 (2009): 73–90.

Sacred Congregation for the Clergy. "Private Letter on 'Pastoral Councils.'" Omnes Christifideles, January 25, 1973. Also published as "Patterns in Local Pastoral Councils." *Origins* 3, no. 12 (1973): 186–90. Accessed February 13, 2020. https://www.pastoralcouncils.com/bibliography/vatican-documents/postconciliar/circular/.

Scicluna, Charles. "Promoter of Justice at the Congregation for the Doctrine of the Faith: The Procedure and Praxis of the Congregation for the Doctrine of the Faith Regarding Graviora Delicta." http://www.vatican.va/resources/resources_mons-scicluna-graviora-delicta_en.html. Accessed September 15, 2011.

Scicluna, Charles. "Days of Covering Up Are Over." https://www.catholicnews.com/services/englishnews/2019/days-of-covering-up-abuse-allegations-are-over-says-vatican-adviser.cfm.

———. "Response to and Prevention of Clerical Sexual Misconduct: Current Praxis." *Origins* 43 (2013–2014): 357–64.

Sherr, R. "A Canon, a Choirboy, and Homosexuality in Late Sixteen Century Italy: A Case Study." *Journal of Homosexuality* 21, no. 3 (1991): 1–22.

Truth, Justice and Healing Council. "Where from and Where to—The Truth Justice and Healing Council, the Royal Commission and the Catholic Church in Australia." Final Report, Volume 1. Accessed February 13, 2020. http://www.tjhcouncil.org.au/.

United States Conference of Catholic Bishops. "Charter for the Protection of Children and Young People." June 2011. http://www.usccb.org/issues-and-action/child-and-youth-protection/upload/Charter-for-the-Protection-of-Children-and-Young-People-revised-2011.

Vaillaint, G. "Restructuring Parishes a Move from Necessity to Audacity." *La Croix International*. August 9, 2018. Accessed February 13, 2020. https://international.la-croix.com.

Waters, I. "The Australian Bishops and Canon Law." In *Health and Integrity in Church and Ministry Conference Papers*, edited by S. Crittenden. 103. Sydney: Franciscan Friars, 2019.

Winfield, N. "Analysis: Pope's Sex Abuse Summit: What It Did and Didn't Do." AP News, February 26, 2019. Accessed February 13, 2020. https://apnews.com.

Woestman, William. "Too Good To Be True: A Current Interpretation of Canons 1041, 1° and 1044 §2, 2°." *Monitor Ecclesiasticus* 120 (1995): 619–29.

INDEX

Abortion, 27–28, 49, 56–57, 177n1
Absolution, 45, 54, 59–60, 73–80, 85, 121, 127–28, 157n38, 193n33, 198n87
Accomplice, 13, 73–80, 166n6
Adminstrative leave, 32–33, 35
Administrative process, 21, 32, 37, 56, 89–90, 140, 156n27, 177n61
Anathema, 51, 54
Anointing of the sick, 36–37, 155
Apostolic See, 13, 32, 47, 70, 75, 76, 78, 97, 101, 113, 139, 165nn78–79, 166nn82–83, 168nn29–30, 171n79, 171n81
"As a Loving Mother," 152n75, 199n108
Australian Royal Commission, 19, 28, 112, 120, 121

Baptism, 52, 102
Benedict XVI, Pope, 1, 5, 15, 26, 27, 49, 79, 89, 102, 107–8, 113, 114, 117, 141
Bishop, 3, 4, 8, 10–11, 12, 17, 28, 42, 62, 77, 83, 93, 94–95, 103, 107–8, 132, 172n88, 179n32
Bishops Conference, 12, 65, 107, 139

Canonization, 9
Cardinal, 11
Celibacy, 19, 63, 133, 134, 137, 140, 141–42, 196n64
Celibacy and John Paul II, 63
Chalcedon, Council, 42
Chastity, 84, 132, 162n53, 181n16

China, 94–95, 106–8
Communion, 27–28, 107–8, 171n68
Communism, 92–94, 96–101, 108–9
Confirmation, 154
Congregation for Bishops, 64
Congregation for Clergy, 47, 198n91
Congregation for the Doctrine of the Faith, 4, 7, 16, 79, 81, 89, 90, 114–15, 117–19, 123, 140, 143
Congregation for the Evangelization of Peoples, 140–41
Consultors, 77
Continence, 132, 138, 196n64
Contrition, 128
Cooperator, 5, 73
Council Legislative Texts, 1
Crimen Sollicitationis, 82–83, 86, 113, 115–16, 136
Crimes, 3, 5, 9, 11, 20, 25, 44, 45, 55, 58–59, 79, 85, 89, 110–20, 132, 136, 139, 144

Defrocking, 130
Degradation, 130, 134, 135–36
Delict, 11, 20, 26–27, 79, 83, 89
Diocesan administrator, 148n20, 175n19
Dismissal from the clerical state, 4, 12–13, 19, 22, 23, 24, 26, 89–90, 124, 130–35, 138
Dispensation from celibacy, 136, 137, 140, 141, 142, 199n97

Dispensation from vows, 158n41
Divorce, 62

Episcopal vicar, 165n80, 172n88
Eucharist, 13, 33, 35–36, 37, 45, 58, 60, 140, 157n35
Excommunication, 12, 13, 40, 49–61, 76, 87, 97, 101, 103, 123
Expiatory penalty, 12, 33, 37, 48, 90
External forum, 53, 59, 66, 69, 128, 137

Francis, Pope, 1, 5, 10, 15, 16, 18, 19, 20, 22, 26, 29, 49, 108

Graviora Delicta, 79, 81
Gregory the Great, Pope, 41

Heresy, 13, 51, 58, 102, 139

Impediments, 155n8
Incardination, 31–32
Interdict, 2, 42, 77, 103, 104, 152n2
Internal forum, 7, 44, 53, 55, 59–60
Irregularities, 17, 27

John Paul II, Pope, 4, 5, 63, 78, 79, 81, 89, 102, 106–7, 113, 115, 116, 117, 123, 138, 139, 140

Laity, 28–29, 119, 133–38
Lateran Council, Fifth, 132
Lateran Council, Fourth, 73, 122, 131–32
Lateran Council, Third, 42, 53, 131
Leo the Great, Pope, 64
Local Ordinary, 5, 7, 56, 82, 86, 87, 133, 148n20, 172n88

Marriage, 30, 98, 141–42
Metropolitan, 10, 148n21

Obedience, 8, 63, 70
Ordinary, 17, 29, 47–48, 59, 66–69, 143, 148n20, 172n88

Parishes, 54, 58, 66
Parish priest, 25, 30, 37, 66, 73–74, 164n70
Particular church, 9, 10, 171n68
Particular law, 17, 32, 65, 66, 67–68, 70, 113, 196n67
Pastoral care, 150n53, 163n57, 170n56
Pedophilia, 113, 114, 115, 116, 131
Penalties, 2–3, 45–46, 47, 58–59, 71, 135
Penance, 30, 45, 51–52, 73, 74, 79, 81–91, 122–23, 128
Pontifical secret, 16–17
Pornography, 5, 20, 22, 26, 117, 120
Precept, 64–65, 67–70, 71–72
Prescription, 110–20, 158n44
Professional standards, 65
Promoter of justice, 157nn29–30

Ratzinger, Joseph. *See* Benedict XVI
Religious, 62–72, 105–6, 119
Religious institute, 21, 31, 36, 71–72, 116, 172n88
Religious leaders, 7, 8, 9, 63
Removal of faculties, 31, 32, 33–37, 40
Remuneration, 12, 56
Rights, 8, 24–25, 39, 41, 56, 69, 111, 134, 150n57

Sacramentorum Sanctitatis Tutela, 4, 19, 20, 29, 81, 89, 113, 116, 117, 118, 119, 123, 139–40
Scicluna, Charles, 8, 11, 89, 116, 117, 123
Seal of confession, 7, 8, 59, 87, 88, 121–29
Secrecy, 16, 122–23, 128
Seminary, 125, 133
Sexual abuse, 110–20, 139
Sexual acts, 20, 193n11
Solicitation, 46, 74, 81–91, 115, 136, 162n53, 181n16, 181n21
Special faculties, 140–43, 144
Suspension, 32, 40–48

Index

Thomas Aquinas, 74, 122
Trent, Council of, 42–43, 53, 132
Trial, 34, 46, 65, 89, 140

Vademecum, 20, 23, 26, 32, 71, 126
Vatican II, Council, 106, 136–37

Vicar General, 56, 132, 175n19
Vietnam, 95–96, 103, 109, 184n25
Vos Estis Lux Mundi, 5, 6–8, 10, 15, 16, 22, 23, 26, 29, 65

www.ingramcontent.com/pod-product-compliance
Lightning Source LLC
Chambersburg PA
CBHW080932020526
44116CB00033B/2319